THE PATH
FREEMASONRY

"Like a drowsy lion, Freemasonry arouses in the outsider both curiosity and mistrust. This landmark book anatomizes the creature without apology or mystification. At the same time, it summons insiders to revive their moribund craft in all the grandeur of its original mission to humanity. Mark Stavish, whose work is informed by a profound knowledge of esoteric traditions, has earned gratitude from both sides."

JOSCELYN GODWIN, PROFESSOR OF MUSIC EMERITUS,
COLGATE UNIVERSITY AND COAUTHOR OF
SYMBOLS IN THE WILDERNESS AND FORBIDDEN FRUITS

"Mark Stavish's *The Path of Freemasonry* provides a comprehensive introduction to the Craft—its history, inner structure, beliefs, objectives, rites, and even its symbolically rich language. Unusually, however, it goes far beyond this brief to encompass the broader social and cultural issues surrounding the tradition; and in particular its relationship with, and profound connections to, the occult societies and esoteric currents toward which some of its most respected members have contributed their energy and organizational and ritual know-how. Indeed but for the disciplinary bedrock provided by Freemasonry it is arguable whether there would be a Western esoteric tradition worth talking of. This commendable work provides the reader with an accessible and engaging overview of this subject."

PETER MARK ADAMS, AUTHOR OF THE GAME OF SATURN,
MYSTAI, AND THE POWER OF THE HEALING FIELD

"Mark Stavish has written a must-read for anyone considering Freemasonry and the esoteric path within it . . . This book will take you on a journey through its unique history, touching upon rituals, symbolism, and diving into the philosophies of its uncharted beginnings and into the modern era. Get ready for a journey and an exciting read into the world's most venerable fraternity."

ERIK W. KROGSTAD 33°, MASTER MASONIC SCHOLAR, LECTURER, AND BLOGGER

THE PATH OF
FREEMASONRY

THE CRAFT AS A
SPIRITUAL PRACTICE

Mark Stavish

Inner Traditions
Rochester, Vermont

Inner Traditions
One Park Street
Rochester, Vermont 05767
www.InnerTraditions.com

SUSTAINABLE   Certified Sourcing
FORESTRY
INITIATIVE   www.sfiprogram.org
SFI-00854

Text stock is SFI certified

Copyright © 2007, 2021 by Mark Stavish

Originally published in 2007 by Llewellyn Publications under the title
Freemasonry: Rituals, Symbols & History of the Secret Society
Appendix A "Sacred Geometry and the Masonic Tradition" © 2004, 2007, 2021
by John Michael Greer. All rights reserved.

All rights reserved. No part of this book may be reproduced or utilized in
any form or by any means, electronic or mechanical, including photocopying,
recording, or by any information storage and retrieval system, without permission
in writing from the publisher.

Cataloging-in-Publication Data for this title is available from the Library of Congress

ISBN 978-1-64411-328-8 (print)
ISBN 978-1-64411-329-5 (ebook)

Printed and bound in the United States by Lake Book Manufacturing, Inc.
The text stock is SFI certified. The Sustainable Forestry Initiative® program
promotes sustainable forest management.

10 9 8 7 6 5 4 3 2 1

Text design and layout by Virginia Scott Bowman
This book was typeset in Garamond Premier Pro with Alchemist and Trenda used
as display typefaces
Illustrations on pages 24, 38, 57, 61, 62, 65, 68, 69, 71, 73, and 106 by Llewellyn

To send correspondence to the author of this book, mail a first-class letter to the
author c/o Inner Traditions • Bear & Company, One Park Street, Rochester, VT
05767, and we will forward the communication, or contact the author directly at
www.hermeticinstitute.org.

This book is dedicated to my wife,
Dr. Andrea M. Nerozzi, and our two sons,
Luke and Nathaniel. They are the cornerstone
upon which all my good works have been built,
and the capstone of my life.

ACKNOWLEDGMENTS

Thank you to Jon Graham, Jeanie Levitan, Patricia Rydle, Albo Sudekum, and the entire staff at Inner Traditions for their support on this project. They are a spectacular group of people to work with and have made a "good book" much better.

Thank you to Carl Weschcke of Llewellyn Worldwide who published the first edition of this book under the title *Freemasonry: Rituals, Symbols, and History of the Secret Society* in 2007. May this new and much improved edition be a testament to the wisdom of both these publishers and their staff.

Contents

Deeper into the Wonderful Mystery

Foreword to the 2021 Edition

Arturo de Hoyos, 33°

FREEMASONRY, THE WORLD'S OLDEST and largest fraternity, has been variously described and defined. The organization defines itself as a system of morality, veiled in allegory and illustrated by symbols. Chief among its objects is the pursuit of "light," which is analogous to truth or reality—or, to use the words of John Locke, "the knowledge of things, as they are to be found in themselves, and not our imaginations."[1] Thus, it encourages mature individual and social responsibility through awareness of the world and our place in it. Within the lodge Masons carefully avoid divisive issues, such as politics and religion. Rather, Masonic "labor" is itself a type of worship that raises humanity by self-improvement (*laborare est orare*, "to work is to pray"). Although Masonry acknowledges the existence of a Supreme Being, it leaves sectarian religious beliefs and concerns to the individual, promoting only brotherhood. Thus, it remarkably transcends all borders, artificial and natural, and unites members who may otherwise have remained distant.

Yet the Craft is much more than that. Albert Pike, the famous grand commander of the Scottish Rite, Southern Jurisdiction, stated, "Masonry is a march and a struggle toward the Light. For the individual as well as the nation, Light is Virtue, Manliness, Intelligence, Liberty. Tyranny over the soul or body, is darkness."[2] And, in his clearest definition, he proclaimed:

> Freemasonry is the subjugation of the Human that is in man by the Divine; the Conquest of the Appetites and Passions by the Moral Sense and the Reason; a continual effort, struggle, and warfare of the Spiritual against the Material and Sensual. That victory, when it has been achieved and secured, and the conqueror may rest upon his shield and wear the well-earned laurels, is the true Holy Empire.[3]

The means by which Freemasonry accomplishes this is through ritual and symbolic instruction. This ancient and time-honored practice has the remarkable ability to bring its initiates into a mythical and symbolic realm where, freed from the thoughts and concerns of the modern world, they gain insights and learn lessons by which they navigate throughout life.

Freemasonry is ancient, and few records survive to give us insight into its original character. The oldest known Masonic document, the Regius Manuscript (ca. 1410), includes the Old Charges or Gothic constitutions—the laws and moral code of conduct observed by medieval stonemasons. Over 120 ancient documents detailing these principles still survive. What today we call the "lodge" was originally just the small private dwelling of the master—the stonemason who held the building contract for a medieval construction project. It was erected near the project, and if a Mason was lucky, he might be invited to enjoy its fellowship. These early Masons were likely read the Old Charges, given a mythical history of their trade, and invested with secret modes of recognition, including special handshakes and passwords. They were religious men, builders of cathedrals, and their stories included tales of the building of the Tower of Babel, Noah's Ark, and, later, King Solomon's Temple. Early Masons were also instrumental in rebuilding London after the great fire of 1666. By the 1640s non-Masons were being admitted into Masonic lodges. This marked a move away from Masonry as a purely operative, trade-based fellowship toward speculative, or philosophic Masonry. In 1717 several lodges met and formed a grand lodge in England, which act is often considered the beginning of Freemasonry as a fraternity. The Old Charges were collated and published as *The Constitutions of the Free-Masons* (1723), wherein we read that Adam was the first Mason, and that the Garden of Eden was his lodge. This work, the first official Masonic book, continues to influence the laws of all regular grand lodges in the world today.

The earliest accounts of Masonic ritual are found in the Edinburgh Register House Manuscript (1696), though it leaves much unstated. Its descriptions of rituals are mostly abbreviated, with little explanation as to what the particular actions actually meant. Yet we know that there were secrets to be learned from the rituals. The Dumfries No. 4 Manuscript (1710) declares that "no lodge or corum of massons shall give the Royal secret to any suddenly but upon great deliberation first let him learn his Questions by heart then his symbals then do as the lodge thinks fit." There's a good deal of debate and speculation among modern Masonic scholars about where some of these practices and symbols came from. Freemasonry has always been eclectic, borrowing what it needed to create and improve its ceremonies, rituals, and instruction. Because members were forbidden from transcribing the rituals and betraying their secrets, we have precious few descriptions apart from early anti-Masonic tracts and published exposés revealing Masonic rituals. Some of these include enigmatic statements. For example, *A Letter from the Grand Mistress of the Female Freemasons* (a mocking attack on Freemasonry published anonymously in 1724 but generally attributed to Jonathan Swift) refers to Masonry's "Caballistical Philosophy," while *The Grand Mystery Laid Open, or the Free Masons Signs and Words Discovered* (an exposé published anonymously in 1726) says that the Masonic secrets "are not divulged to any new admitted Member, because they are Cabalistical." To what do these remarks allude? We don't know precisely. In an 1888 letter to Robert F. Gould (England's premier Masonic historian), Pike noted:

I cannot conceive of anything that could have induced Ashmole, Mainwaring, and other men of their class to unite themselves with a Lodge of working Masons, except this—that, as Alchemists, Hermeticists, and Rosicrucians had no association of [their] own in England or Scotland, they joined the Masonic Lodges in order to meet one another without being suspected; and I am convinced that it was the men who inherited their doctrines who brought their symbols into Masonry, but kept the Hermetic meanings of them to themselves.[4]

After studying Pike's text and arguments, Gould confessed, "There is no one among our British Masonic writers who could have written up to the level of your own performance." He also noted, "Your Lectures on Symbolism impressed me greatly and no part of them more so, than the effective way in which you show how much of the meaning of what is now done in Lodge, has been lost."[5] And there we have it: Freemasonry has much that is of unknown origin, and that is at once both practical and symbolic, or exoteric and esoteric.

In this bold and insightful work, Brother Mark Stavish explores the history, rituals, and philosophies of Freemasonry and its possible relationships with other esoteric traditions, ancient societies, and even modern physics. He looks at a variety of Masonic rites and practices and investigates how the Craft hints at or preserves currents and traditions below the surface of mundane life. But this book is more than an entertaining read. At the end of each chapter, Brother Stavish summarizes key points, provides assignments, and suggests further reading material. In other words, this is a workbook, or practical course, to encourage its readers to look deeper into the wonderful mystery that is Freemasonry.

ARTURO DE HOYOS, 33°, GRAND CROSS, K.Y.C.H.
PAST MASTER, MCALLEN LODGE NO. 1110, AF&AM OF TEXAS
GRAND ARCHIVIST AND GRAND HISTORIAN
SUPREME COUNCIL, 33° SOUTHERN JURISDICTION
(MOTHER SUPREME COUNCIL OF THE WORLD)
THE HOUSE OF THE TEMPLE, WASHINGTON, D.C.

Foreword to the First Edition

Lon Milo DuQuette, 32°

> *Masonry is a progressive moral science, divided into different degrees; and, as its principles and mystic ceremonies are regularly developed and illustrated, it is intended and hoped that they will make a deep and lasting impression upon your mind.*
>
> GRAND LODGE OF CALIFORNIA, *CALIFORNIA CIPHER: A VALUABLE AID TO MEMORY* (1990)

IT'S 4:00 A.M. I creep quietly past the rooms of my sleeping brothers and out to the darkened hallway that leads to the staircase to the atrium. The atrium is a cavernous space, nearly two hundred feet long and over fifty feet wide, built in the style of the Roman Empire. The marble floor is adorned with Masonic symbols inlaid in brass and stone of contrasting colors. The Doric and Ionic columns that flank the great hall and support second-story walkways and chambers are dwarfed by towering Corinthian columns that buttress the vaulted ceiling, three stories high, whose centerpiece stained-glass skylight now bathes the room in soft iridescent moonlight.

There are five bronze statues here whose presence I am moved to honor. Four are the goddess figures of the cardinal virtues: Temperance, Prudence, Fortitude, and Justice. They are positioned at the corners of the room, which I slowly circumambulate as I move from pedestal to pedestal. The fifth goddess stands in the very center of the hall and bears no inscription or emblem. She simply holds her forefinger to her lips as if to hush the universe. It is here at the feet of silence where I sit down on the cool floor and close my eyes. Only a moment, it seems, passes before I hear the warm ring of a temple bowl. The others are awake, and we are being called to dawn meditation.

I slip off my shoes outside the door of the lodge room and tiptoe inside to take my seat. The room is dark save for a single candle on the central altar. After a few quiet words of introduction and instruction, we close our eyes and enter our inner temples. Forty minutes later the sun has risen. We open our eyes and see the room brilliantly illuminated by three large Italian stained-glass panels that form the entire southern wall of the lodge room. Each window dramatically depicts one of the three ages of man: youth, manhood, and old age. My eyes linger on each scene in turn as I weigh the well-lived episodes of my life against those of time misspent.

After breakfast we gather beneath chandeliers of Czech crystal in the spacious reception room and for the first time see who has come this year. I immediately recognize some of the brightest stars in the firmament of modern Masonry. I also see friends and colleagues from years past, writers, scholars, teachers, and students. As always, there are several brothers who have been invited for the first time to present papers and lecture.

We are meeting for three days of presentations and discussions of issues and subjects relating to esoteric aspects of the Craft of Freemasonry. We have gathered secretly and informally under no official warrant, charter, or auspices to explore the Craft as a self-transformational art and science—to labor and strategize how best to proceed to protect, preserve, and advance the esoteric soul of Freemasonry.

Appropriately, the venue for this gathering is one of the largest and most architecturally magnificent Masonic edifices in the world, unexplainably abandoned by its usual team of custodial stewards for the duration of our meetings. The building itself is intoxicating. We are all humbled by its beauty and perfect proportions. One cannot resist being tangibly elevated as we each intuitively attempt to adjust our inner imperfections to reflect the outer perfections of the sacred geometry around us. As we walk the sacred labyrinth, sit quietly studying in the Gothic library, or muse about alchemy at the feet of Assyrian sphinxes, we find ourselves pausing and asking each other, "Is this really happening?"

Yes. It really happens, and *this* is how I always dreamed Masonry would be.

This, however, is not what all Masons think the Craft should be. As a matter of fact, there are a great many who now feel that the esoteric roots of our ancient institution are an embarrassment—queer and unwholesome links to paganism, the occult, and perhaps even Satanism. You might be surprised to learn that there is a concerted effort now taking place within Masonry to once and for all divorce the Craft from its esoteric heritage and make it an organization open only to men professing certain specific religious convictions. Even though Masonic tradition dictates that a candidate need only profess a belief in a Supreme Being and a form of afterlife, today there are jurisdictions and lodges around the world that will not consider the application of a man if they believe his religion to be not "mainstream" enough, or his interest in the esoteric nature of the craft suspiciously intense.

This is why, sadly, I cannot tell you in what country our gathering takes place. Neither can I tell you the names of the participants, or the circumstances that bring us together, or the details of our activities and goals. By necessity, Masonry has for us again become a secret society.

What makes this anti-esoteric movement so ill-timed and suicidal is the fact that Masonry's membership numbers are plunging precipitously. Lodges are closing or merging with other lodges for lack of members. Freemasonry, as we've known it for the last three hundred years, will be dead in just a few years if something isn't done. Ironically (and much to the terror of the anti-esoterics), the only demographic group that is applying for membership in significant numbers is composed of young men who are passionately interested in the esoteric mysteries of the Craft.

Fortunately, at least for the time being, exoteric Masonry is still for the most part a very big tent. Even in the most conservative quarters, leadership still pays lip service to the concept that Masonry opens her doors to upstanding men of all races, religions, political persuasions, and social and economic circumstances.* Aside from the obligatory duties required to advance through the degrees, the individual Mason is free to be as interested or as disinterested as he likes in matters that concern the history, rituals, traditions, and mysteries of the Craft. As it is (and much to the relief of the anti-esoterics), most Masons, once they are raised to the sublime degree of Master Mason (and, if they so choose, go on to complete the degrees in one or more concordant rites), are happy to put the quaint and curious stuff behind them and simply enjoy being part of one of the most active and generous service organizations in the world.

This is as it should be, and please don't think that I am denigrating the contributions and efforts of a brother who wishes to participate at any level. The world needs a generous service organization to sponsor hospitals and clinics and scholarships. Some men need a relatively wholesome place to meet socially once or twice a month with other relatively wholesome men. Add to this the possibility that some men might actually have a psychological need to put on clown makeup and drive tiny cars in parades.

Without men like this, Masonry would not be (for the time being, at least) the largest and wealthiest fraternal organization in the world. These are good men who *are* made better by their involvement in Craft. But there are also those among them who would like to be spiritually transformed by Masonry's deeper secrets, and currently these are the only men applying in any significant numbers. (Still, I'd wager that even some of the clowns in the tiny cars, if properly educated, might be fascinated by the esoteric side of things.)

The sad fact is, most Masons are never adequately exposed to knowledgeable brothers or material that might excite their curiosity beyond wondering, "What's for stated meeting dinner?" It's not that the

---

*Although there are several Masonic organizations, such as Co-Masonry, that accept both men and women, and other rites that are exclusive to women, "regular" Masonry remains for the present a men's fraternity.

information is not available. Plenty of fine books have been written over the centuries, some of which might be found in the libraries of local lodges all around the world. But many of these books were written in the 1800s at a time when interest in esoteric Masonry was at its zenith and when even a high school diploma meant a familiarity with Greek and Latin plus a smattering of philosophy, world religions, and history. Anyone who has ever started to read Albert Pike's *Morals and Dogma* will know exactly what I'm talking about.

What has been lacking for the modern Mason, and what Brother Stavish now mercifully presents us, is a straightforward, and step-by-step, study of Freemasonry and the myriad movements and ideas that gave birth to the Craft in all its manifestations. Moreover, he sets it all vis-à-vis twenty-first-century science, philosophy, and mysticism and challenges the reader to do the same. *The Path of Freemasonry* is a one-volume liberal arts education in Freemasonry, and never before in the history of the Craft has it been more important for individual Masons to be so educated. I wish I could put Brother Stavish's book in the hands of every new-raised brother, not simply for his own benefit, but for the benefit of those individuals throughout his life who will look to him as a worthy example of a knowledgeable and enlightened member of the fraternity.

May the blessing of Heaven rest upon us and all regular Masons! May Brotherly Love prevail, and every moral and social virtue cement us! Amen.

MASTER MASON'S CLOSING PRAYER

LON MILO DUQUETTE, 32°
AUTHOR OF *THE KEY TO SOLOMON'S KEY:
SECRETS OF MAGIC AND MASONRY*

How to Use This Book

While many books explain the rituals and symbols of Freemasonry, none have truly put them in the proper context so that we can understand why they are as important to us today as they were three hundred years ago. *The Path of Freemasonry* shows the reader how to understand the events that gave rise to Freemasonry, why they matter, and how to live a "Masonic" life as a creator, builder, and friend of divinity and humanity, whether or not you ever wear a Masonic apron.

While this book can be read as an overview of Masonic symbolism and ideas and their relationship to Renaissance and classical thought, it can and should be used primarily as a workbook for self-improvement, for self-improvement is what Masonry, esotericism, and the various modern therapies most readers will be familiar with are all about.

Begin each reading session with a prayer to the Divine Architect of the universe, the God of your understanding, to enlighten you on this very special and unique journey. Have a notebook handy and some colored pencils or pens. Read at least one of the books from each chapter's suggested reading list. Pay attention to your dreams as you progress through this book. Allow the ideas to stimulate your creative energies. Practice at least one of the assignments provided at the end of each chapter. Write down ideas, inspirations, and other things that come to you from "out of the blue" as you progress. Eventually, you can take what you have learned and put it to use in the world of action. Join a civic group, or volunteer for a nonpolitical, nonreligious cause. You might be surprised to see how much you are blessed by helping others, and how much you have to give. Give thanks daily for the blessings you have, and spend time in meditation and prayer as often as possible.

What Is the Secret of Freemasonry?

WHEN ASKED IF FREEMASONRY is a secret society, many Masons will simply reply that it is a "society with secrets." That is, there are things within Masonry that are, or should be, known only to members. A true secret society is just that: a secret. It hides its existence and conceals its motives from the public at large—and sometimes from its own members. As such, if Freemasonry is a secret society, it is a pretty poor one. Masonic halls, with their lodge and banquet rooms, dot most urban landscapes. Massive and ornate versions, often called "temples," in that they are temples of learning, can be seen in almost every major city in the oldest and most established sections of town. Thousands of books have been written about Freemasonry, many by Masons (such as this one), and hundreds of websites devoted to Freemasonry in all of its forms and varieties exist. Masons march in parades, support charities, and wear distinctive jewelry and ties and even put bumper stickers on their vehicles so that they may recognize one another when traveling. Despite this, many people often think of Masonry as secretive—something to be feared.

It has always been observed that Freemasonry conceals its secrets from the profane and extracts oaths to maintain that secrecy under pain of the most horrific penalties for oath breakers who violate them.* While

---

*It is interesting to note that the Old English word for an oath breaker is *wǣrloga*, or warlock, a name that, during the eighteenth century, became associated with a male practitioner of magic. This was a period when magic and esotericsm were deeply entrenched in the proliferation of Masonic rites.

1

this is true, it still raises the question of *"what"* exactly Freemasonry's secret is, or at least what it is about. Many authors have turned Masonry into their own personal publishing industry, writing an endless array of speculations about "the secret." For some, the secret is literally a buried treasure to be found somewhere underneath the Temple Mount in Jerusalem, Rosslyn Chapel in Scotland, or the famed Money Pit of Oak Island, Nova Scotia. For others, it is an esoteric secret, a form or style of initiation, possibly obtained by the Knights Templars during their stay in the Middle East and symbolized by their mysterious head of Baphomet. Others will say there are no secrets, except as you are able to find them, thereby making it a personal decision of each Freemason. Of late, many grand masters of various jurisdictions have pointed out that most of the Masonic rituals are published in some form that is more or less accurate, and as such, the only real secrets modern Masonry has are its signs of recognition between its members—funny handshakes, passwords, and other relics of bygone days when dues cards were not issued, membership was outlawed by princes fearing possible democratic challenges to their power, and Masonry was considered heresy by the Roman Catholic Church.

When the owner of Llewellyn Publications, Carl Weschke, first brought up the idea of my writing a book on Freemasonry in 2006, I was both pleased and somewhat taken back. It was no secret that within months, Dan Brown's runaway bestselling novel *The Da Vinci Code* would be released as a movie with a top-of-the-line cast, and everyone would want to get a piece of the action once Freemasonry became the hot topic of the season. The real question in my mind was how to write a book on Freemasonry that addressed the needs of the various readers, some of whom would be Freemasons, some potential Masons, and others simply interested in the topic. The more I thought about it, reflected on my own Masonic experiences, and talked to other members of the Craft—about their expectations from Freemasonry, their experiences, what they would like to see more of—the more it became clear that the message of this book extends well beyond the limits of a single movement, no matter how large or significant it may be.

Above all, it is important for each reader to know that there is no such thing as "*the* book" on Freemasonry. Masonry is defined as a system of moral teachings veiled in symbolism. This means that each Freemason is free to interpret their ritualistic experience in any manner they see fit and that no one can tell them they are wrong. This places Freemasonry in a peculiar situation, but one that clearly reflects the attitude of the age in which it came about. It provides an intellectually liberal framework wherein one can meet with others, while the secrecy protects the organization and its members to some degree from being targeted as challengers to the outside powers that be. If there is no creed of beliefs, other than belief in a Supreme Being, then it surely cannot be a religion, and as such does not compete with the religious establishment of the day.

Even so, those symbols used by Freemasonry that have their roots in religious and mystical practices—primarily those of the Jewish and Christian experience—also include elements, that while not identified, are clearly not biblical. Building, or creating, is the centerpiece of Freemasonry, and it was said for generations that the origin of the fraternity was to be found in the medieval building guilds. Oral traditions state that Freemasons, or their predecessors, were said to have possessed some occult secret carried back from Jerusalem or elsewhere and encapsulated it into the iconography of the great Gothic cathedrals. This theme was particularly expounded upon by the mysterious twentieth-century French alchemist Fulcanelli in *The Mystery of the Cathedrals,* wherein he states that the entire alchemical corpus can be found in the stonework of cathedrals such as Notre Dame and Chartres.

It is easy to see why such an idea could be stated and believed by modern minds. Even as I write this, I am listening to an album of music that was composed in the twelfth century yet is hauntingly timeless—*Vision: The Music of Hildegard Von Bingen*, performed by Richard Souther, with Emily Van Evera and Sister Germaine Fritz as the featured vocalists. When I first heard Hildegard's music many years ago, it became clear to me what the difference was between worship in the High Middle Ages and worship today, and why so many men and women long for a sort of Middle Ages that never was—Masonic and Rosicrucian scholar A. E. Waite among them. In the images of the tarot deck created under his direction, we see idyllic depictions of a rural Gothic world, wherein the quest for the Holy Grail is all-encompassing, and a seamless connection links the daily quasi-pagan/shamanic beliefs of the peasantry with communal church worship and initiatic mysticism.

The beauty, charm, and inspiration of what our forebears built in the name of Our Lady can be seen in every European city and town. The last vestiges of Celtic, Roman, Egyptian, and Germanic paganism were enshrined in Catholic cathedrals in the marble and wood statues of Mary, the Mother of Christ, the Child of the Sun, sending their silent message to future generations. Writing about these fabulous structures and the men who built them in *The Builders: A Story and Study of Freemasonry,* Joseph Fort Newton proclaims:

> Man was not meant to be a cringing being, eaten up by anxiety, shut up a prisoner in silent loneliness, living in blind cruelty. He was meant for great adventures, if he has the insight to see the laws of life and the key of kindness to unlock the doors; and in his quest for the best in others he will discover something in himself not guessed before. For each of us, though we may not be clever or commanding, but only average and unknown, life can be winged and wonderful, full of meaning and music, if we have the faith to trust the God who made us, and the wisdom to live, love, and learn.

Building is what Masonry is all about: building a better person, a better community, a better society, and a better world—all in that order.

We know what a community values based upon what it builds and what it allows to languish or decay. In the High Middle Ages, during the Gothic period, temples of stone and light were created to give praise to the Mother of God. These were once the central structures of a town or city, dominating the landscape, and often were the tallest buildings in the area, visible for miles away. Now we build skyscrapers of poured concrete to warehouse human beings as they move invisible money and information from one digital stronghold to another. These buildings belong to both the private interests that own them, as well as the bloated social services system that has drained creativity and responsibility from people for over three generations now. One need only look at the relationship in size of the Department of Social Human Services building in Center City Philadelphia, and compare it to the Grand Lodge of Pennsylvania (directly across the street from it), the neighboring Trinity Church, Philadelphia City Hall, or any one of a dozen office buildings to understand the message being sent of what is understood to be of value. Possibly the most well-known and least recognized example of architecture acting as an expression of hidden symbolism is the Pentagon in Washington, D.C. While the building takes its name from having five sides, few recognize that the pentagram and pentagon are both symbolically linked to Mars, the ancient Roman god of war. Here again, we know what a culture values by what it builds.

John Anthony West writes in the foreword to *The Return of Sacred Architecture: The Golden Ratio and the End of Modernism* by Herbert Bangs, M.Arch,

> Not so long ago, architecture was typically the highest and most complete artistic expression of a sophisticated civilization. It provided the framework within which the other arts forms manifested. It was where the lion's share of any given society's creativity was directed; the architecture expressed and enshrined the soul. In fact, if we had no written history at all, we would be able to get a very good idea of the living essence of any given civilization simply by looking closely at where its creative energy is expended: Ancient Egypt's creative energy went into its temples, pyramids, and tombs; Rome's went into its roads, massive civic projects, and coliseums; our today goes into an elaborate missile defense system and disposable products designed to feed our materialistic, consumer-driven culture.[1]

Thus, any building represents the ideals of the age in which it was built. The raw functionalism of modern architecture is enough to destroy any sense of the divine—and in turn, destroy any sense of the individual as something other than a walking bag of bones. What inspires us in the United States is the churches, cathedrals, even civic facilities such as museums, and of course Masonic temples, all built before the Second World War, and many in the nineteenth century. While we are still young by European standards, Continental snobbery should not be too proud, in that two world wars, a collapsed sense of national identity, along with the moral and ethical values of rampant social materialism, have done significant harm to them as well.

Through all of this, one of the single constants has been Freemasonry.

At the risk of redundancy later on in the book, it is important to keep in mind that the lessons of Freemasonry are universal in that they deal with human strivings and aspirations for improvement and the search for Light. Masonry also demonstrates the importance of commitment to a single ideal, and how that commitment can allow a movement to not only survive but grow under the pressure of opposition and even persecution. Those interested in community and organization should take note that Masonry is a perfect example of "centralized decentralization." While bound by specific and unchangeable landmarks, or specific Masonic signs, symbols, words, documents, and points, there is considerable variation in how Masonic degrees are worked from rite to rite as well as jurisdiction to jurisdiction. In a Masonic context the jurisdiction is the geographical region of a lodge, and its rites refer to the style and type of rituals as well as the lodge's attendant organizational and administrative structure. Each lodge is obedient to the grand lodge that charters it but has a wide range of autonomy regarding these aspects.

This autonomy, coupled with localization (meaning that members of the lodge come from within that lodge's community), has given a great deal of uniqueness to Masonic expression, for both better and worse. Masonry demonstrates a workable model for new and emerging spiritual movements to use if they seek to be more than Renaissance fairs without admission fees, or counterculture escapism.

Despite promises of perpetual progress, material abundance, and a world without suffering, everything that exists has its moment and then passes. Through its landmarks Masonry teaches, and demonstrates, that which is permanent and unchanging—the essence of a thing—and how to recognize it. For this very reason, the examples in this book have been taken from a variety of published Masonic rituals and jurisdictions. Normally such an approach would appear haphazard or unduly eclectic. However, since all of Freemasonry is united by its landmarks, and its rituals are localized expressions of those landmarks, filtered through the context of a particular place and time, it is possible to widen our understanding of Masonry and its lessons—lessons that can be applied equally by those outside the Craft—by examining those expressions.

If asked to define what characterizes a Mason, there could be no single answer. The virtues of faith, hope, and charity are all embodied in Masonry, as is the golden rule of "Do unto others as you would have others do unto you." If we take our cue from the degrees of Masonic initiation, we could see that a Mason—one who has worked to embody the Masonic ideal and is more than a dues payer or pin wearer—is first and foremost a gentleman. He is slow to anger, quick to forgive, generous with praise, and courteous in his speech. How he treats others is the rule by which he is judged and measured, and the fraternity as well. He is a scholar in that he seeks personal self-improvement and knowledge of himself, humanity, and the world in which he lives. Nothing is truly foreign to him, and the seven liberal arts and sciences (which we'll discuss in chapter 3) are his keys to self-awakening. A Freemason knows that by improving himself, he improves the world, and he becomes an example for his brethren and his community. He is religiously devoted, or, more accurately, mystically inclined. His attention is always drawn toward the ineffable and the sublime, as therein lies the Light of the Oriental Chair, that chair in the "East" of the lodge wherein the Master of the Lodge sits to preside over the work of the lodge. And within himself he constructs the Temple of Wisdom, that personal philosophical structure that allows him to commune with his own conscience, realization of God, and be of service to his fellow human beings. This is done in silence and without sound of hammer, mallet, or chisel, for only in the depths of silence can wisdom speak. He is a mystic last because this is the most private and personal thing about him. The fact that he is a good man, one who is generous to all and who encourages learning and self-becoming, is enough for others to know. He does not hide his Light, but he does not wear it as a badge of honor, either. If others see it in him, then so be it; if not, that is fine as well. Yet when asked, he freely shares his wisdom with others, and, if asked still, he will share how they too may find the Light within themselves, without being a braggart or proselytizing. In this way, the "secret" of Freemasonry is available for everyone to see, but like the Gospel, it is often veiled. As the proverb says, "Let those who have ears hear, and those with eyes see."

Many of my Masonic brethren who read this book will be taken back by the clear connection it makes between the Craft and the esoteric doctrines associated with the practical aspects of occultism—mainly ritual magic, alchemy, and astrology. For many Masons in the United States and elsewhere in the world, Freemasonry's symbols are seen as extensions of the Christian experience rather than what they are: the precursor to it. As even cursory research will reveal, within the context of the Judeo-Christian experience we find lingering traces of the ancient mystery traditions of Egypt, Chaldea, Greece, Rome, Persia, and India. The Masonic ritual experience is rooted in these same traditions, making it distinctly doctrinally non-Christian. For those Masons who object to this connection and fail to see what is before them, I suggest they turn to the King James Bible they were presented with upon becoming a 32nd-degree Mason in the Scottish Rite. Herein, they will find a series of questions and answers, many of which will surprise them if they take the time to read them and research the actual meaning of the words and their context.

The following is found within the first few pages of the Holy Bible prepared for the Scottish Rite, and given upon reception of the 32nd degree. It is published by Heirloom Bible Publishers, Wichita, Kansas.

Questions and Answers Relating to Characters, Places, Words, and Phrases Used in Symbolic Masonry

Taken from material by Mr. Charles H. Merz ("Ask Me Brother"), by permission of the publishers. Macoy Publishing Company, New York, N.Y. Arranged by S. J. Pridgen.

Q. Alexandria: Where was it and for what noted?

A. Egypt, School of philosophy for which Masonic teachers are greatly indebted for many of their splendid doctrines.

Q. "A.U.M." What do they mean, or signify?

A. The trilateral name of God, which is sacred among the Hindus as is the Tetragrammaton among the Jews, is composed of Sanskrit letters, sounding. A.U.M. *A* stands for Creator: *U* for the preserver: *M* for the destroyer or Brahma, Vishnu, and Shiva.

Q. Hebrew language: Why is it of the greatest importance in Free Masonry?

A. Because the alphabet and its numerical values is the key to the greater number of words employed in Masonry as well as the mysteries of the Bible.

Q. Hermes Trismegistus: Who was he?

A. The "Thrice Great," a celebrated Egyptian legislator, priest and philosopher, who lived about the year 2670. From the Hermetic Arts we have in Masonry, Hermetic Rites and Hermetic Degrees.

Q. Masons Wind: What is the fundamental idea?

A. Blowing from the East, in the belief of the Middle Ages, that all good things, such as philosophy and religion, come from the East.

Q. Monarch: What monarch, [is] the son of David, and [what] is the literal meaning of his name.

A. Solomon: Kabalistic composition, its outward form expressed the symbolism as the three principal officers of a Masonic Lodge. Sol, the sun; Om, the meridian sun; On, the setting son — Worshipful Master, Junior Warden, Senior Warden.

Additional questions and answers make reference to some of the ideas presented in this book, such as the mystical biblical patriarch Enoch, and the symbols that Freemasonry shares with the esoteric brotherhood of the Rosicrucians. Other unexpected subjects include placing the origins of Freemasonry in the oldest of ancient mysteries and the astrological sign of Leo, and making reference to the magical creature, or serpent, known as Shermah, which legend says Solomon used to build the Temple.

Once again, those with eyes to see and ears to listen will understand the importance of the above questions and answers both within and outside of a Masonic context. Regardless, some Masons will still hold true to their belief that Masonry is simply an extension of the Jewish-Christian experience, and to some degree this will always be true. However, the ancient mystery traditions are brought forth into the Masonic ritual experience. With this fact in hand, anti-Masons will find further justification for their vilification of the Craft, but then again, be it from this book or another, they would have found their rationale anyhow—even if it meant making it up!

A NOTE TO THE NON-MASON

Most readers of this book will not be members of the Craft. Some readers may know someone—a friend or family member—who is a Freemason and will simply want to know more about Masonry. Others may be interested in the so-called secrets of the fraternity and what they may be. Whatever the case, a non-Mason will, at some point in this reading, have to ask themself, "What does Masonic philosophy have to do with me if I am not a Mason? How can it make my life better?" Answering that question is exactly the reason this book was written. Masonic philosophy is universal, and the lessons it can teach us transcend sect or cult. Any readers who are practicing religious, initiatic, or esoteric organizations will find the exercises beneficial to their particular group. Some may even find themselves "a brother (or sister) without an apron."

Nullius in verba, "on the word of no one," best describes Freemasonry and any attempts to write a definitive book or encyclopedia on the matter. Masonry, as we will shortly see, is a vast topic and, as a living entity, has no official doctrines or creeds, only the requirement that one believe in a Supreme Being. While every effort has been made to demonstrate the direct relationship of the material presented herein to ancient and modern Freemasonry, it is in no way exclusionary. Each Freemason must come to understand the Craft to the best of their ability. This book is simply my effort at fulfilling that oath and obligation I took on my knees before the Altar of Light present at all Masonic initiations.

To be clear to the reader: Despite its philosophical and religious overtones, Freemasonry is not a religion, although it shares the purpose of religion in that it encourages the union of each individual with God. Masonry does not require any specific set of beliefs other than the belief in a Supreme Being, and even this is a fuzzy idea, being individualistic in meaning. While some say Masonry is a religious organization, it would be more accurate to describe it as speculative and philosophic. Masonry has no creed or sacraments, no means of salvation, and it is a human creation, not a divinely revealed one. In the end, Freemasonry is about self-improvement and helping others, because what we do on this earth is an expression of our understanding of our relationship to divinity. The rest is simply details.

MARK STAVISH
DIRECTOR OF STUDIES
INSTITUTE FOR HERMETIC STUDIES
WYOMING, PENNSYLVANIA
ST. JOHN'S DAY
DECEMBER 27, 2006
REAFFIRMED JULY 4, 2020

1

What Is Freemasonry?

The method of initiation, as we can see, is an essentially intuitive way. This is the reason why Freemasonry uses symbols to provoke that understanding which comes through analogy.

PAUL NAUDON, *LA FRANC-MAÇONNERIE*

FREEMASONRY HAS CAPTIVATED the public's attention since its inception because of its reputation as a society of secrets. However, in addition to secrets, or things known only to its members, Freemasonry is also an organization that possesses many mysteries—foremost among them the very origins of the Craft itself. As an organization, Freemasonry defines itself as "a peculiar system of morality, veiled in allegory and illustrated by symbols." And, as such, "Freemasonry makes good men better."

While interesting, these definitions are not terribly informative. To learn more we must examine the history of Freemasonry and how it came to be the meeting ground for men from all walks of life and philosophical persuasions at a time when class structure was rigid and religious wars ravaged Europe. Freemasonry (or, more accurately, the Order of Free and Accepted Masons) derives its system of initiation of three degrees from the techniques and methods of the early stonemasons guild as well as biblical accounts of the construction of the Temple of Solomon. From these two relatively simple resources, a complex structure of ritual, symbolism, philanthropy, and philosophy has risen. The symbolism is in part the mystery as well as the secret. Early on, symbols unique to Masonry, such as the Mason's Word (see page 118) and the legend of Hiram Abiff (see chapter 2), became the source of a great deal of speculation, suggesting that Freemasons were privy to secret esoteric teaching and occult operations. This reputation, coupled with the length and breadth of the organization as it grew, created a perfect climate for Freemasonry to become a vehicle for the promotion of certain spiritual ideas that were outside of the mainstream. While such promotions were more often private affairs rather than centrally directed by a grand lodge, Freemasonry became the happy hunting grounds for esoteric groups seeking members as early as thirty years after the formation of the first grand lodge. The reasons for this are simple: Masons were educated, socially connected, and able to travel relatively freely—and there may perhaps indeed have been some early occult influences in the formation of the first grand lodge.

OPERATIVE AND SPECULATIVE MASONRY

The medieval building guilds, or early unions, had their origin in the construction of the great cathedrals and public construction projects of the day. Given that many trades were passed down from father to son, or from master to apprentice, methods and techniques were jealously guarded not only to ensure proper training, but also to limit the number of workers in any given craft. Rites and rituals of progression developed around these organizations, all reflecting to some degree the dominant theme of religion in daily life and imbuing their trade with a religious or philosophical bent. Roman Catholicism and Eastern Orthodoxy are filled with patron saints, and many of these were linked with a particular trade, serving as a direct link to Christ or divinity and a conduit for divine blessing upon a particular field of work or endeavor.

Members of these guilds had means of recognizing one another during their travels as well as when applying for work on a specific project. That "secret code," as it were, fostered a sense of fraternalism extending beyond simple daily employment. At the same time, the method of transmitting guild knowledge from master to apprentice meant that in some way, even if only tenuously thin, members of these guilds could see themselves as connected to great builders of old, in a lineage going back to the Roman architectural colleges, the temples of Egypt, and even Solomon himself.

Despite their exact and precise knowledge, most of the members of trade guilds were illiterate. Those who were literate would have acted as the contractors on projects and communicated with the church or royal sponsors, thereby giving them some interaction with the ruling elites in the various cities, regions, and countries in which they traveled and worked.

Given this intimate connection and the well-established network of building lodges and related guilds that existed across Europe, it is no surprise that around the year 1640 men who were not operative stonemasons were admitted into Masonic lodges and, as such, were known as accepted or speculative Masons. Preference was given to relatives of operative stonemasons, but the initial reason for admitting nonstonemasons into the lodges appears to have been purely financial. The fees associated with membership were substantial, so along with them must have come benefits to outweigh the costs. What made this development unique—even pivotal—is that a host of middle-class professions suddenly found themselves seated together as never before. Within half a century the majority of masons in most lodges were accepted and not operative. In the 1700s this trend continued, with many lodges composed exclusively of accepted brethren, and not a single bricklayer among them.

This would be of little consequence if it were not for a series of events also occurring in Europe during the seventeenth century. Just as operative building guilds were accepting non-stonemasons into their ranks, the Thirty Years' War was coming to a close. The Rosicrucian Enlightenment—an attempt to promote Hermetic and esoterically inclined leadership across Europe in an effort to end sectarian warfare—had failed, and numerous groups and networks of educated, wealthy men with an active interest in esotericism, alchemy, Qabala, Hermeticism, and Utopian ideals needed a safe place to hide as well as meet. For many, the guild of Freemasonry may have been the perfect place, and not without precedence. As we will later see, the Knights Templar may possibly have used the masons' guild for the same purpose. On the run after the arrest of their brothers-in-arms in 1309, the Templars fled to Scotland, and possibly other areas not under strict papal control, and hid themselves among the stonemasons. This allowed them to still communicate with each other and travel without attracting too much attention.

The same would apply centuries later to Hermeticists on the run or seeking to have a safe means of travel, contact, and lodging when in foreign lands. The speed with which the operative lodges were overtaken by speculative members is critical to this line of thinking, as is the justification given for the formation of the first grand lodge, the Grand Lodge of England. The question we are constantly faced with is, "Why would educated, wealthy men actively seek to associate with other men who were clearly of a lower social class? What is it that the masons had to offer?" The answer, as we will later see, may very well have to do with one word: *geometry.*

During the Renaissance and the early period of the Enlightenment, mathematics was seen as a means to pure knowledge—access to the celestial realms of pure mind and idea. Math, as a repeatable and demonstrable method, gave certitude, which faith alone could not. It was the gateway to the rule of reason (rather than faith), and as a result, along with occult associations of numbers, math was against the law in the medieval era, and zero was forbidden as the Devil's number. It's critical here to understand that at this time, science, philosophy, and esotericism were not separate fields of study but had considerable overlap. Men of learning were at least superficially familiar with Jewish mysticism (Qabala), alchemy, astrology, and the theories of natural magic. Natural magic was the cornerstone of Renaissance philosophy and occultism; it proposed that the universe was composed of a series of interconnected energies, ideas, and planes of consciousness (complete with elemental, celestial, and demonic inhabitants) and that they could be affected through symbols, sounds, and physical acts such as alchemical and ceremonial operations.

Despite the climate of fear that surrounded the study of such things, not all societies investigating the hidden realms of nature were secret at the time. Among the most famous and influential was the College for the Promoting of Physico-Mathematical Experimental Learning, renamed the Royal Society of London for Improving Natural Knowledge in 1663. The Royal Society, as it became known, had King Charles II as one of its benefactors and included some of the most well-known Freemasons as its first members, including architect Sir Christopher Wren (who played a key role in rebuilding London after the Great Fire of 1666),* philosopher John T. Desaguliers, military engineer Robert Moray (an associate of Francis Bacon and René Descartes), and scholar Elias Ashmole.

ELIAS ASHMOLE:
ANGELIC MAGICIAN AND "FIRST FREEMASON"

Elias Ashmole (1617–1692) is often referred to as the "first Freemason" and falsely given credit in some histories as having cofounded the order.† This high praise, while incorrect, does point to the influence he had in the formation of early Masonic ideals, made possible through his love of learning and obsession with antiquity.

Born in the town of Lichfield, Staffordshire, in 1617, Ashmole attended the local school, became a lawyer, and established a practice in London.‡ He became a Freemason on October 16, 1646. Upon his marriage in 1649, his wife's estate allowed him to devote his entire

---

*Forty thousand buildings and eighty-six churches were destroyed in the Great Fire of London in 1666. As a result, operative masons from across England were needed to rebuild the city.

†Robert Moray (1608?–1673), for one, became a Mason before Ashmole. One of the 114 founders of the Royal Society, Moray was an avid researcher into alchemy, the science of the age—or, more accurately, the previous one, since it was increasingly coming under attack by more pragmatic and objective methodologies.

‡A small plaque adorning Ashmole's birthplace reads, "Priests' Hall, the Birthplace of Elias Ashmole, Windsor Herald to Charles II. Founder of the Ashmolean Museum, Oxford. Born 1617. Died 1692. Educated at Lichfield Grammar School."

time to scholarly research, which included alchemy, Qabala, magic, and astrology. He was an avid antiquarian, collecting numerous books and manuscripts. His extensive collection eventually formed the Ashmolean Museum at Oxford University, and among its most famous books were the original notebooks of Dr. John Dee and Edward Kelley detailing their "Enochian experiments"—communications with the spirit world. These notebooks eventually became part of the holdings of the British Museum and formed the core elements of the Enochian system utilized by the Hermetic Order of the Golden Dawn, Aleister Crowley, and later ceremonial magicians. In addition, Ashmole preserved important Hermetic and alchemical texts, including Thomas Norton's *Ordinal of Alchemy,* and authored a book on the early origins of the Order of the Garter, published in 1672. Titled *The Institutions, Laws, and Ceremonies of the Most Noble Order of the Garter,* this was to be his magnum opus.

Ashmole was close friends with astrologer William Lilly; they appear to have assisted each other in staying out of harm's way during the troubled years of the English Civil War and the Restoration of Charles II. Lilly, by all accounts, is the father of English astrology, having earned an amazing sum during his own lifetime from the accuracy of his predictions. His masterpiece of over eight hundred pages, *Christian Astrology,* was the standard reference book on astrology in the English language until the astrological revival of the late nineteenth century.

Like Lilly, Ashmole was not content to be merely a bookish scholar of the occult arts. He eagerly pursued operative methods of alchemy, astrology, and angelic magic—or the attempt to communicate with angels, the messengers of God through various ritualistic and meditative means—in his search for wisdom and knowledge of God.* He even cast a horoscope on October 23, 1667, to discover the most beneficial

---

*Coincidentally, the notion of an "angelic language" or primordial tongue, sought by many during this period, would eventually find itself in later Scottish Rite degrees, even referencing Athanasius Kircher and his discussion of an angelic alphabet, works well known to Ashmole and other Hermeticists.

time for King Charles II to ceremonially place the first stone of the Royal Exchange. Unfortunately, with the 1659 publication of Meric Casaubon's *A True and Faithful Relation of What Passed for Many Years between Dr. John Dee and Some Spirits,* attacks on the works of Dee, known to be in Ashmole's collection, created a whirlwind of controversy that would later be understood as the beginning of the end of the Hermetic worldview.

While much of the antimystical thought of the period was aimed at ending the proliferation of sects and the religious warfare that had decimated central Europe and England, it was also the beginning of a profoundly materialistic, mechanistic, and atheistic worldview that would come to full fruition in the twentieth century, with communism and laissez-faire capitalism as the primary examples.

Over the next three centuries, the scientific model—the basis for modern society—would become perfected but not fully understood. As a result, its technical applications became a replacement for genuine introspection, spawning such false philosophies as modernism, or the belief in eternal progress and a world without limitations, and the so-called scientific materialism of Marxism, atheism, and contemporary "consumerism."*

THE ROYAL SOCIETY

To fully understand the importance of the Royal Society and the contributions of its members, it is important to recognize that like any new organization it did not spring fully formed into existence. It took time to organize and grow, and it had its detractors in the press and church—as well as in that section of individuals who are little more than ignorance and hypocrisy wrapped in a veneer of respectability and known as "society."

The Royal Society was in many ways an extension of the philosophical ideas advocated by Francis Bacon and, in being so, was part

---

*This is most clearly seen in science fiction, particularly the *Star Trek* television series and movies, wherein no problem exists that that cannot be solved technologically.

of a stream of transmission of ideas and formation of groups aimed at transforming society and the world at large. This transformation, outlined by Francis Bacon in *The Great Instauration,* was based upon the fundamental learning of the day, which was all aspects of knowledge in terms of divine, human, and natural. To promote the studies of these things, particularly since divine and natural knowledge often included the study of Qabala, magic, alchemy, and astrology, Bacon created two schools, or groups. One school, the School of the Day, was open; the other, the School of the Night, was private. The secret School of the Night would give rise to the so-called Invisible College, an informal association of individuals involved in the investigation of the secrets of nature, and whose explorations put them in potential opposition to existing authorities of the time, some of whose members would later form the Royal Society and thereby influence the development of Freemasonry.

THE FIRST GRAND LODGE

In the early era of Freemasonry, Masons met in taverns and coffeehouses, naming their lodges after the place where they met. In February 1717 the Apple Tree lodge, the Crown lodge, the Goose and Gridiron lodge, and the Rummer and Grapes lodge met in the Apple Tree tavern on Charles Street in the Covent Garden district of London. Of the four lodges present, three were composed primarily of operative Masons, with some accepted Masons in their ranks. The Rummer and Grapes lodge was a different story, composed exclusively of accepted Masons, all gentlemen, and a few nobles as well. Their discussion centered around the future of Freemasonry in England.

What most concerned the members present was how to distinguish Freemasonry from other clubs and social groups in London at the time. Given that many of these clubs existed solely for the purpose of drinking, eating, gambling, and frequenting brothels, they wanted rules to establish who could be a Mason and codes of conduct expected from members.

The men who met in the Apple Tree tavern wanted to see

Freemasonry grow. They were living in the largest and fastest-growing city in Europe. Social mobility was increasing as workers moved in from the countryside and a merchant middle class exploded to meet their needs. Now, suddenly, skilled laborers, merchants, bankers, and nobles were all sitting together in one place: a Masonic lodge. To govern this body of men of mixed social rank—something unheard of before then—they decided to come together to form a grand lodge, and on June 24, 1717, they elected Anthony Sayer to be the first grand master for the Grand Lodge of England.* Sayer was a gentleman and accepted Mason. With his election to lead the Freemasons, the organization split further from its operative roots and moved into the future of speculative and, as we will later see, occult and philosophical Freemasonry.

ANDERSON'S *CONSTITUTIONS*

During the early years of the Grand Lodge of England, James Anderson, a Presbyterian minister, was asked to write a history of Masonry and in doing so to outline its rules and principles. The result was his *Book of Constitutions,* published in 1723. He used the word *constitutions,* in the plural form, in the title and throughout the work to demonstrate that this was not the idea of a lone individual or lodge but instead a synthesis of precepts, which were, in effect, an updated rendition of the Old Charges or Gothic constitutions. The Charges laid out in Anderson's *Constitutions* were later adopted almost universally by the various Masonic lodges, and even today, their annual reading to the membership is a common practice. In sum, the Charges state how a member of the Craft is to behave in relation to his brethren and society at large, and they extol the importance of religious observance, generosity, moral and ethical propriety, service to God and community, and doing noth-

---

*Given the murky nature of Masonic history, many histories of the organization simply work forward from the date when the first Great Lodge was founded in 1717, as there are few records about the Craft prior to 1717. This can lead to the assumption that Freemasonry has its origins in 1717, but that is inaccurate. For the first grand lodge to have been created, local lodges would have had to have been already in existence.

ing in public or private, with a brother or the profane (non-Masons), that would injure the good name and reputation of Freemasonry.

Among the most important of the rules presented in the *Constitutions* was that in order to maintain peace, harmony, and the good order thereof in lodges and activities outside them, Freemasons were forbidden to discuss politics and religion. The *Constitutions* require that Masons believe in a Supreme Being but do not state what that must be; the document simply refers to the "Grand Architect of the Universe." This nondenominational pronouncement created almost immediate love or hate for Masonry in an era when sectarian strife was always just below the threshold of all social, political, and economic activities. For the first time, through the vehicle of Freemasonry, men of all known sects and social status in England were sitting together in the same room in brotherly love and friendship. In the minds of many, this clearly could lead to no good. The Grand Architect of the Universe was seen as something other than the one God of the "one true faith," and Freemasonry's rituals were condemned as being the last vestiges of occult practices and, as such, contrary to the teachings of the church.

Among the most damning of protests came in 1738 from the Roman Catholic Church, which issued an edict forbidding its members to become Freemasons; later, other Christian sects issued prohibitions stating that Freemasonry was inherently a deist movement, and that leaving individuals to discover God for themselves could only lead back to the sectarian strife that had plagued Europe for generations. The Roman Catholic Church would continue to repeat this ban, as well as reasons for its justification, in ever increasingly hostile language, the most famous of which was Pope Leo XIII's "Humanum Genus," an encyclical (papal letter) published in 1882. The twenty-five-page document stated unequivocally that from the viewpoint of the Roman Catholic Church, Freemasonry was evil, as it was based on reason and not faith. Pope Pius XII picked up the anti-Masonic banner again in the 1950s, when he publicly denounced Freemasonry, along with other civic organizations, for being too liberal in their associations and religious views. In the early 1980s the Roman Catholic Church took a position that was less damning of the Masonry in general but still prohibited its members from joining; should they do so, they would not be able to receive the sacraments and would be in a state of "grave sin." Pope Benedict XVI restated this position in 1983 when, as Cardinal Joseph Alois Ratzinger, he led the Congregation for the Doctrine of the Faith, the successor organization to the office of the Inquisition.

Among other issues, the twin ideas of forbidding members from discussing politics and religion and having men of all classes sit in the same room with each other became a sore spot for others who saw in Freemasonry the seeds of egalitarianism. Here, it was feared, plots against governments would be hatched (and some were), and the right to have a say in representation (republican government) or the right to vote (democratic reforms) would only undermine the inherited rule of royalty. In many countries Freemasonry was forced underground to survive, as some saw it as a threat to the natural order. The Masonic principle that all members must be good citizens of the country in which they live was simply ignored by the Craft's detractors.

MASONIC LANDMARKS AND
THE MAKING OF A MOVEMENT

Among the more interesting aspects of Freemasonry are its landmarks. *Landmark,* in this sense, is defined as an ancient custom, practice, or peculiarity used by Masons in the performance of their rites. For example, in a Masonic rite one often hears Hebrew or Latin mispronounced—but mispronounced uniformly across a particular jurisdiction. This pronunciation is unique to Masonry, and therefore the accepted usage of the term or word. Landmarks are a strange thing in that no one agrees on how many there are; some lists count as few as three and others contain as many as fifty-four. There is no agreement on exactly what they are, either, but the majority of them are agreed upon by the various grand lodges and easily recognized by a visiting brother. As such, the performance of an initiation may be very different in some elements of form, but the key parts and elements will be recognized by visitors who themselves have experienced the same initiation elsewhere. For example, the structure of the lodge room, the placement of the officers, their duties, the methods of performing them, and the general dress and decorum are nearly identical across the Masonic landscape. Landmarks provide for a string or core of connection and continuity in a worldwide system that is quite diverse and independent in many regards.

Some of the landmarks listed by various authorities, such as Albert Mackey, are administrative in nature, such as the requirements to hold regular meetings, to have a personal recommendation for membership, and for petitioners to be able to pay for their membership from their own funds and come of their own free will. This last part is most critical, as no Mason should ever become a Mason unwillingly—because of undue pressure from friends or relatives, or for mercenary or other reasons—as this would make the ideals of Masonry null and their oaths a lie.

Landmarks are subject to change and innovation. For example, a small equilateral triangle was once used to represent the Grand Architect of the Universe; today, a Bible is usually used instead. With the Bible came the adoption of Scripture passages for use in each of the degrees: Psalm 133 for Entered Apprentice; Amos 7:7–8 for Fellowcraft; and Ecclesiastes 12:1–7 for Master Mason. However, these are only the most commonly used passages, and they are by no means uniform across jurisdictions and rites. Some rites and rituals continue to use the triangle in conjunction with the Bible or whatever Volume of the Sacred Law is present. The religious or philosophical text used as the Volume of the Sacred Law (VSL) varies from lodge to lodge and can even be changed at the time of initiation upon a candidate's request; that diversity is part of what distinguishes Freemasonry from a strictly religious or sectarian organization.

In addition to the VSL, two additional landmarks comprise the most rudimentary and basic tools, or furniture, as they are called, for a Masonic lodge to be opened: the square and compass. Together, the VSL, square, and compass are known as the Greater Lights. Despite whatever differences there are between rites, rituals, and jurisdictions, all three Greater Lights are required and must be present for a lodge of Masons to be in session. The Lesser Lights are the sun, the moon, and the master of the lodge, for as the sun rules the day and the moon rules the night, the master rules the lodge with justice and equity to all members. He is a living example of Masonic idealism.

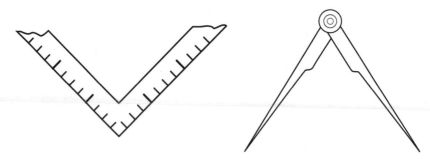

The square and compass

Charity and the Making of a Man

Freemasonry is fundamentally a spiritual organization that encourages individual spiritual research and expression without binding members to a specific creed, doctrine of belief, or practice. Instead, individual Masons must adhere to a moral code to improve their individual characters and, as such, that of the community, one person at a time, rather than through mass movements or legislation.

Action in terms of education comes via rituals that portray specific moral and ethical virtues as illustrated in the sacred literature and historic and mythic events. These initiations, as they're known, instill a particular set of symbols and ideas into the psyche of those who participate in them. Charity is the highest of virtues as it embodies all other virtues in itself. This then manifests primarily in personal conduct, community service, and defending liberties.

All members of the fraternity are equal and may avail themselves of the rights and privileges of membership without prejudice. One is often reminded of instances wherein men of great rank, power, and privilege sat in lodges while their servant presided as master of the lodge, and they subordinate to their servant in that responsibility. It is important to think of the role of master of the lodge as a responsibility, for it is a great one, and not simply a role one plays and then goes home. A great deal of time and attention is required while serving in that capacity. For this reason, past masters, who served and completed their term, are given special respect among members.

ANCIENTS AND MODERNS: THE CRAFT'S FIRST CRISES

In the years following the establishment of the Grand Lodge of England, the ideals of Freemasonry were put to the test. The Grand Lodge of England asserted its dominion over the other grand lodges that followed, particularly those of Ireland (1725) and Scotland (1736). Grand lodges opened in France; the dates are obscured but they appear to have been in existence prior to the mid-1730s. Germany (1737), Denmark (1745), and the Netherlands (1756) all established grand lodges. The first grand lodges in the English colonies were chartered by the Grand Lodge of England and located in Philadelphia (1731) and Boston (1733), with other grand lodges quickly following. Competing grand lodges soon came into the picture as well, forming in various countries to oppose what they perceived as the imposition of the dictates of the Grand Lodge of England on their independence. Many of these grand lodges existed for several generations but were eventually absorbed into the United Grand Lodge of England, while others, such as those in the colonies and on the Continent, maintained their independent status. The most significant of these counter-grand lodges resulted in many of the more interesting aspects of modern Masonry, including the battle between the Antients and the Moderns.

In 1751, within a generation of the publication of Anderson's *Constitutions,* which outlined the rules and regulations for Freemasons, a group of Irish Masons living in London formed the Antient Grand

Lodge. The Grand Lodge first formed in 1717 and forbade Irish Freemasons from attending London lodges in protest against what the Antients considered lax observance of Masonic traditions and landmarks. A crisis erupted between the two camps, with the Antients (or Ancients) advocating for a more elaborate, traditional observance of Masonry, and the Moderns, as they were known, advocating for more flexibility in lodge practice. Among the concerns of the Antients were the Moderns' lack of egalitarianism, neglect of lodge prayers, refusal to acknowledge the Royal Arch degree (discussed in chapter 9), and failure to observe the holy days of the saints John the Baptist and John the Evangelist.

Eventually, in 1813, the two camps would come together in an elaborate ceremony of harmony and union—true Masonic splendor—to form the United Grand Lodge of England. While the unification may seem like a minor point in the history of the fraternity, it is critical to see that Masons of the period were men of conviction and honor, and even when in deep disagreement with each other on issues they considered fundamental to the Craft, they were eventually able to come to a reasonable and workable resolution in true Masonic form and fashion. Their ideals were not simply ideals of convenience, but ones that they stood by—even if imperfectly—when tested.

The crisis of the Antients and the Moderns was another critical turning point for Freemasonry. Just as the acceptance of "gentlemen" into the lodges less than a century earlier had initiated their transformation away from purely operative guilds into wider social organizations, and the formation of the first grand lodge led to a larger cultural and civic movement, the struggle between the ideals of the Ancients and the Moderns would create a third transformation in Masonry: the rise of appendant bodies.

MASONRY AS A METAPHOR
FOR SELF-DEVELOPMENT

Since the days of the medieval guilds, Freemasonry had changed organizationally in its outward as well as its inward appearance. The metaphors embedded in the rituals of stoneworking were easily transformed into metaphors of human development on both the individual and social level. A better person was "built" and "raised," as was a better society. A building was designed for beauty, inspiration, reverence, worship, and function; applying the same process of reasoning to people and society could allow us better lives. The Masons believed that reason, intellect, and study of the seven liberal arts and sciences (grammar, rhetoric, logic, arithmetic, geometry, music, and astronomy) would supplement—and in many instances replace—the blind faith and devotion that the medieval church had required, and which was weakened during the Renaissance. Now, as western Europe stood on the edge of the Age of Enlightenment, God existed, but to know and understand the Grand Architect of the Universe, one had to first know and understand one's very self. Self-reflection, moral and ethical conduct, and self-improvement via the path of knowledge and wisdom and its most precise system—the scientific method—were the tools Masonry would encourage its members to use on their journey of self-discovery.

Embedded within the symbols of Masonry, just as they were embedded within the Gothic cathedrals centuries earlier, were the keys to that improvement—an improvement that was deeply personal, spiritual, and, as some of the key members of the Royal Society demonstrated, deeply esoteric. In the degrees of York and Scottish Rite, as well as numerous other rites long since dormant, mythology, history, and Hermetic symbolism would be preserved and demonstrated to the members. In keeping with true Masonic form, the symbols and ideals would be visible in structures, rituals, and initiations, but they would not be explained. This final note is critical, as each Mason must come to understand what is presented to them in their own manner. The keys of Hermeticism and related topics are ever present and ever hidden (in plain sight) in Masonic rituals, most of which were created during the prolific period of Masonic expansion during the eighteenth century.

What Is Freemasonry?
Key Points

1. Freemasonry defines itself as "A peculiar system of morality, veiled in allegory and illustrated by symbols."

2. The aim of Freemasonry is to "make good men better" through philosophy, charity, and fraternity.

3. The rituals of Freemasonry derive mainly from scriptural references to the building of the Temple of Solomon, specific Masonic mythology, and earlier trade guild practices dating from at least the Middle Ages.

4. Operative Masons are stonemasons engaged in the building arts.

5. Speculative or accepted Masons are members of Masonic guilds who are not operative masons but engage with the philosophical, moral, and esoteric applications of Masonic symbols and practices.

6. Two key figures involved in Freemasonry prior to 1717 were Elias Ashmole and Robert Moray.

7. Elias Ashmole is often referred to as "the first Freemason" and given credit for cofounding the order; though both claims are false, they point to the significant influence he may have played in Craft in the late seventeenth century. Ashmole was an associate of William Lilly, author of *Christian Astrology*, and was an avid collector of esoteric and occult manuscripts. Ashmole's collection of John Dee's materials are in the British Museum.

8. Robert Moray was one of the original founders of the Royal Society and an avid researcher into alchemy.

9. The first grand lodge, the Grand Lodge of England, was founded in 1717. Prior to that date, records of Masonry are scarce, though certainly the Craft was in existence.

10. In 1723, under the direction of the Grand Lodge of England, James Anderson, a Presbyterian minister, published the *Book of Constitutions,* which outlined a history of Freemasonry and its rules and practices.

11. The ancient customs, practices, and peculiarities unique to Freemasonry in the performance of its rites are known as landmarks. Though they can vary from lodge to lodge and there is no

set number for them, many are often easily identified by visiting Freemasons regardless of where they may be from.

12. The first major crisis in Freemasonry occurred in 1751 when a group of Irish Masons living in London formed the Antient Grand Lodge, splitting English Masonry into two camps: the Antients, who claimed adherence to older traditions, and the Moderns, who favored a more elaborate and philosophical presentation of the rituals. This split was eventually reconciled and gave rise to the current United Grand Lodge of England.

Assignments for Chapter One

1. Imagine the social environment of the seventeenth and early eighteenth centuries. Imagine yourself in that environment. How would you attempt to bring people together? What kind of network would you need? What would the rules be? How would you select, admit, and recognize members? What would be the single and most important unifying ideals? How would you begin to put those ideals into action?

2. Reflect upon your current involvement with society. What organizations do you belong to? Are they primarily for business advancement, entertainment, or personal development? Based upon your self-assessment, identify the various service organizations in your community, such as the Lions Club, Rotary Club, Kiwanis, or similar, and resolve to join one as a means of putting your highest ideals into action in a nonsectarian and nonpolitical fashion, without receiving individual credit for your actions.

What Is Freemasonry?
Suggested Reading

The Golden Builders: Alchemists, Rosicrucians, and the First Freemasons, by Tobias Churton (Red Wheel/Weiser, 2005). A well-written and detailed exploration of the earliest years of Freemasonry and its relationship to earlier traditions of alchemy and Rosicrucianism.

Gnostic Philosophy: From Ancient Persia to Modern Times, by Tobias Churton (Inner Traditions, 2005). A look at the broader context of personal spiritual practices and illumination as they relate to the Western esoteric traditions, of which Freemasonry plays a central role.

The Origins of Freemasonry: Facts and Fictions, by Margaret C. Jacobs (University of Pennsylvania Press, 2006). A spectacular and wonderfully readable exploration of the early years of Freemasonry by one of the world's leading scholars.

2

The Temple of Solomon and the Legend of Hiram Abiff

Thus Freemasonry did not claim to be the legitimate heir of the Temple, but it did not deny the existence of established traditional links between the Temple and Lodges.

JEAN TOURNIAC, *PRINCIPES ET PROBLÈMES SPIRITUELS DU RITE ÉCOSSAIS RECTIFIÉ ET DE SA CHEVALERIE TEMPLIÈRE*

WHAT PASSES FOR ARCHITECTURE in the modern world is often little more than a cross between crass utilitarianism, such as the poured concrete housing blocks of the Soviet era, and expressions of psychic neuroses come to three-dimensional life, in such acts of hubris as the Sears Tower (now called the Willis Tower), the entire city of Las Vegas, and the resort for the ultra-rich in Dubai where you can ski indoors despite the average daily temperature outside being well above 100° Fahrenheit. From these creations we clearly, albeit unconsciously, see the truth that each building is a temple of sorts, and each culture pays tribute to its gods by building them the largest and most centrally located temple they can conceive of. During the medieval and Renaissance periods, churches and cathedrals were the largest buildings in cities and occupied the central square. As civic life increased, this space was shared with governmental buildings, and by the nineteenth century we see the early beginnings of both religion and government starting to literally stand in the shadows of commerce and banking. By the middle of the twentieth century, the sky-scraper became the new tower of light to guide human footsteps, and by the end of the twentieth century, many of the largest and most centrally located buildings were for government social service programs.

Each one represents the true and most deeply held unconscious beliefs of its generation, and with each one we see a passing from art to function, from ideal to utility, from inspiration to death in a cubicle. The building is the inner world made manifest, the vision of the cosmos—and nowhere was this more visible than in the classical through medieval periods. The temple is the collective microcosm for everyone to see and participate in; it is the mythic history made flesh.

In the ancient world the dominant assumption was the immanent presence of the divine. In the modern world, whether in the false utopia of communism (as well as its contemporary insidious spawn of political correctness) or the vacuous consumerism and excessive quest for material wealth that capitalism has morphed into, the dominant theme is eternal progress under the direction of scientific materialism. It is no surprise that for decades, and with no end in sight, simplistic and radical forms of religious fundamentalism have attracted followers from not only the lowest classes of society, but increasingly from the middle and upper classes as well.*

THE TEMPLE OF SOLOMON

The construction of the Temple of Solomon is the most important historical event in Masonic lore and is the basis for all degree work—

---

*It is only fitting that in this light we remember the *Shiva Purana,* which states, "The end of the Kali Yuga is a particularly favorable period to pursue true knowledge. Some will attain wisdom in a short time, for the merits acquired in one year during the Treta Age (the second cycle, the Age of Ritual) can be obtained in one day in the Kali Yuga." In traditional Indian philosophy there are four stages of human spiritual awakening that occur in descending order. These are similar to those found in Greek mythology as well. Of them the highest is the Golden Age and the lowest is the Kali Yuga, or Age of Iron. Because few people will practice in the Kali Yuga, more effort is required, and therefore, better results can be obtained than in an easier age. The lesson is that we grow in skill and understanding only through overcoming difficulties.

including the explanatory degrees beyond Master Mason that further elaborate on and explain deeper meanings of the first three degrees and form the basis of Scottish and York Rites. The Temple of Solomon is, in no uncertain terms, the most important building in Western esoteric symbolism. While the Great Pyramid complex, the Temple at Luxor, and even the purely symbolic Vault of Christian Rosenkreutz play important roles, only the Temple of Solomon has continued to be both a historical and spiritual focal point since its construction, for both exoteric and esoteric beliefs and practices.

In *The Temple at Jerusalem: A Revelation,* John Michell, one of the world's leading exponents of sacred geometry, makes the following observation:

> The plan of the Temple as revealed to King David was, like the plan of the Tabernacle that preceded it, a composition of proportions and harmonies that represented the structure of the universe. It was measured by certain "sacred" units, all related to the foot as used today, and also related to the dimensions of the earth. Describing his vision of the Temple, the prophet Ezekiel mentioned three units in its dimensions: the cubit, the cubit-and-a-handsbreadth or greater cubit and the reed of six greater cubits.[1]

A cubit, Michell explains, is 1.728 feet. The cubit's duodecimal aspect (with 1,728 being the product of 12 × 12 × 12) can be seen when it is represented in feet, and it can be directly traced back to the units of measure used in the construction of Egyptian monuments, and the Great Pyramid in particular. He further points out that the various units of measurement from ancient civilizations—Greek, Roman, Egyptian, and Hebrew—relate to each other by simple ratios. Their essential unity and use worldwide suggests that they derive from an older civilization, as of yet undiscovered, that once occupied the planet Earth.*

In this same context, Michell also suggests that while the Temple of Jerusalem is generally seen only in the context of the Abrahamic

---

*For a detailed discussion of this topic, see *Uriel's Machine,* by Christopher Lomas.

religions, it was important to an older faith preceding them, but also issuing from the same cosmological font. He notes:

> Whether by chance or divine intent, Jerusalem has become the temple of four types of religion, issuing like the four rivers of paradise that rose from beneath the Temple towards the four directions, Jews to the east, Muslims to the south, Christians to the West and, in the direction of the north pole, followers of that ancient religious system that preceded the others.[2]

Constructed in the city of Jerusalem (whose name means "new peace") around the middle of the tenth century BCE and made of stone, cedar timbers, and gold, the original Temple of Solomon was a smallish structure designed to house the Ark of the Covenant. Details of the Temple's design and furnishings are given in 1 Kings 5:15–7:51 and 2 Chronicles 1:18–5:1; its dimensions are given as sixty cubits long, twenty cubits wide, and thirty cubits high. A cubit, later standardized in the Middle Ages, is approximately the length from the elbow to the tip of the middle finger, or about eighteen to twenty-two inches. (The word *cubit* derives from the Latin *cubitus,* "elbow.") From this we can see that the Temple was slightly over one hundred feet long, thirty feet wide, and fifty feet high. The central portion of the Temple was forty cubits long and constituted the holy of holies, or inner sanctuary. Here, behind a thick curtain, where only the high priest was allowed to enter, and only once a year, the Ark of the Covenant was kept.

The Ark of the Covenant was critical to early Jewish identity, as it contained the broken tablets of the Ten Commandments as received by Moses on Mount Hebron, and shattered by him when he saw the Jews worshipping before a golden calf. A great deal of legend and lore, both ancient and contemporary, are associated with the Ark, including the claim that it has occult powers.*

---

*The movie *Raiders of the Lost Ark* is the most famous of this genre, with recent publishers turning it and anything related to the Holy Grail, the Temple of Solomon, the Knights Templar, and Masonry into a publishing industry. Much of the material is pure speculation hung on the skeletal framework of a historical timeline and purporting to fill in the missing pieces.

It is interesting from a Masonic perspective that the symbolic ratio of length to width to height of the lodge is 3:1:2, similar to the battery of knocks or raps made by a master with his gavel to undertake business in a lodge. That ratio, as well the raw numbers of 60, 20, and 30, which conform to that ratio, have also been the subject of endless speculation from the symbolic perspective of sacred geometry and its numerology.

A Masonic lodge is laid out according to traditional geographic symbolism, with the entrance in the west, seating along the north and south sides, and the master's station in the east. The master of the lodge is the elected head of the lodge for his term. Senior and junior wardens are elected officers who assist in ritualistic functions and also in training for potentially serving as master in the future. The arrangement of officers is known as the "Line" as generally one first serves as junior warden, followed by senior warden, and finally master of the lodge. The senior and junior wardens have their positions in the west and south, respectively. No officer sits in the north. The Tyler is the outer guardian who sits outside the lodge room to see that no one who is not a Mason is allowed to enter while lodge is in session. This duty traditionally falls to the immediate past master of the lodge once their term of duty is completed, but that is not always the case. Additional officers are placed around the lodge, as well as outside it, and carry out both administrative and ritualistic functions.

Modern Masonic lodges parallel the general theme and layout of the Temple of Solomon. Two large pillars, called Jachin and Boaz, flanked the entrance to the Temple in Jerusalem. The Masonic lodge also holds two such pillars. Depending on the jurisdiction, some lodges have two large pillars directly inside the entrance of the lodge room. In others, the pillars are represented by the columns carried by the junior and senior wardens. Regardless of where they appear in the lodge room, the Masonic pillars are called the Pillars of the Porch, in deference to their location in the historic Temple. This hints at something few may notice about Masonic ritual: All three degrees take place on or around the entrance, and never inside the lodge proper, or the space that stands for the ancient Temple's holy of holies in particular. In the modern lodge this "holy of holies" is designated as an area between the master's station in the east and the altar in the center of the room.*

We find in 2 Chronicles 3:15–17 the following:

> Also he made before the house two pillars of thirty and five cubits high, and the chapiter that was on the top of each of them was five cubits.
>
> And he made chains, as in the oracle, and put them on the heads of the pillars; and made a hundred pomegranates, and put them on the chains.
>
> And he reared up the pillars before the temple, one on the right hand, and the other on the left; and he called the name of that on the right hand Jachin, and the name of that on the left Boaz.

Jachin and Boaz are probably the most well-known and best-recognized symbols of Masonry that give it a powerful link to earlier esoteric traditions, particularly Jewish mysticism or Qabala. In the *Sefer Yetzirah,* one of the earliest Qabalistic manuscripts, these pillars are mentioned in relation to the Tree of Life and the Ten Spheres of Creation, or Sefirot.† These spheres are utilized extensively in Qabalistic practices, and together they are said to represent a ladder to heaven. In Masonic symbolism the ladder, as well as the staircase, represents man's rise from ignorance to illumination, or from crudeness to refinement.

In the *Sefer Yetzirah* we read:

> The appearance of the ten spheres out of nothing is like a flash of lightning, being without an end, His word is in them, when they go and return; they run by his order like a whirlwind and humble themselves before His throne. (Chapter 1, section 5)

---

*Other aspects of the lodge draw more upon Masonic allegory and mythology than historical facts. These include the ornaments of a lodge, whose major symbols are a checkerboard floor, trestle board, and pentagram. These ornaments are by no means universal and, like so many things, will be present in one jurisdiction but absent in another.

†For more information on the Tree of Life and the Sefirot, see *Kabbalah for Health and Wellness: Revised and Updated* by Mark Stavish (2017).

... These are the ten spheres of existence, out of nothing. From the spirit of the Living God emanated air, from the air, water, from the water, fire or ether, from the ether, the height and depth, the East and West, the North and South. (Chapter 1, section 9)

... He created a reality out of nothing, called the nonentity into existence and hewed, as it were, colossal pillars from intangible air. (Chapter 2, section 6)

The First Temple of Solomon stood for approximately five hundred years, or until 586 BCE, when it was destroyed by the Assyrians after a failed revolt by the Jews. For seventy years it lay in ruins, after which much of the population of Israel was deported to Babylon, beginning the period known as the Babylonian captivity. It was during this period that the "Babylonian Talmud" was created, and Jewish angelology and demonology were influenced by prevailing Babylonian traditions and magical practices. When the Babylonians were in turn conquered by the Persians, King Cyrus allowed Ezra and seventy followers to return to their homeland to see what had become of it and its remaining inhabitants. What Ezra found was little more than people living in hovels and ruins, Jews in little more than name only, with no knowledge of their religious beliefs or practices. When the remaining Jews were allowed to leave Babylon and join with Ezra, the Temple was reconstructed, approximating the original design of the First Temple. This Second Temple was later renovated by King Herod, with construction beginning around 20 BCE, and razed by the Romans in 70 CE after another failed Jewish uprising.

The Temple was a source of much myth and mystery throughout the Middle Ages. During the Crusades the Knights Templar established their first headquarters in the old stables of the ruined Temple. This in turn would give rise to endless speculation about their activities, with recent archaeological evidence showing that extensive tunneling was undertaken during the Templar period.

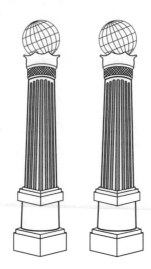

Jachin and Boaz: the Pillars of the Porch

SOLOMON AS MAGICIAN

Solomon, Israel's third king, ascended to the throne upon the death of his father, King David, at the end of the tenth century BCE. The forty years of Solomon's reign (c. 986—c. 933 BCE) was the high-water mark of the Israeli kingdom. This was due in no small measure to David's accomplishments, Solomon's own managerial skills, and the temporarily weakened state of the neighboring empires of Egypt and Babylon.

Solomon's reputed wisdom is well known and recorded in biblical narratives, popular myth, and even modern media. Gnostic references to Solomon also exist, including one of the Nag Hammadi texts. His wisdom encompassed the fields of magic and related occult arts. Books on invocation and magic are attributed to his authorship as early as the first century CE.

One of these books, called the Testament of Solomon, tells how he built the First Temple through magical means that constrained the power of fifty thousand *jinn,* or magical beings (possibly demons), to do his work.

In *Antiquities of the Jews,* written around 93 CE, Jewish historian Flavius Josephus notes, "He [Solomon] was no way inferior to the Egyptians, who are said to have been beyond all men in understanding. . . . God also enabled him to learn that skill which expels demons, which is a science useful and sanitive to men."³

This image of Solomon as magus continued to grow, even paralleling that of Thoth, or Hermes Trismegistus, so that by the time of the Middle Ages and early Renaissance these two figures—one Egyptian or "pagan," the other Jewish—were seen as the archetypal magicians.

In an age when magic was seen as the work of the devil, the pentagram known as the "goat's foot," and witch hunting (and pogroms against the Jews) in one form or another just a memory away, considerable effort was given to sanitize and mainstream these esoteric ideas.

To make them acceptable Hermes was said to be a contemporary of Moses, and, of course, Solomon the Wise was a magician who used his knowledge only for good.

However, this whitewashing was less than universally accepted. A collection of writings known as the Solomonic literature formed the basis for a branch of magic known as Solomonic magic. These books included the Testament of Solomon as well as the well-known *Lesser Key of Solomon* and *Greater Key of Solomon,* the *Book of Solomon on Gems and Spirits,* the *Shem ha-Mephoresh of Solomon the King,* and a variety of books on the notary arts. The notary arts comprise an area of magic that would have been of particular interest to Renaissance scholars in that it is purported to allow one to learn any subject quickly and without difficulty. Solomon is reputed to have received his knowledge directly from God, and yet despite this (or possibly because of it being too Gnostic in tone), the Roman Catholic Church took exceptional rebuke to the notary arts, condemning them repeatedly and destroying copies of books on the subject whenever they were found. Middle Eastern and South Asian folklore supports the view of Solomon as a magician, and much of what we know in this context has come to us from *A Thousand and One Arabian Nights.* Translated by Sir Richard Francis Burton (and published as *The Book of a Thousand Nights and a Night*), the unexpurgated stories are contained in sixteen volumes and were published between 1885 and 1888.

Burton was among the world's most renowned travelers, linguists, and lovers whose adventures took place at the height of the Victorian era. He was a Freemason, initiated into the Hope Lodge of Karachi, in India. His fascination with the ancient tales began early in his career, and he made a point of collecting as much information and variations of the stories as he could in his extensive travels across North Africa, the Middle East, and Asia. Burton's translation is still considered unsurpassed, not only because of its rendering of the poetry, but maybe even more importantly because of his notations drawn directly from his experience with Arabic and Muslim culture, lore, folk magic, Sufi mysticism, and sexuality.

The *Arabian Nights,* as the collection is commonly known, is essentially a series of stories within the framework of a larger story, with magic, mysticism, and various mythical beings playing key roles. The longest of the stories, said to have been told for fifty-three nights, is "The Queen of Serpents," and it is directly connected to the mystical experiences revered in many Asian cultures. Alchemical and magical symbols form the imagery, among them the famous ring of Solomon, the mystic symbol of divine union, by which Solomon keeps jinn, or demons, sealed in a brass vessel. Of interest to Masons and Rosicrucians, however, is that the main focus of "The Queen of the Serpents" is the quest to find the tomb of Solomon, said to be hidden in the sacred mountain of Qaf. Qaf, according to Burton, was a rendition of the Persian Alborz (the Elburz Mountains in modern-day Iran). It is in Alborz that the Zoroastrian redeemer waits for the Second Coming of a "Great Messenger" and the end of the world. According to the legend as told by Burton, it is here in this sacred mountain that the coffin of Solomon rests after having been transported across the Seven Mystical Seas.

Burton further notes that the symbolism used in the *Arabian Nights* is definitively Sufi in many respects, and the symbol of the bird, the Middle Eastern ideogram of the soul, is a common motif. The flight of the bird denotes the human search for divine realities, its pilgrimage across life. Burton translates this wandering as "traveling," and those who undertake it as "travelers," a common term for a Freemason.[4] Similar themes appear in the *Picatrix,* an Arabic text of magic and mysticism dating back to the Renaissance, or possibly older.

PICATRIX

The *Picatrix* is a comprehensive text on sympathetic and astral magic that carried substantial weight in Renaissance circles. It is primarily concerned with the construction of talismans (or physical magical images) based on zodiacal position of the planets, and the creation of prayers, or invocations, to the spiritual power personified by the planets. Over fifty images (possibly of Babylonian origin),[5] along with the appropriate times, places, attitudes, and ritual gestures, are all described so that the operator might successfully invoke the power of their chosen planet. The title of the work, *Picatrix,* is the Latin name given to the 1256 translation of *Ghayat al-Hakim fi'l-sihr* ("aim of the sages by means of magic"), an Arabic text on magic usually attributed to the eleventh-century Muslim Spanish mathematician al-Madjriti.* The Latin text, widely used in the Renaissance, differs slightly from the Arabic original and is shorter. While never printed it enjoyed a wide circulation in manuscript form throughout the fifteenth and sixteenth centuries.[6]†

Precious stones and gems are the preferred substance upon which to make a talismanic image. In fact, gems bearing the images of deities were in use into the medieval period, and even many monasteries had their own cameos, as well as relics, crosses, books, altars, and reliquaries mounted with gems of one sort or another.

However, the knowledge of how to actually carve these images into gemstones was lost somewhere between the second and third centuries. The practice of creating them was replaced with simply possessing the

---

*The title, *Picatrix,* is possibly a corruption of the name Hippocrates, and its images are possibly of Babylonian origin. See *The Survival of the Pagan Gods,* by Jean Seznec (Princeton, N.J.: Princeton University Press, 1981), 53, 60.
†The original Arabic text was translated first into Spanish, under the sponsorship of Alphonso the Wise, king of Castille; unfortunately, that Spanish manuscript has not survived. It was later translated into Hebrew under the title *Takhlit he-hakham.*

corresponding gem itself, and even the passage in the *Picatrix* detailing the creation of such talismans appears to be missing.

CLAVICULA SALOMONIS

The *Clavicula Salomonis,* or *Key of Solomon,* is among the most famous magical texts and continues to exert an influence in magical circles to this day. Purported to have been written by King Solomon, the text gives thirty-six different talismanic images, as well as detailed instructions for their construction, use, and purpose. The talismans are described according to their relationships to the seven classical planets.

Like Moses, Hermes Trismegistus, and others, Solomon is often linked with magical texts because of the extensive mythology that surrounds his kingship. He is said to have possessed a magic ring and used it to control fifty thousand demons for the construction of his famous temple. Despite being pseudo-epigraphical—that is, compiled by someone other than their attributed author—many of these books are still thought to be of magical value.

Rather than having its true origin in the hand of King Solomon himself, the *Clavicula Salomonis* was a much later creation and is a composite of Christian, Jewish, and Arab magical elements. It was in fact translated into Hebrew during the seventeenth century to support this purported antiquity. Similarly, the famous work *The Book of the Sacred Magic of Abra-Melin,* purported to have been written by "Abraham, the Jew of Worms" in the fifteenth century, was in fact originally written in German.[7]

The majority of the talismans described in the *Clavicula Salomonis* use either a five-pointed star (pentagram) or a six-pointed star, often called the Shield of David (*Magen David*). This symbol, though now universally identified with Judaism, was used as early as the Bronze Age and appears in cultures as widely dispersed as Britain to Mesopotamia, with Iron Age examples coming from India and Iberia.[8]

The use of the symbol came into frequency for Jews and their neighbors by the Second Temple period, where it was used alongside the pentagram and along with the swastika by the second or third centuries, though it may have had only decorative purposes. The hexagram does not appear in any of the magical papyri, or Jewish magical sources, and is not associated with such practices until the early medieval period.

In Arab texts the hexagram was used along with other geometrical symbols and was known as the Seal of Solomon, a term later adopted by many Jews and, by the sixth century, Byzantine Christians. From the thirteenth century onward, the symbol appears in Hebrew Bibles from both Germany and Spain.[9]

Arab magicians used the symbol widely, even to some degree using it interchangeably with the pentagram. In Jewish circles its use was much more limited. However, the idea of it having some kind of magical power may have come from Islamic sources. It is in the Qur'an that David is first seen making use of the hidden, inner magical teachings of Judaism.[10]

From the thirteenth through seventeenth centuries, the magical meaning and use of the Shield of David increased in popularity, complexity, and meaning. In the fourteenth century Charles IV allowed Jews in Prague to create a flag for their community. That flag featured the Star of David, thought to be the first time the symbol was used to denote a distinctly Jewish community. By the nineteenth century Jews began to use the Shield of David to represent Judaism as a whole, in the same fashion that the cross represents Christianity, and the symbol took on widespread use. It appeared in books, religious literature, and letterheads of Jewish organizations, in synagogues, and elsewhere.[11]

SHEKINAH: GODDESS OF THE TEMPLE

The Temple of Solomon was unique in that within it the presence of God was said to dwell and be directly experienced by those present. This divine presence, known as *shekinah,* is described as being a great billowing cloud that manifested during rites and was physically palpable and tangible. Shekinah has distinctly feminine attributes, and in oral tradition and in the Zohar, her presence is described in sexual imagery. While some suggest that this may reflect the survival of earlier polytheistic traits within primitive Judaism, others suggest that Solomon may have been secretly involved in a cult of Astarte, and that during the Roman period a temple to Venus was established on the Temple Mount. All of these theories reflect worship of a feminine divinity.

The Temple of Solomon, and even Solomon himself, are linked to the worship, expression, and concrete union with the creative power of the cosmos in distinctly feminine and sexual terms. While this connection is lost to most Jews and Christians, it may find its partial survival in the the "Genius of Freemasonry," the guiding spirit of Freemasonry, who is clearly feminine and is invoked at the closure of every lodge meeting. She is called Wisdom, and is possibly identified with Sophia.

As we will see later, this notion of a feminine presence of deity in and through the immediate material world was of great importance to the Renaissance adepts. In their time, the *anima mundi,* or "soul of the world," was described as being female, and alchemy and geometry were both personified as being female. We even see the great revelations of the period, such as that detailed in the 1616 manifesto the *Chymical Wedding of Christian Rosenkreutz,* being preceded by the visitation of a feminine angel. And in Freemasonry important concepts such as Wisdom, the Word, and Holy Spirit are also feminine in nature and are cornerstones of Craft symbolism.

SOLOMON AND THE DIVINE FEMININE

It is clear that Solomon worshipped at more than just the altar of Yahweh, God of the Jews, perhaps in part as a result of his introduction of workmen from neighboring regions into Jerusalem to assist in the construction of the Temple. The design and construction of the Temple adhered closely to the standards of their own Canaanite and Syrian temples, in particular Tell Tainat, a ninth-century BCE Syrian temple. The excavated remains of Tell Tainat show a temple divided into three sections—entrance, nave, and vestibule—along with two pillars at the entrance. Brass work executed by Hiram Abiff, the architect of the Temple, was also similar to that of other eastern Mediterranean cults. The reason for this was simple: during this period, the fundamental ritualistic differences between the cult of Yahweh and neighboring cults was nominal, the main difference being in moral and cosmological teachings.

Yet despite Solomon having compromised his devotion of Yahweh, biblical condemnations of him are tame by comparison to others who deviated from the one true faith. It is clearly stated in the First Book of Kings, and again in Josephus's *Antiquities of the Jews,* that his introduction of additional cults into Jerusalem was a result of his marriage to foreign princesses; however, the apologists are only partially correct. These introductions were made not when he was old but during the construction of the Temple, and they were essential to it. Political marriages were crucial to Solomon's ability to maintain peace on his borders; in this way, instead of maintaining a large army, he could free up manpower for his massive civil and religious construction projects.

Solomon is said to have worshipped at the altar of Astarte; however, this is possibly a confusion with the goddess Asherah, who was well known to the Jews and introduced into Jerusalem as a result of Solomon's marriage to a Sidonian princess. Asherah was an agricultural and fertility goddess, and like many deities in polytheistic culture, she was often amalgamated, and at times confused, with other deities. Asherah would have been well known to the Sidonian and Tyrian workmen Solomon was importing to construct his temple to Yahweh.

HIRAM ABIFF AND THE
UNIQUE MYTHOLOGY OF FREEMASONRY

While Masonic initiation and allegory quote liberally from the Jewish scriptures, there is in fact little about Masonry that can be historically linked to the Bible. The majority of Masonic ritual is a composite myth or morality tale, created to make a philosophical or moral point rather than an intellectual one. However, since few of the rank and file members of the fraternity are well versed in either religious scriptures or history, this point is often missed, and they will routinely state that Masonry is found in the Bible. It is more accurate to state that the Jewish and later Christian scriptures can be found in Freemasonry. A perfect example of this kind of myth making is in one of the core figures of Freemasonry: Hiram Abiff, the grand master slain by his fellows around whom the entire 3rd degree is devoted. As A. E. Waite writes in *A New Encyclopedia of Freemasonry*:

> The Legend of the Master-Builder is the great allegory of Masonry. It happens that his figurative story is grounded on the fact of a personality mentioned in Holy Scripture, but this historical background is of the accidents and not the essence; the significance is in the allegory and not in any point of history which may lie behind it.[12]

To confound matters the name Hiram is used twice in Masonic ritual and myth: Hiram, king of Tyre, and Hiram the Builder. Together with King Solomon, they constitute the three traditional grand masters of primitive Freemasonry.

Hiram, King of Tyre

King Hiram of Tyre was a friend of King Solomon who, according to Scripture, assisted him in building the First Temple, the temple around which all Masonic initiation is predicated. Upon Solomon's coronation Hiram sent ambassadors and gifts. Solomon requested Hiram's assistance in constructing the temple at Jerusalem, and Hiram in turn sent money, men, and supplies, with the reply:

"I will do all thy desire concerning timber of cedar and timber of fir. My servants shall bring them down from Lebanon unto the sea; and I will convey them by sea in floats, unto the place that thou shall appoint me, and will cause them to be discharged there, and thou shalt receive them; and thou shalt accomplish my desire in giving food for my household" (1 Kings 5: 8–9).

Hiram had timber cut and sent to the port of Jaffa and from there moved overland to Jerusalem.

In return, Solomon gave extensive wheat and oil to support the labor Hiram had sent, and he gave to King Hiram as well twenty cities in the region of Galilee. Apparently, Hiram was not pleased with this gift and personally visited Solomon to inform him of his displeasure.

Hiram the Builder

While King Hiram of Tyre and King Solomon of Israel play important roles in Masonic mythology, they are behind-the-scene players compared to Hiram Abiff. This Hiram, also known as Hiram the Builder, was among the workmen sent by the king of Tyre to assist in the construction of the Temple of Solomon. He is described in Masonic ritual and Jewish scripture as "a cunning man, endued with understanding" (2 Chronicles 2:13) and "a widow's son of the tribe of Naphtali, and his father was a man of Tyre, a worker in brass; and he was filled with wisdom and understanding, and cunning to work all works of brass" (1 Kings 7:14).

The name Abiff is derived from the Hebrew word *ab*, "father," and is a designation of high standing and respect. He was, in fact, an advisor and friend to both kings. This name is used to make a clear distinction between Hiram the King of Tyre, and his loyal architect and friend, Hiram the Builder, or architect. The unique reverence for Hiram the Builder within Masonry gave rise to the now archaic term Hiramites, in reference to Freemasons in general, and those in particular who claimed that the fraternity descended from the architect of the Temple.

The esoteric significance is that Hiram the Builder constructed the two pillars, Jachin and Boaz, and both the Builder and Solomon were filled with wisdom (*hockmah*) and understanding (*binah*), the two spheres of the Tree of Life that cap the pillars. On a spiritual level the two are equal—possibly even unequal, with Hiram being the superior of the two, since it is he who is later slain and he whom the legends of the Craft and its secret wisdom are woven around.

According to the Bible Hiram Abiff "set up the columns at the portico of the Great Hall; he set up one column on the right and names it Jachin, and he set up the other column on the left and named it Boas. Upon the top of each column there was a lily design. Thus the work of the columns was completed" (1 Kings 7:21–22).

The columns were decorated with pomegranate designs, signifying fertility and abundance—the pomegranate being the original apple of the Tree of Knowledge of Good and Evil from the Garden of Eden. If the Tree of Knowledge could corrupt man and cause his fall from grace, then the Tree of Life could provide the means of restoring man to his original glory.

From this we have a peculiar insight into Masonic allegory and its subtle teachings of equality and authority. The three traditional grand masters are all equal in the work, as it takes Solomon's wisdom to envision the Temple, the king of Tyre's wealth or strength to construct it, and the skill of Hiram the Builder to add beauty to the finished design. Herein lie the three pillars of Freemasonry—wisdom, strength, and beauty. These are symbolized by the three principal officers of a Masonic lodge—the master, senior warden, and junior warden. It is these officers who, each in turn, rule a lodge, direct its work, and initiate new members. If they are absent, a lodge cannot be opened.

The Temple of Solomon and the Legend of Hiram Abiff: Key Points

1. Modern architecture is utilitarian and devoid of any spiritual value. That is, it fails to inspire us to greatness or encourage selfless acts or visions beyond materialism.

2. Civilizations can be known by their architecture; a building is the inner world made manifest in three dimensions, in the material world. It is a collective microcosm for everyone to see and participate in, or the myth made flesh.

3. The construction of the Temple of Solomon in Jerusalem is the single most important event in Masonic lore, and in some fashion it is the basis for all of the Craft's rituals and degrees.

4. The Temple is a composition of proportions and harmonics that represent the structure of the universe.

5. Two sacred pillars were built on the porch to the Temple: Jachin and Boaz. A description of the pillars is found in the *Sefer Yetzirah,* an early Jewish mystical text, which links this aspect of Masonic symbolism to both biblical and esoteric interpretations and the Tree of Life.

6. Masonry is constructed upon the three pillars of wisdom, strength, and beauty. These ideals are represented in the lodge through the three key officers: master, senior warden, and junior warden.

7. Masonic lodges have ornaments that distinguish them from other buildings. Among these are a checkerboard floor, a trestle board, and a pentagram. These ornaments are not universal to all jurisdictions.

8. Solomon is known across the Middle and Far East, particularly within Jewish and Arab folklore, as a magician who used occult means to construct the Temple. Many of these stories are found in Sir Richard Francis Burton's sixteen-volume translation of *A Thousand and One Arabian Nights*.

9. Medieval and Renaissance conceptions of Solomon adhered to this image of him as a magician and resulted in numerous manuscripts being attributed to him. *The Greater Key of Solomon* and the *Lesser Key of Solomon* are the most popular of the Solomonic literature.

10. During the rites in the Temple, the *shekinah,* or divine presence, was said to manifest. Its distinctly feminine attributes led many to believe that Solomon was also secretly worshipping the goddess Astarte. During the Roman period a temple to Venus was established on the ruins of the Temple. Masonry, in turn, refers to the "Genius of Freemasonry," the guiding spirit of the Craft, in distinctly feminine terms.

Assignments for Chapter Two

1. What more can you learn about Solomon, magic, shekinah, the Sefer Yetzirah, and Qabala and their connections to Masonry?

2. Examine the buildings in your immediate environment and write down clearly the feelings they evoke within you.

3. Using these feelings, write down the spiritual qualities your architectural environment might embody. What kind of changes might need to be made to improve them?

4. Brainstorm three practical ways you could improve the spiritual qualities in your neighborhood and community.

5. What does your particular spiritual tradition have to say about the concept of the divine feminine? What is the importance of this principle to physical and psychological well-being?

The Temple of Solomon
and the Legend of Hiram Abiff:
Suggested Reading

The Key to Solomon's Key: Secrets of Magic and Masonry, by Lon Milo DuQuette (CCC Publishing, 2006). DuQuette offers an informed and provocative introduction to the suggested relationship between the Temple of Solomon and the traditions of medieval "Solomonic" magic.

The Hebrew Goddess, by Raphael Patai (Wayne State University Press, 1990; orig. pub. 1967). Patai's examination of the divine feminine in Judaism is a seminal work on the hidden role and survival of goddess worship in monotheistic traditions.

The Temple at Jerusalem: A Revelation, by John Michell (Samuel Weiser, Inc.: 2000). One of the most intriguing and important works on sacred geometry, geomancy, and earth energies.

From the Ashes of Angels: The Forbidden Legacy of a Fallen Race, by Andrew Collins (Bear and Co., 2001). A detailed and well-researched look at heretical views related to the interactions of humanity and angelic beings.

3

Masonic Initiation
and the Blue Lodge

*Initiation essentially aims to go beyond the possibilities of
the individual human state, to make possible the transition
to higher states and finally to lead the individual beyond
any limitations whatsoever.*

RENÉ GUÉNON, *PERSPECTIVES ON INITIATION*

MASONRY IS A FRATERNAL ORGANIZATION whose activities are
centered around the lodge rituals. To become a member one must apply
for and be accepted as a candidate for Masonic initiation. It is possible
to apply for lodge membership and undergo investigation by the membership committee only to find that one's application has been rejected,
or blackballed, referring to the use of black (denial) and white (approval)
balls when voting on an application. The vote must be unanimous. A
single black ball is automatic denial. However, in theory, one can only
be rejected from a lodge for Masonic reasons—that is, the applicant
has committed a serious legal or moral offense and is not considered a
good representative of the ideal of Masonry. While the process has been
abused and often falls short of the mark, it has managed to maintain a
basic level of trust and respect among the membership of lodges as well
as across rites and jurisdictions.

Membership in Freemasonry is a privilege, not a right, an idea that
seems foreign to modern society, with its obsession with forced inclu-
siveness and individual rights that are devoid of personal responsibilities.

This sets Masonry apart from many organizations and is in part why it is considered more than just a "fraternity" but a gateway to genuine initiation—not only ceremonial, but also spiritual. Masonry has always been viewed as a select group of men who select of their own free will and accord to undertake membership in an organization that states as its objectives the improvement of each member, their community, and the fraternity and service to a higher ideal of brotherly love and affection in the name of God. Such ideals can only take place under harmonious circumstances, or wherein harmony can be restored through the accepted authority of the rules and regulations—the landmarks—of the fraternity.

INITIATION:
THE MAKING OF A FREEMASON

Initiation is defined as a beginning, but a beginning of what? In modern life ritual initiation can seem mysterious, foreign, and terrifying. Mysterious because it is something rarely heard of, let alone experienced. Foreign because it rarely occurs in our lives except in the most crude and sophomoric fashions, such as pledging into a college fraternity or membership in a special clique or club. Terrifying because to undertake it requires a willing surrender of our personal liberty—to trust another group of human beings whom we do not really know with our well-being and security. This security is not (or rarely) physical but completely psychological and ego centered. Many Masonic lodges have actually destroyed the effectiveness of their own ritual initiations by desacralizing them, openly joking about or even intentionally adopting derisive images of Masonry invented by uninformed non-Masons and other such nonsense, when a profound and deep sense of solemnity and silence should be manifest.

Initiation is distinct from religious worship in that while there is often an element of the divine in initiation rites, particularly those of a mystical and occult nature, they are not a form of worship but a transformation. Candidates take part in a play that is performed for their benefit, so that they may have specific and distinct experiences that will have the potential to transform them on one or more levels. Candidates are both spectator and participant in the events that unfold around them.

Symbols are placed before the candidates, words stated, and stories told that hold within them a veiled truth, a connection to an ancient and mythological period that participates in and transcends human history and knowledge.

Initiation takes candidates beyond time and space and impacts them deeply on a subconscious level. Even if they never again reflect upon the symbols put before them, Masons will find their mind drifting back to one or more of the key experiences and knowing that "something" intangible happened to them at that moment. Be it by an inch or a yard, they were transformed and connected to something bigger than themselves. For some, this bigger something is the lodge and their community; for others, it is the Masonic fraternity as an entity of importance; for a small number, it is the mystical stream of which Freemasonry is a distinct and unique expression; and for the most select, the experience of initiation is a direct epiphany of the cosmos—of their connection to God.

Masonic initiation is designed to change those who experience it on a deep level. It does not make members perfect, nor does it promise salvation; it simply provides to those who seek it out and are accepted the tools and opportunity to make themselves better human beings, each in their own way. Through initiation and lodge work, the nature of the sacred is revealed as an everyday occurrence. For this reason, when Masons meet formally or informally, they recognize the presence of the divine through invocation and prayer, bringing forth the full potential of a spiritual life.

ISOLATION, INDIVIDUALITY, AND THE BEGINNING OF MASONIC AWAKENING

The Chamber of Reflection is a small room wherein the candidate prepares for their initiation into Freemasonry. As the name implies, they are to reflect on their reason for wishing to join the Craft. The main symbols are a mirror, candle, skull, hourglass, pen, and writing paper, and all point toward our mortality. In short, our time and what we do with it. It is a unique aspect of Freemasonry, and though it is not always present in every rite or jurisdiction, it is important enough that no Mason should be unaware of it. In fact, every Mason should replicate such a space in their own dwelling as a means of engaging with the deeper aspects of the Craft.

The Chamber of Reflection sits outside the Masonic temple, and as such, symbolically it sits outside of time and space. This leaves us with nothing more or less than our very consciousness—our awareness—and challenges us to understand why we do what we do and the consequences of our actions. Each of us who requests admittance into the brotherhood does so of our own free will and accord. No one can be forced to join. In the Chamber of Reflection, candidates are asked to reflect upon their reasons for desiring admission and the consequences it may bring. It is worth noting that the Chamber of Reflection came into use at a time when Masonic membership was persecuted, declared heretical to dominant church doctrines, and seen as politically subversive. Membership could mean one's imprisonment, torture, or death, in some instances. Joining was not a choice to be taken lightly.

The Chamber of Reflection is clearly linked to the Renaissance practice of the studiolo, *kunstkammer,* or "chamber of art"—a special room within the household that was highly prized among the wealthy and ruling classes. Here, in their small (and in some instances not so small) room, shut off from the daily concerns of the world, they would surround themselves with paintings, sculptures, wood reliefs, and objects to inspire and impress the imagination.

The purpose of the chamber, however, was not that of a study as we understand it in the modern sense of the word. It was not a place of work but rather a place that allowed one to connect more deeply with both the material and spiritual worlds in a single moment through the suggestive power of art and science.

In *The Pagan Dream of the Renaissance,* Joscelyn Godwin writes:

One of the most attractive inventions of the early Renaissance is the *studiolo,* a small, private, decorated study . . . a place of retreat from the public world into a private universe. As we understand it here, it is not a study for writing, nor a library, a treasury, or a monastic cell, though all of these contributed to its ancestory.

What most distinguishes the studiolo from the cell of a monk or a nun is its decoration. . . . It was not so much to take the owner out of this world, as to situate him within it. The decorations served as mirrors to qualities, aspirations, and knowledge already latent in the individual, but placed in a historical, moral, Hermetic, or cosmic context. The room was a model of its owner's mind and an exteriorization of his—or more rarely, her—imagination.[1]

In the Masonic lodge this chamber of isolation is designed to stimulate the imagination along specific courses of thought, but with the intent of helping the occupant to better engage in his daily activities. In his *Encyclopedia of Freemasonry,* Mackey defines the Chamber of Reflection as follows:

In the French and Scottish Rites, a small room adjoining the Lodge, in which, preparatory to initiation, the candidate is enclosed for the purpose of indulging in those serious meditations which its somber appearance and the gloomy emblems with which it is furnished are calculated to produce. It is also used in some of the advanced degrees for a similar purpose. Its employment is very appropriate, for as Johann Christian Gädicke, author of *Freemasons Lexicon* (1818), well observes, "It is only in solitude that we can deeply reflect upon our present or future undertakings, and blackness, darkness, or solitariness, is ever a symbol of death. A man who has undertaken a thing after mature reflection seldom turns back.[2]

The objects that occupy the Chamber of Reflection can be as simple as a chair, writing desk, single candle, human skull, mirror, and writing paper and pen—simple symbols whose meaning is obvious. In more sophisticated chambers one might find additional symbols taken directly from scriptures, alchemy, and Qabala-Hermeticism, such as a small vial of sulfur and its alchemical symbol, salt, water, the image of the rooster, and the alchemical motto VITRIOL.

While it is easy to confuse the Chamber of Reflection with the more religiously minded monastic cell or a hermit's cave, which are clearly its antecedents, the function of the chamber is most easily identified by its contents, which connect it to the Renaissance studiolo. Symbolically, the contents are designed to anchor the candidate in the present world, in the reality that he is here on Earth to work, and not to escape from it. He is a physical being, but with divine essence, and in working on his rough nature, in building his character through right actions, he achieves the refining of his nature as symbolized by the Smooth Ashlar of Masonic fame: the perfect cubic stone that can be used anywhere in the building process. The process in this case is ultimately that of building a better person and, from that, a better society. This chamber isolates him from the world so that, after reflection, he may better go out and work in it as a laborer for the common good and the divine ideal. Masons live in the world but endeavor not to be a part of it. They recognize their physical mortality and seek to build the immortal within themselves, while still carrying out their daily duties to family, community, and self. Since all initiations are in some way connected with death, or leaving behind the old to embrace the new, it is appropriate that death be the major theme in the Chamber of Reflection. Yet death is just another form of birth, and as Masons soon discover as they pass through the gate of Initiation, we must learn to trust in something other than ourselves if we are to find the Light.

THE TRESTLE BOARD:
MASONIC INSTRUCTION THROUGH SYMBOLS

The trestle board (sometimes spelled *tresle* or *tressle*), a board placed on a tripod for display and instruction, is the most unique aspect of Masonic instruction, and while it is composed of symbols, it is in fact a symbol itself. In operative Masonry it is the place where the master

The trestle board display

draws plans to direct the workmen in their labor. In speculative Masonry the trestle board presents the symbolic plans for the labor of Masons in their growth over the course of their life. It can also take on the added dimension of being a form of the Book of Nature, or means whereby the Supreme Architect of the universe reveals the supreme design for creation.

Trestle boards have their origins in tracing boards, or drawings marked out in chalk or coal on the floor of the room where Masons were meeting. Upon the conclusion of the meeting, the markings could be easily erased with a mop and bucket. The tracing board, or rather the act of its creation, became so integral to Masonry that the act of creating it became known as "drawing the lodge." Tin or other metal templates were often used to speed up the process, as well as to give greater clarity to the images being created.

In the nineteenth century painted floorcloths began to come into fashion, replacing the chalked drawings. These cloths could be rolled up and reused. Eventually, the floorcloths were replaced by smaller, more portable painted boards or framed canvases that could be hung on the walls of lodges—or set on a tripod, leading to the now-famous trestle board.

Coincidentally, when those ornate floorcloths with all of their instructional designs were taken up in favor of trestle boards, the floors of the lodges were then often covered with simple carpets reminiscent of the earlier chalk designs. These carpets on occasion were of a black-and-white checkerboard design, with or without the Blazing Star symbol, and surrounded by tassels. Today, that checkerboard pattern is as intimately associated with Masonry as the square and compass, and it represents the duality of life—the fundamental search for balance in a world of constant change. The Blazing Star is the guiding star of Providence that leads each Mason along their path and bestows light, life, and divine blessing to humanity.

The transition from floor tracing boards to trestle boards did alter Masonic initiations somewhat in that the master no longer walked across the drawings, pointing to their symbols during the ritual. Instead, the candidate was introduced to and instructed in the meaning of the symbols afterward in a lecture.

SYMBOLIC MASONRY: BLUE LODGE AND THE STARRY VAULT OF HEAVEN

A lodge in which the first three Masonic degrees—Entered Apprentice, Fellowcraft, and Master Mason—are conferred is known as a Blue Lodge; this level of the Craft is sometimes known as symbolic Masonry. The degrees belonging to higher-grade Masonry are all based upon and further elaborate what is presented in a Blue Lodge; such practice is sometimes referred to as philosophic Masonry.

The color blue dominates the ceremonial paraphernalia and decorum of a Blue Lodge. Many lodges also conform to the tradition of painting a blue sky, or astrological designs of the heavens, upon the ceiling in representation of the breadth and encompassing nature of the fraternity's insistence on universal friendship and mercy—that is, that Masons are to be as broad and tolerant as the heavens themselves.

Given the Hermetic milieu in which Freemasonry developed, it is appropriate to examine its symbols, including its use of the color blue, within a late Renaissance Hermetic framework. A clear connection to Egyptian symbolism can be made here, wherein the gods were often depicted as blue-skinned to show their heavenly, nonphysical origin and nature (the same is true in some Indian and Tibetan practice). In Qabala the color blue is given to the sphere of Chesed, or mercy, on the Tree of Life, which fits well with the Masonic ideal of benevolence, as well as the universal nature of the Grand Architect's plan. In alchemy Chesed is related to the *prima materia,* or "first matter," the underlying essence of all things; it is the working matter as well as the plan behind creation as we know it. Astrology, well known in the days of the early Craft and even into the early nineteenth century, associates the color blue with Jupiter and the element of Air, signifying breadth, expansion, life, vitality, and clear vision—a plan for the future. All of these ideas are present in the symbolic teachings of the Blue Lodge and are found within the rituals and specific symbols of the trestle board for each degree.

THE ENTERED APPRENTICE:
THE GATE OF INITIATION

The Entered Apprentice is the first degree in Freemasonry and its initiation gives the candidate an overview of Masonic ritual form and structure while instructing members to seek the as-of-yet undefined Light. The Apprentice who has entered a Masonic temple for the first time is prepared for this life-changing moment in the Preparing Room. As part of their due preparation in this room adjoining the temple, the candidates for initiation are stripped of all material possessions and dressed in a strange and peculiar garb that some say resembles the dress of heretics on their way to be burned at the stake—presumably in reference to the death of Jacques de Molay (see chapter 9). This includes a blindfold and a length of rope called a cable tow.

The uniform dress reduces all applicants to the same level and thereby provides the same experience for each Mason, creating a psychological climate wherein each Mason remembers forever the moment they were brought before the altar and made a member of the Craft.

In the lecture of the degree, applicants hear that this uniformity of appearance suggests that Masons learn humility, turning their attention inward rather than toward material wealth.

The blindfold used in the initiation represents secrecy, darkness, and ignorance, as well as trust. Candidates are led into the lodge room for initiation but are not able to see what is happening. They are bound about the waist and arm with the cable tow. A properly drawn trestle board will be enclosed in a cable tow with a tassel at each corner, so in this context the cable tow symbolizes not only the creation of an inescapable bond, but the fundamental unity of the lodge and its members, the fraternity, humanity, and the cosmos.

The most profound moment in each member's Masonic life is when they are first exposed to the Light at the altar of Freemasonry—a profound ritualistic and symbolic revelation of divine wisdom. The sheer impact of its presentation is forever memorable and a point of awe in each Mason's memory. Within the fraternity, this experience—symbolic of the quest and the essence of human life itself—is the moment each candidate becomes a Freemason. This Light is represented, in part, by the compass and square, the universal symbols of Freemasonry, which are presented here to an applicant for the first time and explored in greater depth in the later degrees. If the Jewish or Christian Scripture is used as the Volume of the Sacred Law, it is opened to Psalm 133, whose opening passage reads, "Behold how good and how pleasant it is for brethren to dwell together in unity!" With this prayer the Entered Apprentice is reminded of the fundamental purpose of Masonry—to bring men together, dispel personal animosities for the greater good, and extend the hand of mercy to family, friend, and stranger in distress. Unity of mind, purpose, and action is the strength of any group seeking to accomplish something of value. This unity can only come about when an attitude of forgiveness and mercy predominates and all work is for the common good. Forgiveness and renewal are encouraged and promoted both in daily life and in the life of the lodge.

Yet, oddly, in contrast to the professed notions of forgiveness and mercy, candidates are also told that should they break their oaths

The Entered Apprentice degree

to the fraternity by revealing its secrets, terrible and violent retribu-tion will follow. It is unclear whether this threat was meant only to frighten newly made Masons or whether the penalties may have actu-ally been carried out at some time. However, to make sense of it, we must remember that until very recently membership in Freemasonry was illegal in many countries at various times. To compromise one-self is one thing; to endanger the lives or livelihoods of others— particularly in an organization that can only be joined of one's own free will and upon asking—can be seen as a serious act of treachery. Many modern jurisdictions make clear that these penalties are tra-ditional and symbolic in nature only, representing the candidate's conscience rather than actual harm. Entered Apprentices are invested with an apron, which is traditionally made of lambskin or white leather, both symbols of purity and spiritual strength. The candi-dates hear that the apron of Freemasonry "is more ancient than the Golden Fleece or Roman eagle, and more honorable than [the order of] the Star and Garter." They are then presented with three tools: the twenty-four-inch gauge, a common gavel, and a copy of a Volume of the Sacred Law upon which they took their oath and obligation. The gauge is representative of the hours in a day, the passing of time, and how we use it. The gavel is representative of power and its

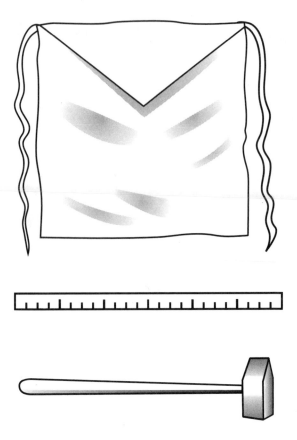

Tools of the Entered Apprentice:
the lambskin apron, twenty-four-inch gauge,
and common gavel

rightful and constructive use in life. The VSL represents each Entered Apprentice's desire to build their life upon spiritual values. It is up to each Entered Apprentice, under the direction of a mentor, to learn how to use these tools properly and thereby demonstrate their worthiness for the Fellowcraft degree. Before passing from this degree to the Fellowcraft one, Entered Apprentices must learn and demonstrate the moral principles of charity, respectable personal conduct, and loyalty to the fraternity.

Entered Apprentices are allowed to sit in lodges that open in

TRACING BOARD—FIRST DEGREE.

For Explanation, fee " The Perfect Ceremonies of Craft Mafonry," p. 54. Alfo 4th, and 5th Sections of First Lecture.

Trestle board for the Entered Apprentice degree. From *The Lectures of the Three Degrees of Craft Masonry* (Complete), 1874.

the Entered Apprentice degree and this degree only.* They may only observe; they cannot speak or vote on any proceedings of the lodge. Symbolically, they are like candidates in the ancient mysteries who were allowed to stand on the porch of the temple but not to enter the inner sanctum.

THE FELLOWCRAFT:
THE MIDDLE CHAMBER

The Fellowcraft (or Fellow Craft), also known as *campagnon* in the traditional building lodges, is the 2nd degree of Freemasonry. Whereas the Entered Apprentice was but a youth who served a symbolic three years before being allowed to be passed on to the second degree, the Fellowcraft builds upon the simple moral teachings given—teachings of the heart—and enlarges them through development of the intellect. Symbolically, candidates now pass from the porch of the temple (Entered Apprentice) into the temple proper (Fellowcraft), but not yet its innermost recesses (Master). During their initiation, Fellowcraft candidates are told of the peculiar biblical account of the Ephraimites, who, having been beaten by the Gileadites, wanted to cross the river Jordan, which was held by their enemy. The Gileadites asked every soldier attempting to cross the river to say the word *shibboleth* in order that the Gileadites might easily identify their friends from their foes based upon the Ephraimites' unusual pronunciation of the word. At first, the story may appear out of place, but for Masons this simple act symbolizes that while the heart must be made charitable and generous, it must also be made wise. Wisdom can only be born from the ability to understand one's experiences. We must be able to know what is beneficial for us from what is harmful, just as we must be able

---

*Each degree has its own opening and closing formula related to its particular initiation ritual. In practice however, most modern lodges open in the 3rd or Master Mason's degree (thereby requiring that all be Master Masons), while some open in the the Entered Apprentice degree, thereby making it easy for all members to attend a single meeting.

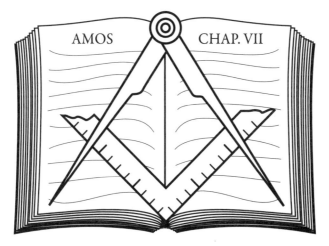

The Fellowcraft degree

to discern friend from foe as the shibboleth story illustrates. To assist in developing this understanding, Masonry turns to the seven liberal arts and sciences.

The seven liberal arts and sciences of traditional learning are divided into two groups: the *trivium*, consisting of grammar, rhetoric, and logic, and the *quadrivium*, consisting of arithmetic, music, geometry, and astronomy. Together, these disciplines create a well-rounded person and creative thinker, someone who is capable of solving problems and understanding the relationships between various issues and subjects.

Grammar allows a person to express themself with the correct use of words. Rhetoric adds beauty to this expression so that it may inspire, uplift, and convey a deeper meaning beyond the words chosen. Logic provides clarity and reason and demonstrates the importance of a life of the mind. Arithmetic is the ability to add, subtract, multiply, and divide, which is essential for daily life and even more so for the operative Mason. Music demonstrates the mathematical relationship or harmonies that exist in the world and directs the mind to the ultimate harmony of the ancients: the Pythagorean "Music of the Spheres," a mathematical expression of universal harmony (see chapters 5 and 6).

Geometry, or "the queen of science," as it was known, is the practical application of mathematics to the material world and allows for the precise measurement of objects both far and near. Astronomy—which would most likely have been astrology in the classical, medieval, and Renaissance periods—extends this ability to measure to realms beyond the Earth, enlarging our view of creation.

These fields of study, along with the teachings of the previous degree, form a winding staircase that will slowly and progressively lead candidates toward the inner light of the sanctum sanctorum—the holy of holies.

The image of the winding staircase is found in 1 Kings 6:5–8, and it leads to an antechamber for the holy of holies. In Masonry this antechamber is called the middle chamber. The middle chamber symbolizes a time of learning, of experiencing the material world and shaping it according to what we have learned.

Just as the tools of the Entered Apprentice are for shaping material stone, the tools of the Fellowcraft are for shaping the inner life, or the life of the mind, in preparation for the Master's work on the life of the soul. The Fellowcraft tools are an instructive tongue, attentive ear, and faithful breast or heart. They represent the need of the Fellowcraft candidates to be constructive in their words to the others, to apprentices in their care, and to the lodge; attentive in listening to instructions from the master; and faithful in their adherence to the knowledge and instructions they receive.

A Fellow of the Craft will spend five years in the middle chamber. This time is symbolic in the speculative lodge, as that would have been the time one spent as a fellowcraft in an actual apprenticeship.

The Scripture passage used in the 2nd-degree initiation is Amos, chapter 7, where the symbolism of the plumbline is given to represent the divine standards to which each Mason aspires to adhere to that they may enter the holy of holies. The plumb is one of the working tools of a Fellowcraft, along with the square and the level.

TRACING BOARD—SECOND DEGREE.

For Explanation, see "The Perfect Ceremonies of Craft Masonry," p. 105. All 3rd, 4th, and 5th Sections of Second Lecture.

Trestle board for the Fellowcraft degree. From *The Lectures of the Three Degrees of Craft Masonry* (Complete), 1874.

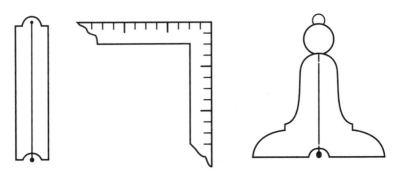

Tools of the Fellowcraft:
the plumb, square, and level

THE MASTER MASON:
THE HOLY OF HOLIES

Master Mason is the 3rd and final degree in Masonry. (At the risk of being repetitive, it is important to recognize that any additional degrees are considered instructive in nature, further elaborating on the basic Masonic framework given up to and including the 3rd degree.) All Master Masons are equal and may sit in any degree, speak on issues relevant to the lodge, and vote. In this initiation the greatest of Masonic truths are symbolically revealed, and the sublime nature of the soul and its immortality are inculcated. It is here that the mysteries of life and death are revealed.

This revelation is in part done through the mystic chain, or the linking of brethren arm in arm, as a newly made Master Mason is raised from the stinking stench of death to the bonds of fellowship. The proverbial veil has been pierced, and after the symbolic term of seven years' labor, Master Masons are masters of life, able to shape themselves inwardly and outwardly, to serve their fellows, and to hear the voice of God within.

The Scripture passage used in the Master Mason initiation is Ecclesiastes 12:6: "Or ever the silver cord be loosed, or the golden bowl be broken . . . " This line is famous for its allusion to the so-called astral cord experienced by many who have had out-of-body experiences. In

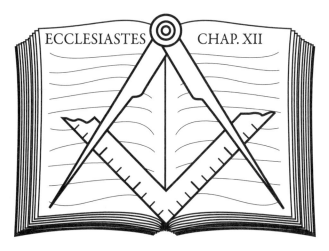

The Master Mason degree

this degree the veil of the sanctum is pulled back. The spiritual world lies before Master Masons upon their raising. It is up to each to take the step that will allow them to cross over.

Life for Master Masons is built upon the three pillars of strength, wisdom, and beauty. Just as the lodge is sustained by these qualities as expressed through the actions of the Three Immovable Jewels—the master, senior warden, and junior warden—so do individual Masons build their individual life upon these ideals, knowing, as it is stated in Ecclesiastes 14, "For God shall bring every work into judgment, with every secret thing, whether it be good, or whether it be evil." All that we do is known to us and to our Creator. Nothing can escape the rule of conscience or universal justice. This knowledge is the ultimate culmination of the first question each Entered Apprentice is asked: "In whom do you put your trust?" The Master Mason knows that answer is simple: "God." Only with a complete trust in divine omnipotence, omniscience, and omnipresence can life be truly lived.

To have this trust and to build this life, all the tools of Masonry can be used, but one tool above all else represents the power of the Master Mason: the trowel. Just as a trowel spreads cement to hold stone together, so the Master Mason spreads brotherly love in daily life, thereby helping to complete the building of the temple of life.

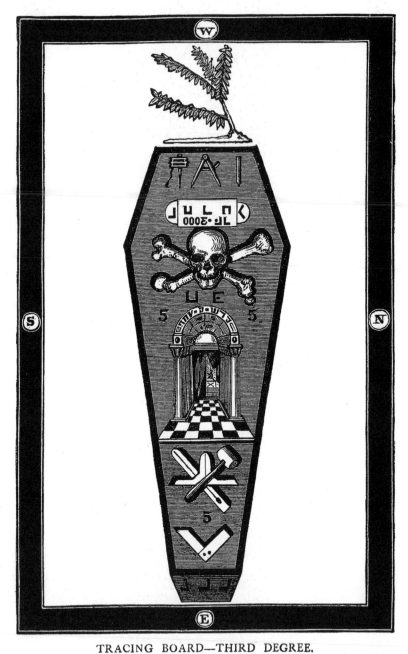

TRACING BOARD—THIRD DEGREE.

For Explanation, see " The Perfect Ceremonies of Craft Masonry," p. 142. Also 3rd Section of Third Lecture.

Trestle board for the Master Mason degree. From *The Lectures of the Three Degrees of Craft Masonry* (Complete), 1874.

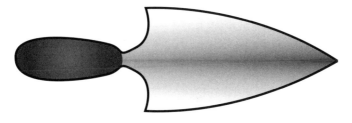

The Trowel:
A Master Mason's tool to spread brotherly love

In summary the three degrees of Freemasonry instruct members to:

1. Listen to those who have gone down the path before them so that they may learn from their experience and tutelage.
2. Study the seven liberal arts and sciences so that through them they can improve their intellectual knowledge, understanding of creation, character, and spiritual life.
3. Explore the Divinity within, symbolized by the search for the Lost Word that Hiram Abiff possessed and died to keep inviolate, the only true source of peace, power, and understanding. This is expressed in daily life through a broad and tolerant love of humanity. The Grand Architect of the Universe is omniscient, omnipotent, and omnipresent, and through our spiritual unfolding we can share and participate in that totality—but only through the power of love.

A MASON IN THE WORLD

Despite tradition nowhere in Master Mason initiation do we hear that a Master Mason must memorize the rituals, perform each act exactly as those before us without error, or even attend lodge meetings, for that matter. While we can justifiably argue that only through lodge contact and listening to those who have gone before us can we understand and undertake those actions, it is clear that to be a Master Mason, what goes on outside the lodge is more important than what goes on inside it.

To become better we must leave the old self behind. The death of the little self, or our self-imposed concepts of limits and controls, allows us to be of service—first to our family, then to our community, and finally to Masonry—with our work in each each realm being an expression of our service to God as we understand it. This provides a unique framework wherein we are given a yardstick with which to measure our actions and the fruits of our actions with one simple question: "Who does this serve?" In doing this the Master Mason finds the Lost Word, the name of God invoked before any undertaking, within themselves, their fellow human being, and all aspects of life itself.

While hardly flashy by modern esoteric standards, this stance provides a means to make us think and reflect upon what we are doing, why we are doing it, and what will come of our actions. In short, what kind of world are we building by doing such-and-such an action? Service teaches humility and egoless action. In promoting service Masonry is one of the largest charitable organizations in the world and yet is heard of the least. Anonymous charity is true charity. Getting your picture in the paper, your name on a wall, or an auditorium or building named after you is nice, but it is not charity from the heart. This kind of charity comes from working in the world as an Unknown Superior—someone who performs their works anonymously and as an act of spiritual devotion. True Masons do not draw attention to their actions but help others understand that helping a community, religious organization, philanthropic service, or stranger in need is simply normal everyday behavior and not something that needs to be rewarded with applause or special acknowledgment.

In the words of the journeyman known as La Volonté de Vouvray: "You can stay a simple workman and yet be a great workman. In this way, I have known some journeymen and some workmen who have not completed their tests, who were in my eyes masters and teachers of the trade, for they loved the trade with all their heart. They were also teachers of life, for they loved their fellow man, doubtless without even being aware of it. This is how they came to have the gift of teaching and handing on."[3]

THE PENTAGRAM

One of the more controversial and misunderstood symbols of Masonry is the pentagram. While Masons will state that the Blazing Star of Freemasonry represents the Five Points of Fellowship, the means whereby a Master Mason is raised as well as recognized, the occult aspects of the pentagram were well known by the time it was included in the ritual work of Masonry, as was the case for many other symbols. According to Heinrich Cornelius Agrippa, the pentagram was the most important of all esoteric figures in that it represented the powers of the cosmos present in man, or the microcosm. With it, the energies of the visible and invisible worlds could be contained and harmonized in the life of its possessor. Individuals could raise themselves from mere human status to cosmic peace and harmony with the divine mind—with God.

In his book *A New Encyclopedia of Freemasonry*, A. E. Waite gives ten Masonic interpretations of the pentagram in Masonry: (1) the star of the Magi; (2) the glory of divine presence; (3) divine providence; (4) a symbol of beauty; (5) light from God on the path; (6) sign of a true Mason; (7) emblem of the sacred name of God, thus God Himself; (8) the sun as the grand luminary of nature; (9) the Dog Star of Anubis; and (10) nature as "a volatile spirit animated by the Universal Spirit."[4] Pythagoras (c. 570–c. 495 BCE) considered the pentagram an important symbol of mental and physical harmony. The brotherhood that he founded used it as an identifying symbol, often with the Greek letters for "health" at each of the five points, and wore it on a signet ring.

The Pentagram:
The Blazing Star of
Freemasonry

Masonic Initiation and the Blue Lodge:
Key Points

1. Membership in Freemasonry is a privilege and not a right. It can be requested but not demanded. With it comes responsibilities and obligations.

2. No one can be forced to become a Mason. Each must come of their own free will.

3. Membership in a Masonic lodge is requested by petition. Candidates for membership are interviewed by two or more members of the lodge; petitions are reviewed and voted on in the open body of the lodge that has been petitioned.

4. Masonic membership is defined by having been accepted and initiated into all three degrees of the Craft, thereby making the member a Master Mason. All Master Masons are equal in their standing within the Masonry.

5. Initiation confers symbols, experiences, and knowledge that is distinct from those of religious worship. Initiation has the potential to be a transforming event in the life of the candidate.

6. All Masonic activity begins with a prayer or invocation to the Grand Architect of the Universe.

7. Some Masonic rites require a candidate to spend time in a preliminary chamber, known as the chamber of isolation, prior to initiation. This chamber has its origins in ancient initiatic rites and the chambers of art prominent during the Renaissance.

8. The three degrees of Freemasonry are Entered Apprentice, Fellowcraft, and Master. Each has its own set of symbols and teachings revealed on trestle boards. It is the duty and obligation of each Mason to study these symbols and find meaning in them for his life.

9. In the Entered Apprentice degree, candidates are admonished to listen to those who have gone down the path before them—to listen and to learn.

10. In the Fellowcraft degree candidates are admonished to study the seven liberal arts and sciences and to improve themselves that they may be of better service to their community, family, lodge, and God.

11. The seven liberal arts and science are divided into two sections, the *trivium* and *quadrivium*. The trivium consists of grammar, rhetoric, and logic, and the quadrivium consists of arithmetic, music, geometry, and astronomy (or astrology).

12. Masonry is concerned with how one acts in the world to make it a better place. All philosophic and mystical speculations must be put to the test of daily living to see if they are of value.

Assignments for Chapter Three

1. Invoke the divine presence before undertaking any work. Ask others if they will do this with you. Notice their responses, as well as the effect it has on the quality of the work resulting. Is there increased productivity? Creativity? Group harmony?

2. Copy the Entered Apprentice trestle board on paper or, better still, on pavement with chalk. Examine your thoughts and feelings as you do this.

3. Commit the symbols on the Entered Apprentice trestle board to memory. What effect does this have on your imaginative process, meditations, and dreams? Write down any ideas, dreams, or inspirations that come to you as a result of this work.

4. At the end of the day, reflect on your actions of the day and how you might have done better. Commit yourself to any new course of action suggested by your reflection, particularly if this new course of action would improve your relationships with other people.

5. Create a sacred space within your home for meditation and prayer. Set aside a period of time each day to spend alone there. Meditate on themes such as the nature of physical life, your personal mortality, what it is you want to become and to accomplish, and whom those accomplishments will serve. What will be your legacy to your community, family, and self?

6. Begin a systematic study of the seven liberal arts and sciences and see how quickly your intellectual and spiritual life is enriched.

7. Each day, imagine that as you rise from sleep, you have risen from death itself. Greet each day as a new opportunity.

Masonic Initiation and the Blue Lodge:
Suggested Reading

Hidden Wisdom: A Guide to the Western Inner Traditions, by Richard Smoley and Jay Kinney (Quest Books, 2006). A detailed exploration on the various Western esoteric currents and their survival from the classical period to the present. A very important and informative text.

The History of Magic and the Occult, by Kurt Seligmann (Gramercy Books, 1997). One of the most singularly important books on magic in the twentieth century. It is extensively illustrated, with many images from what were at the time of publication in private collections.

How to Think Like Leonardo da Vinci, by Michael J. Gelb (Delacorte Press, 1998). As the title states, this book tells you how to train your mind to think like a Renaissance genius and thereby better understand the Renaissance mindset and worldview and why it is important to us today.

Memory Palaces and Masonic Lodges: Esoteric Secrets of the Art of Memory, by Charles B. Jameux (Inner Traditions, 2019). A concise and critical examination of the art of memory and its role in both Renaissance magic and Masonic ritual.

4

The Worldview of the Renaissance

The World Is Alive, and Magic Is Afoot

The occult philosophy in the Elizabethan age was no minor concern of a few adepts. It was the main philosophy of the age, stemming from John Dee and his movement.

FRANCES YATES

IT IS DIFFICULT FOR US TO UNDERSTAND the nature of the Renaissance mind, let alone that of its magi. Their relationship to the world, Creator, and creation, in particular through the medium of imagination, art, and symbols, which they called magic, is completely misunderstood by modern terms. As Hans Kayser points out in the preface to his 1921 anthology on Paracelsus, the world in which Paracelsus lived is "quite alien to our time, and only rarely comes into contact with it."[1] This is even more true at the dawn of the twenty-first century.

While it is difficult to give a stereotypical profile of what the average Renaissance magician was like, they held many character traits in common. All were independent thinkers who looked within and to the world for experience and knowledge. They sought to understand nature and didn't separate divinity from creation or its inhabitants, as did their medieval predecessors and their contemporary theologians. God was everywhere and in everything, and as such, divine power was literally in the hands and hearts of the magis who chose to use it. Plants, stones, and the stars were all a part of this divine power and creative expression and could be called upon by magicians to assist them in their redemptive work. This work was aimed at ultimately healing the soul—the rift of "the Fall" in biblical terms—and put magicians in a precarious situation in which they mediated between heaven and earth, a power desired by kings and popes, but also one that they could not control except by sword and flame.

The greatest tool of magicians was, and still is, their creative imagination: the ability to create in the mind's eye images of reality not yet experienced or of an ephemeral, transcendental nature. Through the use of such images, magicians could enter into the ethereal realms like Ezekiel in his chariot, control the destiny of nations, and command the very elements of creation itself. Through judicious use of imagination, will, and confidence in this inner power, the magi believed that anything was possible.

As they ascended in power and knowledge through the celestial spheres, the magi would enter into communion with beings of a highly specialized and sacred nature. Through them and the words they would convey to the magis, they could command the heavenly legions as well as spirits in the deepest bowels of the earth.[2] The Sacred Word (or Sacred Name), the first vibration of creation, was their tool to use, and in using it, the magi identified themselves with God. But power was not everything, and often merely a by-product of the mages' accomplishments. The true revelation came in realizing one's relationship to the godhead and in having direct communication, free of interlopers and priests, with the Creator. This was done through love—a love so pure, etherial, and abstract that it was the veritable incarnation of the Platonic ideal of love. In this love, Creator and creation were one and expressed and experienced each other directly. This divine union, reminiscent of Gnostic, Hermetic, and even Buddhist and yogic doctrines, is best expressed by Johann Scheffler (1624–77), writing under the pen name Angelus Silesius:

> *I know that without me*
> *God can no moment live;*

Were I to die, then He
No longer survive.

I am as great as God,
And he is small like me;
He cannot be above
Nor I below Him be.

In me God is fire
And I in Him its glow;
In common is our life,
Apart we cannot grow.

He is God and man to me,
To Him I am both indeed;
His thirst I satisfy,
He helps me in my need.

God is such as He is,
I am what I must be;
If you know one, in truth
You know both him and me.

I am the vine, which He
Doth plant and cherish most;
The fruit which grows from me.
Is God the Holy Ghost.[3]

Theosophy via theurgy became the predominant focus of the Renaissance magi. This theurgy was different from its medieval predecessor in that it stressed the individual's role in repairing the rift between humanity, creation, and the Creator. Ritual and invocations were no longer meant to summon evil spirits but instead to assist in human redemption. Magic became a kind of social sacred ceremony, a Mass in which all benefited, but in which the magician was the sole participant. The tools of the magician combined with the love and compassion of the mystic, creating a synthesis greater than either could accomplish alone.[4] This successful combination of two seemingly opposing esoteric views, in a climate that was at best lukewarm to the idea of the existence of either, led many Christian leaders, Catholic and Protestant alike, to seek out magi such as Paracelsus, Agrippa, and Giordano Bruno to heal the many rifts in Christianity—a function that Masonry would also in part play through its nonsectarian approach to membership.

This love is borne out in the fact that despite the richness of their works, those who sponsored them (on occasion), and the never-ending stream of wealthy and poor seeking help, most of the prominent Renaissance magi died in poverty.

It is intriguing but also understandable to note that the majority of the great writers and practitioners of magic and alchemy in this period were either church-trained or active churchmen. Some have made much of their apparent orthodox Christian calling or activity. But the Roman Catholic Church in particular offered the easiest access to many of the "forbidden books" in its libraries, as well as the needed education and leisure time to read them. And until the end of the fourteenth century, almost any practice was acceptable in Christian circles as long the Holy Trinity was invoked and members considered themselves "Christian." Then the witch trials began to occur, thereby institutionalizing church intolerance and making it the norm.[5] With the Jews being forcibly removed from Spain in the same year that the last Arab stronghold in Europe fell (1492), and those remaining forced to convert or hide, Europe was essentially officially a "Christian" continent, albeit a heavily divided one. Some magi sought to reinvigorate the church with pre-Christian classical wisdom and learning, driven by an appreciation of Nature and observation of her truths. The teachings of the church, the sacraments, and the rituals—these were merely the outer cloak that gave meaning and form to the magi's inner truths. God spoke to them through Nature, but the church gave the language of the day to express it. Since taking any title other than Christian would have brought a death sentence, we cannot know what they would have called themselves given the freedom to do so openly. Since natural philosophy is what united them, some chose to be called by the humble title "philosophers of nature."

> As such the magician operates in a manner wholly different from that of his precursor: where the one had a direct line to the god or gods of his tribe, the other [i.e. Renaissance magus] works with different techniques, different contacts, yet is always seeking to break through into the inner realm itself, to speak directly to God, as his ancestors [i.e. tribal shaman] had once been able to do. Thus his magic is a practical extension of a philosophical/mystical underpinning, and without that foundation, it would not exist. To look at the magician without taking into account his dream of unity, however partial or superficial, with deity, is to mistake his whole purpose.

And:

> Magic and ritual are microcosmic expressions of the macrocosm: man's tiny torch of desire uplifted to the fire of the stars. We plug into the universe through the enactment of ritual—beginning with . . . the propitiation of the elements and a desire to enter the womb of the world-mother. The Hermetic approach, as adopted by the magician, is more intellectually motivated, celestial rather than chthonic. The astrological calculations of "star-led wizards" of Milton's *Ode on the Morning of Christ's Nativity* are a far cry from the instinctive actions of the tribal shaman—yet each in his way is motivated by the same needs and desires, only their methods have changed with the movement from tribal to individual consciousness.[6]

THE WORLD OF NATURAL MAGIC

From the point of view of the Renaissance magi, nature is born out of the cosmic night, the Ain Soph Aur (or Ein Sof) of the Qabalists, the creative power of the Demiurge of the Gnostics, the primordial waters of the Egyptians. Nature is alive and filled with energy, matter, and intelligence. Like man, it has degrees of self-consciousness. What else explains why a rock is a rock and not a snake? Or why one rock is quartz and another a diamond or ruby? While modern science can explain the difference in terms of chemical compositions, this is simply another manner of stating that one stone vibrates at a different rate than the other. This "cosmic melody" of creation, this harmony of the spheres made concrete, is the essence of matter—of material form and life. From the Hermetic and Renaissance perspective, it is disingenuous to speak of "energy" and "matter" as separate concepts because they are in fact one and the same—simply different perspectives of the same thing.

When we speak of "natural magic," we are really speaking of the ways in which the energies of the invisible world impact the physical world—even creating it. Spiritual laws, or laws of nature exist, wherein the magician is able to effect the world of causes—something beyond the physical world of the senses—and create effects in the physical world. That is, as do researchers in quantum physics, magicians believe that their very consciousness can affect the physical and metal worlds of themselves and others. Everything is in contact and sympathy with everything else, both visible and invisible, and it is only ignorance that keeps one from experiencing this fundamental unity directly.

This worldview is no different from that of Tibetan Tantrism, wherein, after taking various initiations, the adept can see the physical world as a "Buddha field" filled with enlightened beings, and all objects are material reflections of pure light, wisdom, and energy. The magician has the same experience in the ritual circle, and the architect in the design of the temple or building. During the Renaissance the garden was a particularly unique expression of this kind of ideal, becoming a place where heaven and earth were united and the designer was not the master but the handmaid of nature.

Nature and Natal Charts

The word *nature* derives from the Latin *nasci*, "to be born"; *nasci* is also related to *nativity* and *natal*. One's natal chart or horoscope is cast for the moment of birth to show the positions of the heavenly spheres in relationship to the location of the birth and thereby—through those relationships, or the angles that are formed—understand the cosmic influences that will influence the newborn's life. The natal chart is, in effect, not only a map of the heavens but a sort of schematic diagram, like an electrical chart, showing how the energies illustrated will flow and the effect they will potentially have.

ANGELIC MAGIC

Angels have played an important role in the development of Western religious, mystical, and esoteric practices. Angelic magic is the theory and practice of communicating, or at least attempting to, with invisible beings—namely angels. In theory, angels, being God's messengers, could provide information to a magician who was able to establish a relationship with them. In this way they functioned as a sort of giant consulting firm, encyclopedia, or cosmic search engine if you will.

While Freemasonry makes no specific reference to them in its rituals or symbols, the fundamental relationship Freemasonry shares with Middle Eastern traditions makes the link an embedded idea. We often hear of the "Genius of Freemasonry"—the guiding spirit—referred to as "she" and discussed in anthropomorphic terms, expressing human qualities, but on a perfected or archetypal level. This may be confusing to moderns who think of "genius" in terms of mental acuity rather than as an individual; however, the word *genius* is from the Latin *gignere*, meaning "beget"; *gignere* is also the root of *gen-* words like *generate*. There is the possibility of it being a loan word from the Arabic root for *genie*, or *jinn*. The jinn are considered to be beings of spiritual fire that Arabic magicians sought to control, and as previously discussed in chapter 2, Solomon, considered the greatest magician of all time, built his temple through the employment of fifty thousand jinn. With this in mind, consider the image of a woman sitting alone in a cell designed for contemplation wherein the mysteries are revealed, which is presented in the closing charge recited at that end of every lodge meeting. This symbol then takes on a deeper connection to both a literal spiritual force protecting Freemasonry as well as the Gnostic notions of the divine Sophia, or Wisdom—the bride of God.

John Dee (1527–1608) and Edward Kelley (1555–1597)

Of all the Renaissance magi, the most famous angelic communicators were John Dee and Edward Kelley. At some times comic, and other times tragic, this pair of celestial scryers are known to more modern practitioners of magic than all of their contemporaries combined. While that may say more about modern occultists than it does about the work of Dee and Kelley, the fact remains that Dee and Kelley have come to be the modern archetype of the Renaissance magi and a major influence on Freemasonry in the era before 1717.

John Dee was the Renaissance incarnate. Whereas we often think of Leonardo da Vinci as the seminal "Renaissance man," or polymath, in truth, despite da Vinci's genius, it was men like Dee who defined the cosmological milieu in which the architectural, artistic, literary, and scientific achievements of the Renaissance occurred.

In their work on the Western mystery traditions, John and Caitlín Matthews compare the magician to his ancient predecessor, the tribal shaman. In this context the authors state:

> If Merlin is an inner resonator who generated the literature which gathered about his name, then Dr. John Dee must be considered almost his outer manifestation in the real world. He is probably the single most influential aspect of the magician ever to have lived and a worthy successor to the Arthurian mage. Though his abilities have often been called into question, his influence has continued to be felt right up to the present time.[7]

Born in 1527 Dee rose to prominence quickly. As a student he received acclaim—and laid the foundation for his lifelong reputation as a sorcerer—by building a mechanical beetle for a production of Aristophanes's *Peace*. At the age of twenty-three he was lecturing in Paris on mathematics, and a year later he was awarded a pension by Henry VIII for his skill in astronomy. When Mary Tudor ascended the throne in 1553, Dee was received at court and invited to draw up her horoscope. When Elizabeth I succeeded Mary six years later, she asked Dee to choose her coronation date, which became January 14, as Dee saw it as astrologically auspicious.

Dee's love of learning prompted him to amass at least 2,500 books, one of the largest private collections at the time. Many of the manuscripts formerly in his collection now reside in the British Library. In 1564 Dee himself published *The Hieroglyphic Monad,* said to have been written in two weeks, and dedicated it to Emperor Maximilian II, king of Bohemia and Hungary. In addition to his occult studies, Dee was also sought out for his practical and mundane knowledge in such diverse topics as astronomy, navigation, geography, perspective, optics, and mathematics. Dee, as an ambassador for Elizabeth, was also believed to have been a spy, as well as possibly a tutor to a young Francis Bacon and the prototype for Prospero in Shakespeare's *The Tempest*.[8]

Across his life Dee was patronized by some of the most influential monarchs and nobles of his day; Count Albert Lasky of Poland, King Stephen of Poland, Count Rosenberg of Trebona, and even Sir Walter Raleigh sought his services.

Dee's life moves on an almost fatal course after his meeting with Edward Kelley. Kelley, or Talbot, as he is also known, came into Dee's employ in 1581. While it is not clear whether Kelley and Talbot are the same person or separate people, that issue is irrelevant, as the key portions of Dee's diaries were written during his association with "Kelley." The problem is less about his true identity than the fact that we have only Dee's perspective on him.

Kelley became the source for the majority of the visions that comprise the core of Enochian magic. Rumors circled around him, associating him with everything from forgery to necromancy. He is painted as a scoundrel preying on Dee's credulity. Despite their troubled relationship they stayed together for seven years and experienced many adventures, and they have survived as a symbiotic pair—as esoteric Siamese twins, perhaps, or maybe Laurel and Hardy.

Systemically, the methods employed by the two were similar to what was typical in Renaissance magic, except for three things: Dee did not celebrate holy Mass as part of the ritual, there was no ceremonial circle, and there was no "license to depart" or verbal command sending the spirits back to wherever they had originated from—a near universal safety measure of the time. This is highly unusual given the terrific fear that the process of evocation and most ceremonial operations could lead to being dominated by spirits and having them negatively affect one's life, or even outright possessing of one's mind and body. For years, however, the two experimented, recorded, and rewrote the details of their sessions. Promises of long life, riches, and fame poured forth from the "angels" they communicated with. Their relationship was tumultuous—Kelley threatened to leave Dee on several occasions, but he always stayed.

Yet in the end Dee's life was in shambles. His house had been partially destroyed, along with the precious library he had worked so hard to build, by a peasant mob after they heard of his magical practices. Despite this, Dee continued to practice magic until the end of his life and was even willing to stand trial for witchcraft, certain that the courts of James I would see that his quest was an honest, Christian, and spiritual one. After finally splitting with Dee, Kelley boasted of possessing the philosopher's stone and was imprisoned for life for murdering a man in a rage. He died after falling from a tower while trying to escape and breaking his leg.

At least two plays have been written about Dee: *Doctor Faustus,* by Christopher Marlow, which put an end to Dee's influence at court as it associated him with devil worship, and Shakespeare's *The Tempest,* for which Dee served as the protype for the outcast and betrayed magus Prospero.[9]

THE END OF THE RENAISSANCE

Many postmodern critics have pointed out that it was not science that put an end to the magical operations of the Renaissance. The end of magic did not come from the rational replacing the "super-rational." Instead, it was the irrational. It was fear that put an end to the Renaissance's scientific explorations into the cosmos and consciousness. Protestant witch hunts and the Inquisition of the Roman Catholic Church, and the drive to destroy anything that did not mirror, subscribe to, or obey religious authority and worldview, would deliver the crippling blows. Only with the establishment of the Royal Society at the end of the seventeenth century do we see official sanction for exploration and inquiry into creation, and with this official sanction, some protection. From this small coterie of scientists, inventors, and scholars of all types, this notion of freethinking extended into Freemasonry and the formation of the Grand Lodge of England.

The Worldview of the Renaissance:
Key Points

1. The metaphysical worldview of the Renaissance and the period leading up to the formation of the first grand lodge in 1717 is misunderstood by many scholars and ignored by contemporary Freemasonry.
2. Dame Frances Yates states it best: "The occult philosophy in the Elizabethan age was no minor concern of a few adepts. It was the main philosophy of the age, stemming from John Dee and his movement."
3. According to this occult worldview, a variety of nonhuman spiritual beings existed and could be contacted. The mind, imagination, symbols, and ritual action were all seen as having an impact on the physical world. The arts, sciences, philosophy, religion, and the so-called occult practices were seen as extensions of one another and not separate entities.
4. Within this world, the dominant religious organizations, primarily the Roman Catholic Church and various Protestant denominations, held sway over which intellectual, artistic, and spiritual

practices and researches were deemed acceptable. To step outside those bounds without powerful patronage was to risk death.

5. The primary occult practices of the age included the study of Jewish mysticism or Qabala, ritual magic, alchemy, and astrology.

6. These practices were often cast in the light of two schools of magic: natural and angelic. Proponents of natural magic work with the energy, cycles, and intelligence in nature. Proponents of angelic magic converse with angels, or good and holy servants of God, and eschew demonic magic or sorcery as being counter to the will of the Creator.

7. John Dee, astrologer to Queen Elizabeth, ambassador, and spy, was the seminal Renaissance magus. He embodied the totality of the occult view, and for him, conversing with the angels of God was the highest form of magic and best source of information about material and spiritual realities.

8. Edward Kelley was Dee's assistant, and a man of peculiar talents and low scruples. He died after breaking his leg in a prison break. He was the source of many of the visions that form the core of Enochian magic.

9. Despite opposition to research into the possible validity of esoteric doctrines and associated occult practices by the Royal Society, it was not reason that put an end to the Renaissance worldview, but witch hunting.

Assignments for Chapter Four

1. Spend time outside contemplating the power and presence of nature. Go a week without recorded entertainment (videos, news, television, music) and social media. Limit your computer and cell phone use to only work-related activities. Plan ahead so that you can limit your automobile and mass transit use as well. Now imagine what it would be like to live in a world in which nature is all-powerful, everything you know is within walking distance, and you have little information about the outside world. How does this make you feel? What are your concerns and how can you address them?

2. After having done the above assignment, imagine that the world you live in is alive, even populated with invisible beings of both good and evil natures. How does this affect your sense of security? Who or what can you turn to in order to get control over your life?

3. Explore the nature of holism in modern life. Take education and health care, for example. Are they really holistic? List the ways in which you can begin to make your life more holistic and in harmony with the forces around and inside of you while still living in a twenty-first-century environment.

The Worldview of the Renaissance: Suggested Reading

The Occult Philosophy in the Elizabethan Age, by Frances A. Yates (Routledge, 1979). A detailed introduction to the pivotal role occultism played in the Renaissance by one of the twentieth century's leading Renaissance scholars.

Giordano Bruno and the Hermetic Tradition, by Frances A. Yates (University of Chicago Press, 1964). Bruno was central to the Renaissance, and his role as a martyr for free thought makes him relevant to the modern era. Yates resurrected Bruno from scholarly isolation and transformed him into a cultural icon with this book.

The Art of Memory, by Frances A. Yates (University of Chicago Press, 1966). A critical look at a critical topic: the mind in Renaissance intellectual and spiritual philosophy and practice.

Eros and Magic in the Renaissance, by Ioan P. Couliano (University of Chicago Press, 1987). Essential reading for anyone who wants to understand the survival of Renaissance ideas into the modern age and their influence on the world at large.

The Magus of Freemasonry: The Mysterious Life of Elias Ashmole— Scientist, Alchemist, and Founder of the Royal Society, by Tobias Churton (Inner Traditions, 2006). A spectacular introduction to the life and works of one of the most important men of the period: both as a Freemason and scientist.

5

Sacred Geometry, Gothic Cathedrals, and the Hermetic Arts in Stone

Numbers are the sources of form and energy in the world. They are dynamic and active even among themselves. . . . [They are] almost human in their capacity for mutual influence.

THEON OF SMYRNA

IN MANY WAYS attempting to understand Freemasonry from the viewpoint of the early twenty-first century is not unlike trying to understand lions by watching one in a zoo. While the zoo lion is a lion, and truly a dangerous animal, it most likely was born and raised in captivity, and while it has all of its natural instincts, walls forbid it to run free, to hunt game, to mate, or to raise its young. It has adapted to its world, and as can be seen in the eyes of so many lions in the zoo, it suffers from the apathy that its environment creates. Freemasonry is little different. Modern Masons have much in common with their predecessors; however, many—grand lodge officers included—lack the critical worldview that dominated the intellectual landscape in which Masonry gestated and flourished in the seventeenth and eighteenth centuries. As a result, much of contemporary Masonry has been reduced to fraternal and charitable activities, with philosophy being totally forgotten.

The most obvious aspect of this can be seen in one of Masonry's

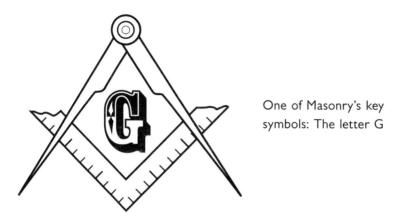

One of Masonry's key
symbols: The letter G

key symbols: the Roman letter *G*. So often newer members and non-Masons ask, "What does the G mean?" Some less informed brethren will answer "God," not knowing that this would work only in English and other Germanic-based languages. The initial for "God" would be the letter *D* in French, Italian, or Spanish lodges, with similar changes made elsewhere. (Even so, the appearance of the letter *G* is not universal in Freemasonry.) In actuality, the *G* stands for geometry, the most critical field of learning for any educated person, and particularly one who would be in the building trades. The word *geometry* means "the measure of the earth." The Greeks learned this science from the Egyptians, master builders of the Great Pyramid complex and thousands of temples and tombs great and small. Geometry can be seen as the study of archetypes and their physical manifestation in life. It is the cornerstone of the seven liberal arts and sciences, uniting the other six. Through geometry, order, harmony, and synthesis are achieved, not in the abstract, but in the concrete and material world.

The earliest form of sacred architecture in western Europe during the High Middle Ages was the Gothic style. Gothic buildings were massive, with wide open spaces, towering windows of stained glass, and impressive acoustical structure, and their construction spurred the growth of the building guilds that in part would give rise to Freemasonry. It is interesting to see images of Christ in manuscripts and stone holding a compass to measure the world, symbolizing divine harmony at the heart of all things.

Just as Renaissance artists moved out of the flat and two-dimensional representations of their predecessors into elegant, refined, and detailed use of perspective, we see the building trades, wherein the master mason was both architect and contractor, moving away from the small, squat, fortress-like structures of the Romanesque design into houses of worship that elevated the senses and with them spiritual consciousness. Early Cistercian architecture was transitional between the Romanesque and Gothic styles.

St. Bernard of Clairvaux (1090–1153), advocate for the architectural style of the Cistercian Order, believed that there should be no decoration in structural designs, and that buildings should rely on the use of proportion to achieve visual, spatial, and acoustic harmony.

Regardless of their style the buildings of this period, many of which remain to this day, are in fact spiritual energy made concrete, no different from the popular methods of Chinese feng shui. Nor are the methods used in their construction unavailable to the modern person or layman.

In *Sacred Art in East and West,* Titus Burckhardt points out that sacred art creates "a vision of the cosmos which is holy through its beauty; it makes men participate naturally and almost involuntarily in the world of holiness."[1] This subtle and unconscious pull into the divine can be felt to this day by nearly everyone who has entered into the realm of sacred art and architecture. Given that our ancestors were for the most part illiterate, the play of light and shadow, colors, and acoustical quality exercised a profound impact on the individual and collective imagination. This was not lost on the secular, ecclesiastical, or even heretical authorities of the day. Just as Albert Einstein is often quoted as saying that imagination is the most important tool we possess, his Renaissance predecessor, the father of Western alchemy, Paracelsus, states:

Imagination is like the sun. The sun has a light which is not tangible; but which, nevertheless, may set a house on fire; but the imagination is like a sun in man acting in that place to which its light is directed.

Man is that what he thinks. If he thinks fire, he is fire; if he thinks war, then he will cause war; it all depends merely on that the whole of his imagination becomes an entire sun; i.e., that he wholly imagines that which he wills. (De Virtute Imaginativa)

Man is a twofold being, having a divine and an animal nature. If he feels, and thinks, and acts as divine beings should act, he is a true man; if he feels and acts like an animal, he is then an animal, and the equal of those animals whose mental characteristics are manifested in him. An exalted imagination caused by a desire for the good raises him up; a low imagination caused by a desire for that which is low and vulgar drags him down and degrades him.[2]

In this context the sights, sounds, and actions accompanying Masonic rituals, but initiations in particular, take on a new significance. Everything is done to uplift the imagination and bring the full impact of symbols—in form and in action—into play, for symbols have but one area of the human mind wherein they work, and that is the subconscious. Masonic ritual, temples, and tools are designed to stimulate the subconscious mind of those exposed to them and thereby stimulate what Paracelsus calls our "divine nature" and "raise" us up.

In his *Three Books of Occult Philosophy*, Agrippa writes:

The doctrines of mathematics are so necessary to, and have an affinity with magic, that they that do profess it without them, are quite out of the way, and labour in vain, and shall in no wise obtain their desired effect. For whatsoever things are, and are done in these inferior natural virtues, are all done, and governed by number, weight, measure, harmony, motion, and light.

And:

Hence a magician, expert in natural philosophy, and mathematics, and knowing the middle sciences consisting of both these, arithmatic, music, geometry, optics, astronomy, and such sciences that are of weights, measures, proportions . . . knowing also mechanical arts resulting from these . . . do many wonderful things, which the most prudent, and wise men may much admire.[3]

The most striking characteristic of Gothic architecture is the volume of stained-glass windows that are utilized. Chartres alone has over 6,500 square feet of glass. The method of creating stained-glass appears to have originated out of Muslim lands, where glass was affixed to plaster casings and reinforced with plant fibers. This technique appears to have been perfected in France, quickly spreading, with lead being used to hold the glass together and to attach it to the surrounding iron framework.

The most famous windows in Gothic history are, of course, those of Chartres. The red and blue colors of Chartres have been the subject of much speculation, including from modern alchemists who sought some metallic secret within their construction. The oldest windows date to 1150 and to an earlier building destroyed in 1194, yet nearly seven hundred years after their construction, the colors of the newer windows remain vibrant, particularly those where the red and blue colors were utilized.*

The most famous expositions on the esoteric symbolic meaning of the great cathedrals is found in the writings of the mysterious twentieth-century alchemist Fulcanelli. Little is actually known of who Fulcanelli was, although there has been and continues to be a great deal of speculation. Legends have grown up around him as well as the book attributed to him—*The Mystery of the Cathedrals*. First published in 1925 the book examined the sculptures of the major cathedrals in France, focusing on Notre Dame of Paris and Notre Dame of Amiens, and states that they represent the alchemical process as encoded and

---

*It is a miracle that we even have Chartres today. The cathedral barely escaped demolition after the French Revolution and the anticlerical attitudes that followed. The city was occupied by Prussian troops for a brief period of time after France's defeat in the Franco-Prussian War but was undamaged, as it remained despite the destruction that would follow from 1914 to 1918. Some damage occurred to the city and minor damage to the cathedral during the Second World War, but the windows we so admire were removed in 1940 and put in storage to prevent their possible destruction.

preserved in stone. The preface to the book's second edition is most interesting in that it refers to Fulcanelli as not yet having received the "Gift of God," or full Illumination, but being close, he kept with tradition and maintained anonymity in his writings so as not to attract the attention of the merely curious and the foolish.* Among those suggested as having been Fulcanelli is R. A. Schwaller de Lubicz, author of numerous books on Egyptian symbolism and temple architecture, and Jean-Julien Champagne, an erudite student of esotericism who fits the description given of Fulcanelli as a man who dressed and acted as if he were in an earlier age.[4]

Regarding the Gothic cathedral Fulcanelli writes:

> The gothic cathedral, that sanctuary of the Tradition, Science and Art, should not be regarded as a work dedicated solely to the glory of Christianity, but rather as a vast concretion of the ideas, of tendencies, of popular beliefs; a perfect whole, to which we can refer without fear, whenever we would penetrate the religious, secular, philosophic or social thoughts of our ancestors.
>
> The bold vaulting, the nobility of form, the grandeur of the proportions and the beauty of the execution combine to make a cathedral an original work of incomparable harmony; but not one, it seems, concerned entirely with religious observance.[5]

It is interesting to note that during this time, many, if not all, of the great cathedrals, and to a fair extent the smaller ones as well, were dedicated to "Our Lady" or the Virgin Mary, the mother of Jesus Christ. Several cathedrals also feature images of "the Black Madonna" an expression of Mary that has esoteric significance that is often overlooked, but well known in alchemy. Herein we see the material world giving birth or expression to divine ideals, taking them from the abstract and making them tangible, concrete, and living. The previous chapter

---

*"Curious and foolish"—polite names for those whom we now refer to more accurately as "psychic vampires." They take and take for their own satisfaction and give nothing in return, nor are awake enough to realize the fundamental degree of their selfishness.

points out that this reverence for things feminine continues in Masonry, in which the closing charge, said at the end of each meeting, refers to the Genius of Freemasonry: "Wisdom seeks the secret shade and the lonely cell, designed for contemplation. There she sits, delivering her sacred oracles." This "Genius" is the guiding spirit of Freemasonry and every Mason who seeks to understand its mysteries. In an earlier age, the one in which Masonry arose, this spirit would have been thought of as a real power and intelligence, not unlike a guardian angel, whose existence and influence were very real, and not simply poetic license. Later esoteric groups would think of it in terms of an *egregore,* or collective consciousness of Freemasonry, that both gives and receives from the actions of its members. Like "Geometry" and "Wisdom" in the form of Sophia before it, the tendency to turn abstract forces and ideals into anthropomorphic images, particularly of a feminine form, suggesting pre-Christian sources in classical paganism.

One Medieval woodcut shows geometry personified as a beautiful woman, complete with the letter *G,* and surrounded by the working tools of the building trade—a "lewis" hoist for blocks, a square, a setting maul, a measuring stick, and a brick. She is even depicted using the compasses, while two assistants nearby use astronomical equipment to survey the heavens depicted above.

This form of personified expression of geometry as a woman is reminiscent of the Egyptians, who saw their gods, or *neters,* as powerful abstract forces who became accessible when transformed into the pantheon we know as the Egyptian gods. Given the relationship of geometry to Egypt, there may be some connection here to the ideals of geometry as a tool for understanding divine order and harmony.

The importance of geometry cannot be understated, as it was an applied science among the ancients. Daily life was ruled out—literally in terms of measure as well as laws—according to perceptions of divine proportions. The Egyptian temples are among the finest examples of this. It is no surprise that the cornerstone of the Renaissance would rest upon the Hermetic arts and science for the revival of classical learning. Herein, the Emerald Tablet of Hermes, the Egyptian god of magic, wisdom, and learning, would reveal the entire secret in a few lines:

That which is above is as that which is below, and that which is below is as that which is above, for performing the miracle of the One Thing.[6]

For us, the key lines to consider in relation to sacred geometry are the first: "That which is above is like that which is below, [and] that which is below is like that which is above," which illustrate the connected nature of the so-called material and spiritual dimensions. Here, in the hard reality of material life, the work of becoming a better person, of creating an earthly paradise, a utopia, as so many Renaissance dreamers wrote about, takes on true meaning only in the light of earthly inertia. To overcome the baseness of human nature—the sheer weight of habit, training, and cultural mores, be they beneficial or not—and to shape and form the world so that our conscious daily interaction with it and others is a reflection of divine laws is really the Masonic ideal, as well as the Hermetic one. It is reflected in the words of Jesus when he tells his disciples that they are to "become perfect as your father in heaven is perfect" (Matthew 5:48). Just as the Word is "made flesh" through Mary, ideal becomes form through geometry.

This interrelationship of worlds is also the cornerstone of natural magic, in which these relationships can be manipulated—be it in the building of a temple, creation of a talisman, or design of a garden, city, or political state.

The notion of measure, building, numerology, creation, the feminine role in morality and divinity, and earthly rulership is expressed in Edmund Spenser's *The Faerie Queene*. Spenser was in contact with leading members of John Dee's inner circle and sought to reform Hermetic philosophy to better suit his Puritan views. Despite this, his works are profoundly Neoplatonic and reflect the Hermetic philosophy of the period. Frances Yates calls *The Faerie Queene* "a great magical Renaissance poem, infused with the whitest of white magic, Christian Cabalist and Neoplatonic, haunted by a good magician [i.e., Dee]. . . . Spenserian magic should be read not only as poetic metaphor . . . but also in relationship to contemporary states of mind."[7]

The frame thereof seemed partly circular,
And part triangular, O work divine;
Those two the first and the last proportions are,
The one imperfect, moral, feminine:
The other immortal, perfect, masculine,
And twixt them both a quadrate was the base,
Proportioned equally by seven and nine;
Nine was the circle set in Heaven's place;
All which compacted made a goodly diapase.[8]

The metaphor of ancient philosophers was continued in the medieval and Renaissance eras—one in stone, in the construction of cathedrals, and the other in verse, in the language of poets and playwrights. Both are united in geometry, the study of number, shape, form, and measure, but also on a more subtle level—that of numerology.

Fulcanelli states that there was a verbal Qabala based upon, but distinct from, Jewish mysticism in that it played on words in a phonetic manner, whereas Qabala used an alphanumeric relationship between letters and numbers within words, sentences, and even paragraphs to suggest hidden meanings—pointing a Masonic student of these topics back to the idea of the Lost Word (see chapter 6).

The world of the men and women of the classical world, the Middle Ages, and the Renaissance, up to and including the early period of the formation of the first Masonic grand lodge, was significantly different from ours. This difference was not so much that of technology, environment, or even understanding, but one of perception and belief. While modern men and women worry much about the impermanence of human life and their own fleeting mortality, the people of earlier ages saw little difference between the material and spiritual dimensions. Physical bodies came and went, but life was eternal. The world was not a fixed and static place but one in which the elemental spiritual forces of nature, angelic beings of the celestial heavens, demons from the pits of hell, and even the dead could come forth and interact with the so-called living.

Referring to pre-Christian texts that permeated the medieval Christian era, Claude Lecouteux writes:

What clearly emerges out of their study is that their authors were simply incapable of drawing a clear line between this world and the hereafter, between "life" and "death." This does not imply that they were indifferent to what must be called a change in condition or status, or that they did not conform to what is an obviated observation, that is . . . the "dead person" does not have the same type of reality as the . . . living person. . . . There is a mentality in which a dead person can come along at any moment and adopt the shape of the living, the living can animate the deceased, and a surprising (for us) movement is established between the two realms.[9]

These themes were echoed throughout the Elizabethan era, particularly in the plays of Christopher Marlowe and William Shakespeare. Only at the end of Renaissance, with an increasing emphasis on humanism, or the philosophy that place man as the measure of all things, does the magical worldview of millennia begin to fully unravel and become replaced by the god of Reason.

While these ideas are generally lost to the twenty-first-century reader, it was something well known to the average literati during this period leading up to and well past the formation of the Grand Lodge of England in 1717. Esoteric and occult ideas based on the Renaissance magical and alchemical practices played a major role in popular folklore and even university education in Europe and its colonies into the early decades of the nineteenth century.[10]

TEMPLES, TALISMANS, AND THE SURVIVAL OF THE STONE

The notion of sacred geometry was applied on a grand scale to cathedrals, chapels, private estates, and, some even suggest, the ground plans for the cities of Paris and Washington, D.C. However, even a landless individual, or one living in the cramped confines of seventeenth- or eighteenth-century urban living, could avail themselves of the significance of symbols and proportions. This physical act of moving from the two-dimensional drawing on the trestle board to the three-dimensional expression of actual construction meant that the symbols of geometry came alive as Platonic solids.

One of the leading proponents of this kind of unified knowledge theory was Francesco Giorgi (1466–1540). Giorgi was a Franciscan friar whose main publications were *De harmonia mundi* (1525) and *In Scripturam Sacram Problemata* (1536). Clearly influenced by Neoplatonism and the writing of Giovanni Pico della Mirandola—who sought to unite all schools of philosophy under one umbrella and advocated that people should use magic to transform themselves into angelic beings—he was also a Qabalist with access to Hebrew source material through the Jewish community in Venice, a community that expanded considerably after the expulsion of Jews from Spain in 1492 by the Catholic monarchs Isabella and Ferdinand. Like his predecessors in the Florentine Neoplatonic movement, Giorgi saw Qabala simultaneously as a means of proving the validity of Christianity and as a direct connection to the writings attributed to Hermes Trismegistus. In addition, Giorgi fully integrated Pythagorian-Platonic numerology, demonstrating the essential harmony of the world, and Vitruvian architectural theory, which Giorgi saw as being directly connected to the Temple of Solomon.

Giorgi further refined the angelic systems Pico had presented and their essential harmonies, which allow man to climb to the font of creation itself. Number was the key to understanding for Giorgi, for number was proportion and harmony. Through number, the unalterable cosmic principles of sacred geometry were revealed.

Platonic solids are the five basic shapes mentioned by Plato in *Timeaus* that are believed to have given rise to all known shapes and forms. These basic shapes are the tetrahedron, octagon, cube, icosahedron, and dodecadron. (This theory would have been clearly known to the early operative and speculative Masons, and not lost on them, as it forms part of the seven liberal arts and sciences.) Johannes Kepler linked the five Platonic solids to the five planets that orbit the sun—Mercury, Venus, Mars, Jupiter, and Saturn—and through them, to the classical elements of water, earth, air, fire, and ether.

The most significant aspect of Masonry for the non-Mason is the various regalia worn by Freemasons in their public and private ceremonies. Close examination of this regalia will reveal symbols that are often geometric, expressing abstract ideas in graphic form. Others of these symbols decorate the collar jewels and aprons of the officers. Through these designs the tools of the work are revealed to the members present, and they represent the spiritual and moral function of the officers in the lodge. Of course, wearing special clothing for ceremonial purposes is nothing new and has been done since time immemorial to set culturally significant operations and proceedings apart from worldly or mundane affairs. In the context of Freemasonry, ritual garb creates a special atmosphere and grants recognition to participants by virtue of the particular jewel or emblem of the office they are wearing.

As we saw in chapter 2, in the early days of the Craft, the symbols of initiation were drawn on the floor and wiped clean after the ceremony was completed. This gave way to the creation of special carpets or floor cloths that could be easily transported and rolled out when needed. By the mid-eighteenth century, as Masonry moved out of rooms above taverns and into buildings exclusively dedicated to Masonic work, these cloths in turn became more or less elaborate paintings depicting Masonic initiation and were placed on easels for easier instruction.

These Masonic temples became living, three-dimensional representations of the ideas presented on the trestle boards and, in doing so, special places where the mystery of the Mason's Word became flesh in the laying of the first foundation stone and in the making of the candidates in the temple raised upon it. These were special places, and everyone, members and general public, knew it. They were talismans of Masonic virtue.

The word *talisman* derives from the Greek *telesma,* meaning something consecrated. (*Telesma,* in turn, derives from *telein,* "to initiate into the mysteries.") Freemasons are regularly reminded that where they walk is "holy ground," and that the space around the altar, the entire temple itself, is dedicated and consecrated to a specific act: that of making Freemasons and bringing them together for the act of mutual assistance and self-improvement.

Just as the cathedral can be seen as a giant three-dimensional talisman, as described by Agrippa, so too can we see the same in a Masonic temple when a lodge of Masons is in session.

Amulets, often confused with talismans, are more general "good luck" pieces and are not ritualistically created. If we look at the manner in which Freemasonry, or any similar organization, for that matter, utilizes its ritual regalia, we see that the items used fall somewhere in between. While not magical in the classical sense of the word, they do create a psychological context that is more uplifting and formalized— and thereby special and of importance—than if they were not worn and lodge actions were performed in street clothes.

This emphasis on special clothing, in existence since the very inception of the first Grand Lodge and earlier, is a link to the ancient mystery traditions that should not be dismissed or overlooked. The special clothing and jewels of the officers, as well as the simple aprons worn by attending members, all pertain, in part, to the legend of Hiram Abiff and the building trade. Even if we accept that the jewels were used earlier in the stonecutters' guilds for easier recognition by their members, the connection or similarity with even earlier traditions is not lost.

Masons wear special tools for the work they perform. That work has now become little more than learning and performing the basic rituals as the sum total of the Craft, whereas at one time it meant something else—something deeper.

It is important to remember that in the worldview of the pre–grand lodge eras, calling upon God or any of the invisible beings said to inhabit the heavenly realms was considered a literal act—that is, call on them and they come—and not a formal but empty gesture. When a blessing was made, it was believed that an aspect of divinity was lit up within the person or persons receiving the blessing. When a building or structure was blessed, it was believed that an aspect of divinity, possibly even an angelic force, was made present and tangible in the structure.

When Freemasons ask for the blessing of God, the Grand Architect of the Universe, or the "Genius of Freemasonry who presides over all our actions," in the environment of the Renaissance this would have been seen as a literal invocation of divine power no different from charging a dead battery with electric current. No explanation to the members would have needed to be given. The *Fourth Book of Occult Philosophy,* attributed to Agrippa, states:

> But now we come to speak of the holy and sacred Pentacles and Sigils. Now these pentacles, are as it were certain holy signes preserving us from evil chances and events, and helping and assisting us to binde, exterminate, and drive away evil spirits, and alluring the good spirits, and reconciling them to us. And these pentacles do consist either of Characters of the good spirits of the superiour order, or of pictures of holy letters or revelations, with apt and fit versicles, which are composed either of Geometrical figures and holy names of God, according to the course and manner of many of them; or they are compounded of all of them, or very many of them mixt. . . . And if we will draw about him any angular figure, according to the manner of his numbers, that also shall be lawful to be done.[11]

This emphasis on geometric shapes and forms is not unique to medieval and Renaissance European magic but is also found in earlier Middle Eastern practices upon which they drew, as well as in Eastern mandalas—that is, geometric images designed to present cosmological views in symbolic form. These mandalas were not limited to paper, stone, or cloth. Tibetan sand paintings as well as the three-dimensional construction of structures such as *stupas* (similar in some ways to the old herms, or road markers of the classical period) demonstrate that ancient societies around the world held that putting archetypal patterns into material form was vitally important, allowing them to transform and enhance our lives.

Ancient civilizations symbolized the relationship between these pure ideas and the energies they directed through the function of the angle, which is, in essence, the fundamental relationship between two numbers. When personified, these ideas became the gods. Thus, the angelic forces invoked in religious rites or esoteric practices are essential cosmic principles personified; they are, in their own manner, the creative Word made concrete.

While the Temple of Solomon was a divine revelation, it was not a singular historical event, but rather with cyclic regularity was renewed, and in doing so, reinvigorated the world. The Temple was the key to understanding the laws of the universe: number, measurement, and harmony.

That is why the Templars and other mystical idealists devoted lives to discovering the secrets of the Temple. It is like the philosopher's stone, a talisman that turns base metal into gold, that brings new light into the world and restores its natural condition as an earthly paradise.[12]

Given this context it is peculiar that one of the most commonly known as well as commonly ignored symbols within Freemasonry is the Blazing Star, or pentagram. According to Agrippa geometric figures are as powerful as the numbers they represent, with the number five belonging to the pentagram:

A pentangle [pentagram] also, as with the virtue of the number five hath a very great command over evil spirits, so by its lineature, by which it hath within five obtuse angles, and without five acutes, five double triangles by which it is surrounded. The interior pentangle contains in it great mysteries, which also is to be inquired after, and understood.[13]

Elsewhere, Agrippa illustrates that man—the human body—is the perfect pentagram, and that within the human body are energies that are in harmony with the invisible energies of the planets and the stars under the direction of divine providence.

Freemasons meet each other upon the Five Points of Fellowship, which is often the meaning given to the pentagram. While an important moral lesson, it robs this ancient symbol of its great power, both for the fraternity as a whole, as well as for each individual Mason. The average Mason remains unaware of this ancient usage of the pentagram and its occult significance until the 28th degree of the Scottish Rite.

It is not until this degree, known as Knight of the Sun, Prince

Adept, that we hear of the esoteric and practical importance of the pentagram:

> In the West, over the Warden, you behold the holy and mysterious pentagram, the sign of microcosm, or universe, called in the Gnostic schools "The Blazing Star," the sign of intellectual omnipotence and autocracy, which has been partially explained to you heretofore. It represents what is called in the Kabala microprosopos, being in some sort a human figure, with the four limbs, and a point representing the head. It is the universe contained with the Deity.
>
> It is a sign as ancient as history and more than history; and the complete understanding of it is the key of the two worlds [spiritual and material]. It is the absolute philosophy [Hermeticism] and natural science [alchemy].
>
> All the mysteries of Magism, all the symbols of the gnosis, all the figures of occult philosophy, all the kabalistic keys of prophesy, are summed up in the sign of the pentagram, the greatest and most potent of all signs.[14]

Though this specific ritual is no longer in current use today, the reference to the ability of this symbol to keep evil spirits away is of significance to Masonry in that, as was mentioned earlier, according to legend King Solomon commanded fifty thousand spirits to build the Temple. Thus, in this simple image, we have an allusion to the great occult power of the fraternity's traditional grand master, the Hermetic-Pythagorean-Qabalistic reference to number, harmony, and form, and finally, the idea that under the star of illumination, wherein the inspiration of God touches the members present, harmony is produced.

THE FORTY-SEVENTH PROBLEM OF EUCLID: THE GREAT SYMBOL OF MASONRY

Geometry is so important to Masonry and its understanding of the cosmos that the symbol of the Forty-Seventh Problem of Euclid adorned the cover of Anderson's *Constitutions* when it was published in 1723.* While this carries little meaning in an age of near universal education, and when almost everyone learns the most rudimentary elements of algebra and geometry before high school, in the sixteenth century, geometry was the key to almost every conceivable art and science of material importance and directly linked to the teachings of the Greek and Egyptian mystery schools—the sources of Hermetic knowledge—through Pythagoras. In addition, through the study of numbers, the secrets of the ancient texts, long suppressed through religious intolerance and secular power, could be understood using the Qabalistic systems of *gematria, notarikon,* and *temura.* These systems of letter-number substitution allowed for the creation of new words, connections, and magical devices. We see among many ancient cultures—the Jews, Greeks, Egyptians for example—that numbers were the keys to heaven and earth, and through them, the locks that kept man in spiritual and intellectual ignorance could be removed.

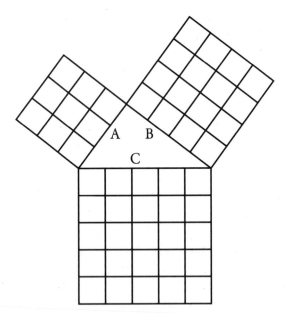

The Forty-Seventh Problem of Euclid

---

*Euclid of Alexandria wrote what is considered the first textbook on geometry and published 465 axioms, equations, postulates, and theorems in his thirteen-volume *Elements.*

On the level of operative Masonry, the Forty-Seventh Problem of Euclid is the most practical equation in construction. It states: "In right-angled triangles, the square on the side subtending the right angle is equal to the squares on the sides containing the right angle," or $a^2 + b^2 = c^2$. Through its application, it is possible to create perfectly squared angles (important for buildings), to survey mountains (important for maps), to calculate longitude and latitude (important for sailors), and to determine the distance of the sun, moon, and planets from the Earth. Tunnels can be built using it, allowing entrances to be started on both sides of a mountain and to meet exactly in the center. From a purely speculative point of view, a symbolic image of the Forty-Seventh Problem of Euclid is worn by past masters of a lodge to remind members to be lovers of the arts and sciences, thereby improving themselves, their communities, and their lives. It also reminds the more insightful that it is possible to start at very opposite places in life and arrive harmoniously at the center.

Sacred Geometry, Gothic Cathedrals, and the Hermetic Arts in Stone: Key Points

1. The letter *G* in Masonic symbolism refers to geometry.
2. *Geometry,* whose name means "the measure of the earth," was imported into Europe by the Greeks, who learned it from the Egyptians.
3. Through geometry, order, synthesis, and harmony are achieved in a concrete expression of archetypal ideas.
4. The earliest form of sacred architecture in Christendom is the Gothic style of the High Middle Ages.
5. St. Bernard of Clairvaux was the main advocate of this style of construction.
6. The intent of sacred architecture is to allow observers to participate in the sense of holiness taking place around them.
7. Mathematics was linked to the occult arts in the Middle Ages, and the Roman Catholic Church forbade its study. The most famous occultist of the Renaissance, Heinrich Cornelius Agrippa, stated

that "the doctrines of mathematics are so necessary to, and have an affinity with magic," that without them magic is in vain.

8. Mathematics are essential to geometry and architecture and therefore, some believe, link the great Gothic cathedrals to the Hermetic arts and sciences.

9. The mysterious twentieth-century alchemist Fulcanelli authored several books, of which *The Mystery of the Cathedrals* interprets Chartre, Notre Dame, and others according to the alchemical practices of the Great Work, being another term found in Masonic literature and ritual to designate each Freemason's philosophical quest, and the fraternity's link to the ancient mystery schools by way of the medieval stone guilds.

10. Most of the great cathedrals were dedicated to "Our Lady," or Mary, the mother of Jesus. The Black Madonna that is seen in several of these cathedrals has esoteric significance that is often overlooked but well known in alchemy. It also links these structures to the Temple of Solomon, the presence of the shekinah, and his purported worship of Astarte-Venus.

11. Washington, D.C., and Paris are said to have been laid out according to the principles of sacred geometry, making each a giant talisman, or magical device.

12. The Forty-Seventh Problem of Euclid is the great symbol of Freemasonry, and it is the most practical of all equations in material construction.

Assignments for Chapter Five

1. Collect images of the great temples, cathedrals, and buildings from the classical, medieval, and Renaissance periods. Place them in locations where you will see their beauty daily, even if unconsciously. Write down any thoughts that arise related to their presence in your environment.

2. Sit with one of those images of a great cathedral or temple and visualize yourself inside it. What is it like as you approach the doors? What do you see and feel? What is it like inside?

3. Find a house of worship near where you live, and regardless of its

simplicity or ornateness, approach it as if you were a pilgrim seeing it for the first time after a long journey to pray there. What is the first thing that strikes your eye? What is your first impression of the building and its environment?

4. Obtain an inexpensive set of drafting tools and, using what you can learn from appendix A in this book, undertake a study of sacred geometry. Notice the effects it has on clarifying your thinking and creative process. Reflect on how the practice of geometry under-scores the importance of details. What kind of synthetic effects does it have on your consciousness?

5. Using your studies and meditations from Assignments 1 and 2, and practical study from Assignment 3, reflect on your own living space. Make a plan for adjustments to your living space to incorpo-rate sacred geometry and other qualities from great architecture.

Sacred Geometry, Gothic Cathedrals, and the Hermetic Arts in Stone: Suggested Reading

Sacred Geometry: Philosophy & Practice, by Robert Lawlor (Thames and Hudson, 1982). A wonderful introduction to sacred geometry for those who would like to work directly with the forms themselves.

Cathedral of the Black Madonna: The Druids and the Mysteries of Chartres, by Jean Markale (Inner Traditions, 2004). An informed exploration of the French cathedrals and their role in the survival of earlier European goddess worship.

Fulcanelli, Master Alchemist: Le Mystère des Cathédrales, by Fulcanelli, translated by Mary Sworder (Brotherhood of Life, 1984). A modern classic that interprets the French cathedrals in the light of practical alchemy.

6

The Lost Word and the Masonic Quest

Architecture is frozen music.

ARTHUR SCHOPENHAUER

IT IS THROUGH MARY that the Word is "made flesh," and through geometry that ideal becomes form. The Word is the power of creation itself. In the medieval worldview Mary is the Seat of Wisdom, the foundation of all creation, and the Word is her offspring. In other words, the power of creation is found in wisdom.

Harmony expressed in sound produces music, and in word a certain rhythm, or even a chant. This idea of words expressing power over their listeners is embedded in the word *enchanted,* which derives from the Latin *incantare* (*in* means "against"; *cantare* means "to sing").

Rhythm and rhyming can affect the consciousness of both the speaker and the listener and are an effective memory device as well as a tool of suggestion or hypnosis. It is no surprise that we see rhyme and rhythm playing an important part in magical incantations of the early homespun variety—known as witchcraft—or in the oaths and obligations of members of another craft—that of Freemasonry. Through particular wording and rhythm, extensive rituals can be committed wholly to memory and passed on orally for centuries.

In Masonic initiation, as an example, the candidate for initiation would be blindfolded for the greater part of the ritual; only through intense listening to the words of the lodge officers would he know what was happening. This detail may sound insignificant to anyone who has not undergone the experience, but for those who have, even decades after their initiation, entire lines from it are memorable because of the concentration given to what is happening around them—and the peculiar resonance of words and rhythm with consciousness. Through these uncommon and archaic modes of speech, Masonic rituals link those who experience them across the limitations of history, of time and space, to something approaching the eternal.

Those who have found the Lost Word have heard the voice of God within, and can truly be called Master Masons in both essence and form. The Lost Word has been recovered and is the True Word. The Substitute Word is no longer needed. The master Hiram Abiff, who is slain by three fellows of the craft, represents the desire for humans to have power or privilege that is unearned. It is the false send of self, derived from identification with the material world that slays and cuts us off from communion with our true Inner Master, and as such, until we can humble ourselves at the Porch of the Temple, we can not enter, nor receive the Word. Until then, a substitute word is given. This substitute is religion.

Religion comes from the root, *relig-*, meaning "to *unite*," and the goal of most religions is to unite the human consciousness with divinity in some fashion. However, most fall far short of this goal, and instead are mediums of inculcating moral and ethical virtues into their adherents through the process of ritual and collective work. As such, true uniting can only occur on an individual level and in the privacy of one's own chamber, such as used prior to the Entered Apprentice degree and symbolized by Hiram's daily meditations in the Porch of the Temple. Anyone who has truly understood the "plan" or lessons that are prepared for them, be it by predestination, chance, or *karma,* becomes like Hiram: unafraid in the face of certain death for failing to reveal a secret that cannot be revealed from man to man, but only from Self to self.

JEWISH MAGIC

Within Qabala the possibilities of magic are clearly stated, particularly through the use of divine names. However, magic was considered to be a rare event, performed by a pious person only in times of emergency, and at physical and spiritual risk to himself. While Qabalistic writings have warnings against the use of magic, there are no universal condemnations of it. This issue is further complicated by the distinction made between purely physical or material magic and inner or spiritual magic, when such distinctions in practice are not always clear-cut.

Spanish schools of Qabala made a distinction between schools of practice received from the Lurianic tradition using the Tree of Life and those perceived as being derived from magical practices based on the Name. It is on the practices of the *ba'ale Shem,* or "masters of the Name," that much of medieval and later surviving magical practices are based, including German and Pennsylvania Dutch folk magic. The distinction between "practical" or magical uses of Qabala—and at times reproach for the former—is historically significant, since it is like a child disowning its grandparents, as practical Qabala is older than the speculative or philosophic schools.

The practical application of spiritual knowledge is derived from magical practices of the Talmudic period through the Middle Ages. They are distinct and separate from the philosophic schools that use the Tree of Life and in no way are dependent on them. Yet the use of power, even naturally forming power, can corrupt but the most ardent soul, which gave rise to nefarious or "black magical" practices in which the "unholy names" of the fallen angels were employed to do harm, effect personal gain at others' expense, and disrupt the natural order of creation. With the widespread diffusion of Jews across Europe and North Africa, Jewish magic also took on some of the practices of its neighbors, especially Arab demonology and German and Slavic witchcraft. In turn, the practices of these people were also affected by Jewish magical doctrines, as belief in the efficacy of Jewish magic quickly became legendary. The idea of "the Jew" being a powerful magician, capable of conjuring up angels and devils, amplified others' awe of practical Qabala, as well as anti-Semitic fears. The *ba'al Shem,* "master of the Name," became the archetypal magus of the medieval period; many Christians sought to imitate this model, despite direct prohibitions by the Roman Catholic Church against magical practices.

Magical Writing

The use of special alphabets attributed to angelic or divine sources is a cornerstone of phonetic Jewish magic. It also influences those practices in which talismans and magical drawings are also used, in that many of these images are composed of carefully crafted constructions made up of Hebrew letters.

The earliest of these so-called magical alphabets or *kolmosin* ("angelic pens") is attributed to Metatron, the archangel of the Countenance (or Throne of God), who is connected in oral tradition to the biblical figure Enoch. Additional alphabets exist and are attributed to other angelic and archangelic beings, such as Raphael, Michael, and Gabriel, in the same fashion that various magical texts are attributed to Hermes, Solomon, Moses, and other important figures. Several alphabets are similar to Babylonian cuneiform, while others more closely resemble early Hebrew and Samaritan scripts. These alphabets are often referred to as "eye writing" in that they are composed of small dots and lines, closely resembling the human eye. This manner of writing was occasionally used in writing divine names in nonmagical texts, but it was mainly used in the creation of talismans. These magical images descend from Greek and Aramaic theurgical practices from the first century CE.[1]

Reuchlin and the Miraculous Name

Johannes Reuchlin (1455–1522), born in Germany in the town of Pforzheim, received a doctorate in philosophy from the University of Basel in 1477 and a degree in law from the University of Poitiers in 1481. He traveled to Rome as part of the diplomatic corps before settling in Stuttgart. In 1492, at the age of forty-seven, Reuchlin learned Hebrew. This was a difficult year for Jews, as it marked the beginning of several pogroms. Under orders of the new Catholic king and queen, Ferdinand and Isabelle, Jews were ordered to leave Spain, convert to Catholicism, or risk death. Neighboring Portugal would follow suit within two years.

Reuchlin's knowledge of Hebrew allowed him to study Qabala directly from the original texts, and within two years he had produced his principle work on the subject: *De Verbo Mirifico*. *De Verbo* became a sort of bible on what would eventually be called "Christian Cabala."* In it, Reuchlin claimed to have reconstructed the "true" name of Jesus in Hebrew by taking the Tetragrammaton, or "four-lettered name" of God in Hebrew—Yod-Heh-Vau-Heh, or YHVH—and inserting the letter Shin in the middle to yield YHShVH.

> The main subject of Reuchlin's first book on Kabbalah, *De Verbo Mirifico,* was to expose the miraculous powers of the hidden divine name, the Pentagrammaton, formed from the insertion of the letter *Sh,* in the middle of the Tetragrammaton; this name formed, according to Reuchlin and his source Pico della Mirandola, the secret name of Jesus. . . . In the Jewish Kabbalah we can find formations of "divine" names that cannot be detected in classical Jewish texts, which are as bizarre as the form YHSVH [sic].[2]

This miraculous name was quickly adopted to show that the true mission of Jesus was that of savior, but also to show that within Qabala, there were many secrets that had been forgotten since the time of the first Christian churches. This attempt to "Christianize" Qabala made it a politically safer topic for Reuchlin and others to study.

However, Reuchlin did eventually end up before the tribunal of the Inquisition. The position of Jews in Christian Europe was always a precarious one. Not accepting the Christian faith was bad enough. Being blamed as a people for the death of Christ, the Son of God, only made things worse. When Emperor Maximilian I ordered all books in Hebrew burnt on August 15, 1509, few might have really been surprised. However, authorities did ask Reuchlin—in what might have been an effort at entrapment for his Jewish-leaning sympathies—if he felt it admissible to burn all Jewish books, sparing only the Torah. Reuchlin answered no and was ordered to appear before the Grand Inquisitor in Mainz to defend himself against charges of heresy. Fortunately for

---

*Spellings of *Qabala* vary. However, strictly Hebrew mysticism is increasingly using the spellng *Kabbalah,* Christian variations *Cabala,* and Hermetic schools *Qabala.*

Reuchlin, he was a well-liked man. Representatives from fifty-three towns in the province of Swabia (in present-day Germany) spoke up on his behalf. To thank him for the great risk he took in their defense, the rabbis of the town of Pforzheim supplied him with the documents he would later use in writing *De Arte Cabalistica.*

After its publication in 1516, *De Arte Cabalistica* quickly became a preferred text for Christian cabalists. It was dedicated to Pope Leo X, who had an interest in Pythagoreanism. The basic format of *De Arte Cabalistica* is that of a dialogue between a Pythagorean and a Muslim, mediated by a Jew, who explains how Qabala contains the oldest of divine wisdom. This wisdom states that the sacred letters and names of things—in Hebrew, of course—are not just symbols but carry the very spiritual essence of the thing they are related to. The same doctrine was held by the ancient Egyptians regarding hieroglyphs and their sacred writings. To substantiate his claims Reuchlin references the Zohar and the magical text *Sefer Raziel* (Book of Raziel), whose authorship has been attributed to the archangel Raziel. The name Raziel means the "secret of God," and he is the archangel of the sphere of *hockmah* (wisdom) on the Tree of Life. This makes Raziel the guardian of the secret wisdom of God, the archangel that revealed the mysteries to Adam, Enoch, Noah, and King Solomon. *Sefer Raziel* describes the "Fifty Gates of Wisdom," of which even the great king and magus Solomon was able to penetrate only unto the forty-ninth, with the final "gate" being closed even to him.

Distinctions between Magic and Mysticism

While magic was seen as filled with dangers and used mainly for creating effects in the outer world, mysticism, which employed many of the same principles, was seen as a means of increasing one's personal holiness and relationship to God. Through prayer and meditation, it was believed, the individual could ascend the celestial spheres and attain increasing knowledge, love, and wisdom.*

---

*These spheres could be seen as a mirror of the biblical stories of Jacob's ladder and Ezekiel's vision, and its latter adaptation in Lurianic Qabala as the Tree of Life.

Gershom Scholem states:

> The Kabbalah regarded prayer as the ascent of man to the upper
> worlds, a spiritual peregrination among the supernal realms that
> sought to integrate itself into their hierarchical structure and to
> contribute its share toward restoring what had been flawed there.
> Its field of activity in kabbalistic thought is entirely in the inward
> worlds and in the connections between them. . . . The ontologi-
> cal hierarchy of the spiritual worlds reveals itself to the kabbal-
> ist in the time of prayer as one of the many Names of God. This
> unveiling of a divine "Name" through the power of the "word" is
> what constitutes the mystical activity of the individual in prayer,
> who meditates or focuses his *kavvanah* [meditation] upon the par-
> ticular name that belongs to the spiritual realm through which
> his prayer passing. . . . Such "inward magic" is distinguished from
> sorcery in that its meditations or *kavvanot* are not meant to be
> pronounced. The Divine Names are not called upon, as they are
> in ordinary operational magic, but are aroused through meditative
> activity directed toward them.[3]

We see that for the pious Jew practicing Qabala, the so-called
divine names were not a starting point or an end point but something that was revealed from within during periods of prayer and
meditation and that acted as signposts along the way. They were
not functional tools in and of themselves, nor were they meant
to be. Only in later years did specifically Qabalistic prayers and
meditations develop.

The end goal of these prayers and meditations was complete
absorption into the godhead. In doing so, the breach between God
and humanity, symbolized by "the Fall," was repaired, and God
became accessible once again. This often revealed itself in the form
of ecstasy, which was sometimes even contagious to those around
the one praying, and heightened states of awareness, such as proph-
esy, healing, and clairvoyance. These phenomena, however, were
regarded as side effects of the state, and not a goal in themselves. They

were viewed similar to Paul's advice on the "charismas," or various spiritual experiences associated with the powers of the Holy Spirit among the early Christians: they are a sign of grace, but not the act of grace.

FLUDD AND THE ROSICRUCIAN CONNECTION

Robert Fludd (1574–1637), or Robert de Fluctibus, as he preferred to be called, left us a remarkable work on medical theory, *Anatomiae amphitheatrum* (1623).* Fludd, a physician and member of the Royal College of London, believed that the root cause of all diseases could be found in original sin. He believed that disease was caused by demons and healed, or at least combatted, by angelic forces. Thus, prayer was seen as effective as medicine in bringing health to patients.

Fludd was the son of a Kentish squire and traveled on the Continent in his youth, returning to study medicine at Oxford and graduating in 1605. Fludd probably met Michael Maier during his visit to England sometime after 1612. It is from this possible meeting that Fludd may have come into contact with the Rosicrucian stream of Hermeticism that was beginning to flourish abroad, especially in central Europe. While the connection of Fludd to Rosicrucianism via Maier is clearly circumstantial, what is not is Fludd's publication of a defense of Rosicrucianism and the "Rosy Cross Brotherhood" in 1616: *Apologia Compendiaria Fraternitatem de Rosea Cruce,* or "A Compendium Apology for the Fraternity of the Rosy Cross."

Fludd published this compendium, and all of his important works, abroad with a publisher who had exhibited occult interests. Fludd also may have been a Freemason, and thus responsible for introducing Rosicrucianism into the early formation of Freemasonry. The first written suggestion linking these two forms of Hermetic

---

*For more information see: *The Greater and Lesser Worlds of Robert Fludd: Macrocosm, Microcosm, and Medicine* by Joscelyn Godwin (Inner Traditions, 2019).

initiation—Rosicrucianism and Freemasonry—occured one year after Fludd's death in Henry Adamson's *Muses Threnodie:**

> *For what we do presage is not in grosse,*
> *For we be brethren of the Rosie Cross:*
> *We have the Mason's word and the second sight,*
> *Things for to come we can fortell aright.*[4]

THE MASON'S WORD

Albert Mackey tells us:

The mythical history of Freemasonry informs us that there once existed a WORD of surpassing value, and claiming a profound veneration; that this Word was known to but few; that it was at length lost; and that a temporary substitute for it was adopted. But as the very philosophy of Masonry teaches us that there can be no death without a resurrection,—no decay without a subsequent restoration,—on the same principle it follows that the loss of the Word must suppose its eventual recovery. . . .

The WORD . . . I conceive to be the symbol of Divine Truth; and all its modifications—the loss, the substitution, and the recovery— are but component parts of the mythical symbol which represents a search after truth.[5]

In several of the degrees in Scottish Rite and Royal Arch, also known as Capitulary Masonry or Capstone Masonry, the Lost Word is revealed to the Master Masons who are present. This "Word," so long hidden, has also lost much of its significance despite the massive amount of clues given in the dramatic and symbolic material presented during the performance of the initiation rituals.

Prior to this revelation of the Lost Word, the Master Mason is given

---

*This poem can also be found in the *Encyclopedia Britannica* under the entry for "Rosicrucian."

another word, known as the Substitute Word. Unfortunately, the oral nature of this part of the Masonic tradition has meant that during the transmission of this important word by which Masons may recognize each other, the pronunciation has been garbled, giving rise to two actual words in use. One is predominant in continental Europe and the other in England, the United States, and other primarily English-speaking countries. According to Mackey the second word came into existence and use during the formation of the High Degrees (those degrees from 4th to 33rd that are often the subject of much speculation by non-Masons) and the influence of the exiled Stuarts on Freemasonry. What is intriguing about this is that both words have come to have their own unique and specific meaning, making both of value to the Mason who is on the path of illumination and not simply a card carrier. This value lies in part in the essential Hebrew origin of the words; it also lies in the simple meaning of a word or spoken phrase in Freemasonry and esotericism in general as well. However, in some instance this meaning must be injected into the word, or the word that the sound most closely approximates, because so many Masons were lacking education in ancient languages and thus the meaning and pronunciation of many terms has shifted.

While some Masons will object to "revealing" the Master Mason's Word, it must be pointed out that these words are easily found on the internet as well as in numerous books on Masonry. It is hoped that those objecting will realize this, as well as the certainty that without knowing the additional means of identification, or which word belongs to which jurisdiction, simple knowledge of the sounds will not allow people to pass themselves off as Master Masons.

Albert Mackey tells us that the proper word has four syllables, not three, as claimed by others (and we'll examine those claims in a moment). He says:

> The correct word has been mutilated. Properly, it consists of four syllables, for the last syllable, as it is now pronounced, should properly be divided into two. These four syllables compose three Hebrew words, which constitute a perfect and grammatical phrase,

appropriate to the occasion of their utterance. But to understand them, the scholar must seek the meaning in each syllable, and combine the whole. In the language of Apuleius, I must forbear to enlarge upon these holy mysteries.[6]

Pike states:

The True Word of a Mason is to be found in the concealed and profound meaning of the Ineffable Name of Deity, communicated by God to Moses; and which meaning was long lost by the very pre-cautions taken to conceal it. The true pronunciation of that name was in truth a secret, in which, however, was involved the far more profound secret of its meaning. In that meaning is included all the truth [that] can be known by us, in regard to the nature of God.[7]

A second version of the word has received a great deal of attention in some of the popular books pretending to be exposés on Freemasonry. Their authors claim that it is a synthetic word referring to "Ja" or Yod-Heh (the prefix of the Tetragrammaton), "Bal," and "On," thereby show-ing that Freemasons are in fact not good Christians, Jews, or Muslims, as many profess, but indeed worshippers of strange deities. Even if there is some truth to the origin of the three parts of the threefold name, all it demonstrates is that Masons see all gods as one. Collectively, they call this supreme power the Grand Architect of the Universe; individu-ally, they call their god by different names; and in their hearts many see all gods as being a partial and imperfect human expression of the One True God.

Tetragrammaton:
the unspeakable name of God

For the majority of Masons, even these Substitute Words are little more than a means of recognition, no different from the words given to craftsmen for traveling purposes in the Middle Ages. For the mystically inclined brother, they are the keys to self-awakening, to the construction of the inner temple that each must build in their own heart and therein hear the voice of the soul.

The Mason's Quest

The identification of the Master Mason's Word as the Substitute Word is of critical significance to the Freemason who is paying attention. The ancient religious, philosophical, and esoteric notion of the Word is that of divine truth: unquestionable and omnipotent power and the authority to create. Thus, if the Word is divine truth, then the Lost Word must be that truth either forgotten, ignored, or transformed in some manner during the act of its very expression—just as clay remains clay but is still modified when it is turned into a piece of pottery. The Substitute Word can be seen as twofold: either as a failure to find the truth, as the Fellowcraft who went in search of Hiram failed to find the Word, or as a temporary bridge to assist the aspirant on their search for truth. It is a comfort to aid them until the Word is found. The suggestion of a "substitute word" is found in various rituals of the eighteenth century, but it is not identified as such until later. If the Word is then divine truth, the quest for this truth is the very reason for the existence of Freemasonry, and each Mason's obligation and work is to find that Truth. While variations of the Word do not change its essential character, the idea of it is critical to the very existence of Masonry. Without the Word Masonry is dead: "The letter killeth, but the spirit giveth life" (2 Corinthians 3:6).

The Creative Power of the Word

Each Mason is tasked with finding the Lost Word, lost when the Master Hiram was slain, and from which was tasked the twelve Fellowcraft Masons who went in search of his body, to return and tell of the first sound they heard, as that would act as a substitute for the Lost Word. The symbolism here is particularly subtle in that the Lost Word cannot be heard without but only within. It is our inner Word—the Word of God, of the cosmos, of the Grand Architect of the Universe—that speaks to our heart. This voice of God within is the true Word. It is unfailing, ever-guiding, and life-affirming, not only in the symbolic sense, but literally as the power of creation itself.

Ptah, the eldest god of the family of dieties called the Memphis Triad, was known to the Egyptians as the Grand Architect of the Universe. In Egyptian mythology it was he who spoke the Word from which all of creation came into being.

The Egyptians had complete confidence in the divine origin and creative power of speech. All living beings, of the material or spiritual worlds, and objects had their origin in the utterance of sound. The entire universe was understood to be under the control of men and gods who knew the sacred speech. For the Egyptians material creation was sound made substantial. Every sound had substance and life—creative power—when uttered properly. In sacred speech there was complete harmony between the spoken and the incarnate, between the ideal and the material form. For these reasons (among others), the ancient philosopher Iamblichus (245–325 CE) regarded the Egyptian language as closest to the original primordial language of the gods, even more so than his native Greek.

The Egyptian god Thoth, equivalent to Hermes of the Greco-Egyptian period, is said to have written down the words Ptah spoke. They comprised forty-two books, which were closely guarded. Thoth was the lord of wisdom, writing, and magic. It is from Thoth-Hermes that we derive the name for that body of ancient theosophy known as Hermeticism, of which Freemasonry is an expression.

It is important to note that the Egyptians had no word for religion, only *heku,* or, poorly translated, "magical or creative power." The more creative power one had, the closer one was to the gods. This creative power, as we have seen, was closely linked to speech and writing. Written words or hieroglyphs were seen as living things, not unlike an animal, plant, or human being. Defacing them was tantamount to defacing the message they contained. Given that few people could read and write in primitive cultures, it is easy to see why the written word was held to be sacred, for it was memory, wisdom, and direction for its people.

However, Thoth's real power came from the spoken use of the words, not simply their static, engraved, fixed, or ritualistic use. Through the power of speech and the vibrations it creates, words were said to give power to men, nature, and the invisible worlds. The names of the gods were held in secret, and even two names were had for each of the gods: one for public use, and the other for private ceremonies.

This belief in the power of names and words carried over into Judaism, with the sacred four-lettered name of God, or, in Greek, Tetragrammaton, being only whispered into the ear of the initiate. If it were pronounced aloud, adherents were told, all of creation could be undone. The *Encyclopedia of Freemasonry* states that the Lost Word is none other than the true pronunciation of this name: Yod Heh Vau Heh.[8]

Of course, this doctrine of sacred or esoteric speech finds some of its most sophisticated development in the work of the alchemists and Qabalists, who often referred to it, respectively, as the "green language" or the "language of the birds," which Solomon was said to be able to understand. Given the symbolism of the color green for life and the well-known use of various birds in Egyptian and Asian mystical schools (and even in Christianity as a symbol of the consciousness or soul), we can easily see the idea that Solomon understood the language of the birds as a metaphor for his attunement to his inner voice, or the Word of God.

By the time in the early Christian era that the first line of the Gospel of John was penned, "In principio erat Verbum . . . " or "In the beginning was the Word," the idea of the creative power of the spoken word to affect all of nature, seen and unseen, was highly developed across the Middle and Far East. In India and Tibet, for example, we find the meditative practice of *mantra yoga,* with *mantra* being a Sanskrit word that literally means "mind tool." In mantra yoga words and sounds, whose meaning may not always be known, are repeated either vocally or mentally to focus the mind for meditative purposes. Repetition of such names of power was commonplace across the Classical World and found their way into Medieval and Renaissance magical manuscripts, albiet often in highly corrupted form. It is possible that the proper use of the name of God as a meditative device was being suggested in early Masonic symbolism and ritual. If so, it would clearly link Masonry with several schools of Qabala wherein meditation on the Tetragrammaton and its variations was the core practice. Here, in the use of words to turn the mind inward and listen for the inner voice, we see the use of sacred speech reach its pinnacle of development.

By the time of the early Christian era when the first line of the Gospel of John was penned and we are told, "In principa erat Verbum . . ." or "In the beginning was the Word," the idea of the creative power of the spoken word, to effect all of nature, seen and unseen, is highly developed across the Middle and Far East.

To understand this emphasis on speech, we need only look at these ancient cultures and reflect on the following facts:

- Words reflect our inner psychic as well as subconscious state.
- Words trigger emotions and ideas that, once initiated, cannot be taken back.
- Words are our foremost means of creation (after sex, of course), and it is no wonder that the thyroid is a secondary sexual organ, and considered among esotericists to be critical to the effective communication with the Divine.

This last point is important when we remember that with Hiram's murder, the first blow was to his throat. It is often said that this was so he could not cry out for help. But help from whom? And if the assailants were there to get the Word from Hiram, why would they render him speechless, unable to tell them the Word? Why destroy their very chance of receiving the Word?

Maybe the one who struck the first blow realized that Hiram would not give them what they sought but could in fact use it against them. As Jesus asked, "Thinkest thou that I cannot now pray to my Father, and he shall presently give me more than twelve legions of angels?" (Matthew 26:53). Could it be that the first blow was struck to stop

Hiram from calling on the angelic legions to protect him, just as Jesus said he could do?

In the New Testament we read that those in need approached Jesus and proclaimed, "Speak the word only, and my servant will be healed!" (Matthew 8:8). We also read of Jesus telling his closest disciples to go out among the multitudes and to heal the sick, raise the dead, and perform what we in the modern world call miracles, all "in the name of the Holy Spirit."

Such notions are radically foreign to modern thinking but must be reconsidered if the esoteric aspects of Masonry are to be fully understood. It is a proven fact that the very miracles described in the Scriptures are possible. They have been done, are being done today, and can be done and are in harmony with the known laws of modern physics.

Jean Dubuis, a twentieth-century French alchemist and well-known esotericist, wrote:

> According to mystics, a long time ago, on earth, there used to be a unique language called the original language which is sought today as the "Lost Word."
>
> The true Verb [Word], the Verb [Word] of the Bible's "Fiat Lux!" is the energy which is ceaselessly radiated by the formless being. The Fiat Lux is simply the vibrations of this energy as they are subjected to the law which is dictated by The Being, the Harmony where Beings, the Elohim came from, and all those who use this energy to create the worlds, the bodies of men and light of the sun which is but a pale reflection of this energy. Putting order into this energy results in Time, form, space; without these operations there can be only the Void, the Non-Manifest. Our body, our flesh, our blood are but vibrations which are subject to the ultimate law of vibrations: Harmony. Harmony exists in all realms, but we can get a clear idea of it in the realm of music. We see that some notes, while different, seem to have analogies between them.
>
> Let's imagine a keyboard, extending to the infinite of space. Let us strike the note of G, and increasingly move upward in octaves.

Each G is recognized as being similar to those that went before it, yet different, of a higher vibration. The number of vibrations per second for G is 384, and doubles with each increase in octave.

Given this increase in vibration, after the first six or seven G's we go beyond the realm of human hearing—but the note G still exists and vibrates. If we could build a keyboard with these higher octaves we could strike a note that would disrupt radio, television, even radar. We could even produce heat, and after the forty-second G a red light would be generated. Then, neither sound or light. A C note would produce hydrogen, an A note produce oxygen, and a chord would generate physical water.

We see in the Old Testament the idea that Adam named the animals, but can clearly understand now, that the First Being, or Adam, did more than name them. Through speaking he actually brought them into existence. Moses as well new the true name of water, and as such, brought it forth from the rock.[9]

This original language is all but lost, and it is the duty of initiates of the mystery traditions, of which Freemasonry is an heir, to restore it. Just as the twelve Fellowcraft went in search of the Word and found it not, but brought back a Substitute Word, initiates also use a substitute language, or series of languages, until this inner language can be reestablished. Many mystics consider several of the ancient languages— Hebrew, Egyptian, and in some instances Latin—to be closer to the original tongue, thereby making them the preferred means of prayer and invocation.

Given this meaning, the biblical story of the Tower of Babel and the Masonic symbol of the Lost Word are more easily understood. In many ways, the Tower of Babel is a fitting story for Masonic study, as it more closely fits the Masonic myth than does the Temple of Solomon, for that temple was completed and destroyed twice. The Tower of Babel, on the plains of Shinar, however, was not completed. For Masons, like humanity after the collapse of the tower, are confined to speaking many languages and, as such, encounter difficulty in the world of matter. The unity that humanity is said to have originally had is a faint memory, but still informs the desire for cultural, racial, and linguistic purity we see across the spectrum of political, religious, and social movements. The promise of a return to a Golden Age, to Edenic purity, to establish some form of heaven on earth is a powerful attraction and always a path to hell when imposed from without. A clue to the importance of this can be seen in the fact that Masonry has an injunction against "babbling" or meaningless speech both inside and outside the lodge.

The only way that this unity can be established is individually, in and through each of us. The working tool to rebuild this tower is the same as for the Temple: the trowel, for it spreads the cement of brotherly love and affection.

Only love—the emotion of the heart, the true organ of human consciousness and spiritual perception—can allow us to unite the many bricks needed to rebuild the tower that reaches to heaven. Only love can open the door to the inner temple, the true sanctum sanctorum, that each Freemason must complete and build for himself.

The Original Language, or Word, is a vibratory image of the Divine Plan. When one reintegrates their consciousness with the inner unity symbolized by the Pillar of Wisdom and the station of the Lodge Master in Freemasonry, this language becomes a reality.

One does need to be a Freemason to begin the search for the Lost Word; the quest is most easily done by examining our own use of language. Are our words meant to be beautiful and harmonious, or are they sarcastic and divisive? Do we use clear, precise, and simple speech or excessive, vague, and complex phrases to hide our true meaning? Are we vulgar and profane or cultured and inspiring?

Attitude is also a clue to where work must be done. A positive attitude is critical to successful work in both the material and spiritual realms. Only by having a firm, steadfast, and unwavering conviction can we accomplish anything, and in the realm of our self-becoming, a positive attitude is even more important.

If upon reflection we find ourself tending to complain, talking about illnesses, troubles, or problems (while not seeking a genuine solution) on a regular basis, then given the power of our speech, how can we expect anything else from life?

Masonry teaches that it is imperative to focus on the beautiful, the strong, and the wise and to invoke the spirit of harmony into daily life. Through the teachings of "the Work," Masons learn that all things, no matter how difficult they may seem, are only passing, and that as Shakespeare said, "There is nothing either good or bad, but thinking makes it so" (*Hamlet,* Act 2, scene 2). Through our speech—the spoken expression of our inner convictions—and our attitude toward life, we bind ourselves to happiness or sorrow, health or illness, and success or failure, and as creator of that bond, we are the only one who can change it. This is the ultimate purpose of the search for the Lost Word.

The Lost Word and the Masonic Quest: Key Points

1. The Lost Word is what every Master Mason is charged with seeking. During his raising to the 3rd degree, he receives only a Substitute Word.

2. Harmony expressed in sound produces music, and in word a certain rhythm or chant. Words, or sounds, express a power over their listeners.

3. Masonry uses in its rituals peculiar wording and language that link it to an earlier historical period as well as exert a positive influence over the psyche of those participating.

4. Freemasonry speaks of three words: the Lost Word, the Substitute Word, and the true Word. Each is a reflection of the others and represents stages in human spirituality. The Lost Word is ignorance, symbolized by the fall of Adam and Eve from grace in Genesis and the murder of Hiram. The Substitute Word is the use of religion, law, and authority to bring harmony and order to human condition. The true Word is direct revelation or personal experience of the divine, the God within.

5. The name of God known as the Tetragrammaton, or YHVH, plays an important role in Jewish mysticism and magic. During the Middle Ages rabbis known as "masters of the Name" were said to have been able to perform miracles through the use of this and other divine names.

6. Special writing and divine names are linked to each other as well as the angelic cosmology of Judaism. Angelic alphabets are often attributed to Metatron, who is also identified with Enoch. Enoch plays an important role in Masonic lore.

7. Johannes Reuchlin's book *De Arte Cabalistica* demonstrated how the sacred letters and names of things in Hebrew are not just symbols but are thought to carry the very spiritual essence of the thing they are related to. According to Reuchlin (and others of his time), knowledge of the letters and words gives the power to create.

8. Within Jewish mysticism prayer is considered more important than magical acts or the use of divine names.

9. Robert Fludd, an apologist for the Rosicrucian movement, advocated the use of prayer in healing.

10. The Egyptian god Thoth is identified with Hermes Trismigestus, the founder of the Hermetic arts and sciences, and is a master of the Word, or the creative power of magical speech.

11. A positive attitude is critical in all work, be it spiritual or material, and our words reflect our attitude.

12. Positive speech is essential to human harmony, spiritual well-being, and physical health.

Assignments for Chapter Six

1. Pay attention to the frequency of your speech. Limit your speech to only what is essential for one week. Notice how often you are tempted to speak simply to be heard, or to say something meaningless, sarcastic, or simply unnecessary.

2. Pay attention to the quality of your speech. Do you use positive action words, or are they passive? Do you speak negatively and in terms of limitations or positively in terms of possibilities? What does this say about your fundamental worldview?

3. How does your particular religious practice use speech? What does this reflect about the practice?

The Lost Word and the Masonic Quest:
Suggested Reading

Encyclopedia of Freemasonry, by Albert Mackey, rev. ed. edited by W. J. Hughan and E. L. Hawkins (Masonic History Co., 1924). This can easily be found online, and older secondhand copies are commonly available. It is an essential reference for understanding Freemasonry.

Masonic Presentation Bible (such as those published by Heirloom Bible Publishers). These bibles, specially printed for presentation at Masonic rituals, can often be found from secondhand stores or used book dealers. They often contain illustrations as well as a glossary of terms and their particular meaning within Freemasonry.

Meaning of Masonry, by W. L. Wilmhurst (Barnes & Noble Books). Wilmhurst is a modern master of Masonic symbolism and its power to "make good men better."

Symbols of Freemasonry, by Daniel Beresniak (Editions Assouline, 1997). A beautiful book of Masonic symbols and lodges, mainly European. Simply a joy to behold.

7

Scottish Rite and the Rise of Esoteric Masonry

The Occult Science of the Ancient Magi was concealed under the shadows of the Ancient Mysteries: it was imperfectly revealed or rather disfigured by the Gnostics: it is guessed at under the obscurities that cover the pretended crimes of the Templars; and it is found enveloped in enigmas that seem impenetrable, in the Rites of the Highest Masonry.

ALBERT PIKE

SCOTCH RITE, OR SCOTTISH RITE, as it is more commonly known, originated in France in the early eighteenth century. Its name in part derives from the claim that Scottish Rite was established in France by Scots fleeing the English invasion and seeking asylum on the Continent. Claims are often made linking various Masonic rites through Scottish Rite to "Bonnie" Prince Charles of Scotland and his Jacobite supporters in exile. Like many things in Masonry, these claims are easy to make and almost impossible to prove, making them more legend than history. The name ultimately owes its origin to the Scots Master (or Scottish Master) degree, worked in London since 1732. From there it went to France and Germany, where other high degrees were framed around its traditions. However, as Scottish political interests played a part in the creation of many of these various rites and degrees, attempts to establish a connection between the two reflects the social and political culture of Masonry in the eighteenth century.

Critical to the formation of many Continental lodges and Masonic rites was the assertion by Chevalier Andrew Michael Ramsay of Scotland that Freemasonry was a direct descendant of chivalric and mystical societies brought to Europe by returning Crusaders. Most of the Masonic rites that appeared in France after 1737 were founded upon Ramsay's assertion, along with the added notion that it was connected to the Knights Templar, who, it was claimed, had fled in part to Scotland after their persecution by King Philip IV of France and Pope Clement V in the early fourteenth century. The French currently refer to these degrees as Huats Grades, or "High Grades," rather than Scottish Rite.

Scottish Rite came to the New World with the appointment of Etienne Morin in 1761 as "Grand Inspector to all parts of the New World." With the missionary zeal common to eighteenth-century Masonry, in 1763 Morin established the Rite of Perfection, consisting of fourteen degrees, in Santo Domingo, in the Dominican Republic (at that time a French colony known as Saint-Domingue, in the West Indies). From this Caribbean foothold, the Rite of Perfection spread to North America and grew into the worldwide movement of Scottish Rite. The Rite of Perfection was established in New York in 1765 with the arrival of Henry Francken, an associate of Morin and a resident of Jamaica. It was later established in Charleston, South Carolina, in 1783 by Isaac Da Costa. It was here in South Carolina at the beginning of the nineteenth century, far away from the traditional Masonic strongholds in the metropolitan centers of Europe, that things began to get interesting. In 1801 Dr. Frederick Dalcho and John Mitchell arrived in Charleston with a document granting the bearer the right to establish new chapters of Freemasonry, allegedly under the authority of Frederick the Great, King of Prussia. The constitutions of these new chapters went on to add an additional eight degrees to the existing rite, and it referred to it as the "Ancient and Accepted Scottish Rite." It was dated 1786 and apparently had the desired effect, for on May 31, 1801, the Mother Supreme Council of the 33rd Degree of the Ancient and Accepted Scottish Rite of Freemasonry was formed. Scottish Rite spread slowly across the South but would soon become a dominant force—at least for a while. In the North, York Rite, with its additional degrees and bodies (see chapter 9), was dominant, and the various Scottish Rite bodies there became embroiled in bitter disputes as to authenticity and jurisdictional authority. This devastating weakness of Scottish Rite in the North would continue until after the Civil War, when in 1867 the Northern Masonic Jurisdiction (NMJ) merged with the Cerneau Scottish Rite to become the recognized authority to coffer the degrees in fifteen states.

Ordo ab Chaos

The motto of Scottish Rite is *Ordo ab chaos,* or "order out of chaos." Nothing could be a more fitting description. While it is difficult for someone living in the early twenty-first century to understand why all of these groups existed, with the various degrees and rites, it is important to recognize the profound cultural differences between eighteenth-century European and American life and what we experience today.

In a world in which it took two months to cross the Atlantic or two weeks to go from Philadelphia to New York City, social connections were critical to personal success in life. Belonging to an organization that provided instant contacts in distant cities was in itself a major benefit, despite political and religious persecution that may have accompanied it at times. In addition, without a vast network of colleges, adult education classes, or near instant access to information via the internet or mail-order delivery, Masonry and its degrees provided a forum for personal improvement. It also allowed members to have a means of "prequalifying" or screening potential business, social, or even esoteric contacts through a network of established channels and signs of recognition. The world of the eighteenth and nineteenth centuries was slower, more distant, and disconnected than it is today. Freemasonry served as a major vehicle in bringing distant points together.

THE DEGREES

Scottish Rite is the second largest rite, after York Rite. Both confer the three degrees of symbolic Masonry in Blue Lodge, which are given only by lodges duly and lawfully chartered by a grand lodge.

From there, however, the number of degrees in the Scottish Rite expands considerably, up to and including the famous 33rd degree, or that of the Sovereign Grand Inspector General, which is conferred by the Supreme Council—the administrative head of the rite for the jurisdiction under its authority. The twenty-nine degrees below the 33rd are divided into groups, each with its own governing body, subservient to the Supreme Council. In general, the 4th through 14th degrees are conferred in a Lodge of Perfection, the 15th and 16th degrees are conferred in a Council of Princes of Jerusalem, the 17th and 18th degrees are conferred in a Chapter of Sublime Princes of Rose Croix, the 19th through 30th degrees are conferred in a Council of Kadosh, and, finally, the 31st and 32nd degrees are conferred in a Consistory of Princes of the Royal Secret. Of course, like all things Masonic, there is some variation in these assignments according to jurisdiction.

Lodges of Perfection: These degrees elaborate on King Solomon's Temple and the search for the Lost Word or unspoken name of God. They are similar to Royal Arch degrees in York Rite.

Council of Princes of Jerusalem: These degrees focus on the rebuilding of the Temple of Solomon. This particular division does not exist in all Masonic jurisdictions; these degrees may instead be included in the Chapter of the Rose-Croix.

Chapter of the Rose-Croix: While Christian in tone these degrees contain alchemical symbolism and suggest a Rosicrucian influence in Masonic development.

Council of Kadosh: This is a particular classification for governing the 19th through 30th degrees within the Southern Jurisdiction. *Kadosh* is Hebrew for "holy" or "consecrated to God," and its use denotes the nature of the philosophic instruction of these degrees. There is a Templar connection as well.

Consistory of Princes of the Royal Secret: This is an administrative designation for meetings of members of the 31st and 32nd degrees for the Southern Jurisdiction and 19th through 32nd degrees for the Northern Masonic Jurisdiction. There is a distinct Templar association with the 31st and 32nd degrees, and the Council of Kadosh is included in Consistory meetings in the Northern Masonic Jurisdiction to reduce this redundancy.

The size and scope of these degree meetings constitute small theatrical productions and are a form of initiation combined with a morality or teaching play. In the United States these degrees are rarely given to a single member but instead to groups of men, often in an auditorium or theater specially designed for the purpose. In Europe and elsewhere, the degrees are conferred on a smaller scale, with less theatrics, but the fundamental nature, teaching, and lesson of the degrees are the same.

ALBERT PIKE AND THE RENEWAL OF SCOTTISH RITE

It would be impossible to discuss Scottish Rite without taking a look at the life and work of Albert Pike (1809–1891), one of Masonry's most profound and controversial figures. Pike was born in Massachusetts and as a child demonstrated exceptional skill in school, learning Greek, Latin, and Hebrew before the age of twenty. He passed his entrance exams and was accepted to attend Harvard University, completing two years of his undergraduate program in one year, but as the son of an alcoholic shoemaker, he was unable to afford the remaining tuition. In 1831 he left Massachusetts and headed west, ending up in Fort Smith, Arkansas. There, his natural talents came to the forefront as he taught school, edited a newspaper, practiced law, and even became a state Supreme Court justice. Pike married Ann Hamilton in 1834 and, with his wife's financial backing, entered politics. His military career began in 1846, and the following year he led a volunteer unit at the Battle of Buena Vista against the Mexican army. Pike was popular with the local Native American tribes and represented them in court against the

United States government. Pike continued to practice law later in life as well, and he argued several cases before the United States Supreme Court.

Pike became affiliated with Freemasonry during his time in Arkansas, joining Star Lodge #2, in Little Rock, in 1850. In 1852 he assisted in establishing Magnolia Lodge #60 with sixteen fellow Masons, serving as master in 1853 and 1854. Pike took the ten York Rite degrees and was active in that rite on a state level. In March 1853 he traveled to Charleston, South Carolina, where he received the 4th through 32nd degrees and was appointed deputy inspector of Arkansas for the Scottish Rite.

At the time, Scottish Rite was among the smallest of the existing Masonic bodies; membership records show fewer than one thousand members in the United States in 1853. Pike's extensive training in the classics and his scholastic skill made him a natural candidate for the position that would soon define his life's work. The Supreme Council of the rite's Southern Jurisdiction established a five-man committee to revise the rituals as part of a plan to reinvigorate itself. The committee never met, but Pike undertook the task himself. As part of the process for this massive undertaking, Pike immersed himself in Hermetic philosophy and esotericism, hand-copied all of the rituals on file and available to him, and completed his draft in 1857. With the resignation of Albert Mackey as Supreme Commander that same year, and with only six years of membership under his belt, Pike became the head of the Southern Jurisdiction of the Scottish Rite in January 1859, holding the office until his death in 1891.

In 1861 Jefferson Davis, president of the Confederacy, appointed Pike as commissioner of Indian affairs, investing him with the rank of brigadier general. In 1862 Major General Thomas C. Hindman declared martial law in Arkansas, and ordered Pike to turn over weapons and Native American Indian treaty funds. Pike refused, believing Hindman had no right to this request. Hindman ordered Pike's arrest. Fleeing to Texas, Pike was briefly jailed. Pike resigned his post and commission and published a letter stating that the Confederate government was in violation of its treaty agreements with and obligations to Native

American tribes. He was released as the Confederate military in the West collapsed in late 1862.

Without friends or family, in danger from both Union and Confederate forces, and bankrupt, Pike retreated to the Ozark Mountains, where he remained until 1868. Studying Qabala, alchemy, Hermeticism, Eastern scriptures, and philosophy, he revised the rituals of Scottish Rite even further than he had in his earlier draft, and in doing so, he included a large part of the Western esoteric traditions. With his work completed he left the Ozarks for Washington, D.C., where he remained for the rest of his life, living in a small apartment provided for him by the Supreme Council. He dedicated his entire life to the development of Scottish Rite and other Masonic bodies.

MORALS AND DOGMA:
THE UNOFFICIAL BIBLE OF SCOTTISH RITE

To those who are familiar with him, Pike is best known for his massive tome *Morals and Dogma of the Ancient and Accepted Scottish Rite of Freemasonry*, or just *Morals and Dogma* for short. Few books have been so widely read, flipped through, misunderstood, and misquoted as *Morals and Dogma*. In fact, this book alone is often the single most misquoted source for those wishing to demonstrate something insidious and malefic about Freemasonry in general and Scottish Rite in particular. The reason for this is simple: Pike was a scholar who understood the fundamental esoteric teachings that are present in Masonic symbolism but went unnoticed or were misunderstood by most of its members.

Using the existing literature of his period, and drawing heavily upon the early works of the French occult revival (he quoted heavily from Eliphas Levi's 1854 *Dogma and Ritual of High Magic*), Pike sought to demonstrate that Masonry was more than just the gentlemen's social club it was morphing into but, instead, that the organization was the inheritor of a secret tradition of human unfoldment that was thousands of years old. What came from his research was largely published in *Morals and Dogma* and was meant to be used as a series of lectures for each of the degrees, making it a textbook of sorts for the candidate. Copies of *Morals and Dogma* are easily found in secondhand bookshops these days, as it was given to almost every 32nd-degree member of the Southern Jurisdiction until 1974. Despite his importance to Masonry and the Scottish Rite, Pike's works are not universally adopted nor appreciated by many within or outside of the Northern Masonic and Southern Jurisdictions in the United States.

THE ROYAL ART:
FREEMASONRY AND HUMAN EVOLUTION

Freemasonry often refers to itself as "the Royal Art." According to Albert Mackey's *Encyclopedia of Freemasonry,* Anderson's *Constitutions* referred to Freemasonry as the Royal Art as early as 1723, and Mackey goes on to say that this name was first used in 1693, when William III was initiated into the Craft. He also spends two pages explaining that Freemasonry differs from a handicraft in that the Freemason is no mere technician but a genuine artist who understands all aspects of his chosen expression—this expression being the perfection of himself in relation to humanity and God, a perfection achieved through love. Quoting a German Masonic catechism from Prague (1800), he states, "Every Freemason is a king, in whatsoever condition God may have placed him here, with rank equal to that of a king and with sentiments that become a king, for his kingdom is LOVE, the love of his fellow-man, a love which is long-suffering and kind, which beareth all things, believeth all things, hopeth all things, endureth all things."[1]

Like alchemy, the Royal Art was preoccupied with the Great Work: the metaphorical transformation of "lead" into "gold"—that is, in one sense, the perfection of human capacity by an act of will upon oneself and nature. (As the saying goes, the goal of Masonry is "making good men better.") Mackey states:

> Freemasonry and alchemy have sought the same results (the lesson of Divine Truth and the doctrine of immortal life), and they have both sought it by the same method of symbolism. It is not, therefore, strange that in the eighteenth century, and perhaps before, we find an incor-

poration of much of the science of alchemy in that of Freemasonry. Hermetic rites and Hermetic degrees were common. . . . The Twenty-eighth Degree of the Scottish Rite, or the Knight of the Sun, is entirely a Hermetic degree, and claims its parentage in the title of "Adept of Masonry," by which it is sometimes known.[2]

Regarding the Knight of the Sun, Prince Adept, Albert Pike states:

Like all the Mysteries of Magism, the Secrets of "the Great Work" have a threefold signification: they are religious, philosophical, and natural. The philosophical gold, in religion, is the Absolute and Supreme Reason: in philosophy, it is the Truth; in visible nature, the Sun; in the subterranean and mineral world, the most perfect and pure gold. . . . The Great Work is, above all things, the creation of man by himself; that is to say, the full and entire conquest which he effects of his faculties and his future. It is, above all, the perfect emancipation of his will, which assures him the universal empire of Azoth, and the domain of magnetism, that is, complete power over the universal Magical agent. . . . So that the Great Work is more than a chemical operation; it is a real creation of the human word initiated into the power of the Word of God. The creation of gold in the Great Work is effected by transmutation and multiplication. . . . The Great Work of Hermes is, therefore, an operation essentially magical, and the highest of all, for it supposes the Absolute in Science and in Will. There is light in gold, gold in light, and light in all things.[3]

When we compare this to to Eliphas Levi's writings, we see a clear and present influence in the writings of Pike, to the point of Pike lifting entire passages from Levi for use in *Morals and Dogma*. Levi is often viewed as the father of the French occult revival of the nineteenth century, a period in which fringe Masonry and occultism intermingle full bloom. It is simply impossible to understand Pike and his profound influence on Scottish Rite if we do not understand Levi, whose writings had a profound effect on Pike. For men like Pike

Masonry's obsessive search for the Lost Word could be fully explained by the writings of Levi.

Levi states:

Magic is contained in the word and a word well pronounced is more powerful than the combined powers of the Heavens, Earth and Hell. Nature is commanded by a Name; in the same way we can conquer power over the different kingdoms of Nature. The occult forces which compose the invisible Universe are submissive to whoever can pronounce, in full knowledge of the CAUSE, non-communicable names.[4]

Michel Caron and Serge Hutin would later write on alchemy:

The fire principle plays a predominant part in many alchemical treatises, for it is the soul of the Microcosm. The elemental atoms of this fire, certain alchemists tell us, pervade the universe in the form of currents; these produce light when they intersect in the heavens, and gold when they meet beneath the ground.

Light and gold are sometimes considered to be fire in its concrete state: to "materialize" this gold, which is sown profusely throughout the world, one need only condense widely scattered atoms.

Properly speaking, gold is not a metal—gold is light.[5]

It is no coincidence, then, that the Emerald Tablet of Hermes refers to the Great Work as "the Work of the Sun."

Levi further states:

There is in Nature a . . . Universal Agent, whose supreme law is balanced and whose command answers to the Great Arcana of Transcendental Magic. . . . When it radiates it is called light. . . . The will of intelligent beings acts directly on this light, and through it on all Nature which then undergoes the modifications of the intelligence. Through the direction of this agent, we can even change the sequences of the seasons, produce phenomena of the day during the night, instantly correspond from one point to the opposite end of the earth, heal at a distance, provide speech with universal results and consequences. To know how to master this agent, so as to take advantage of its force and direct its currents, is to accomplish the Great Work, to be the master of the world and the depository of God's power.[6]

While such claims may appear outlandish on first reading, we need only consider that among those interested in practical alchemy and magic and involved with the development of Freemasonry, particularly in the higher degrees, were the most prominent scientists of the day. Both early science and Freemasonry were obsessed with geometry and mathematics, as these fields allowed for the study of optics, which in turn allowed for the study of light. Modern physics, particularly quantum physics, has demonstrated that the state of mind of the scientist conducting an experiment on the subatomic level—the level of light— can and does change the outcome of experiments.

In his book *The God Theory*, Bernard Haisch describes this background of light on the subatomic level as Zero-Point Energy, or the fundamental energy that is the basis for everything. He writes:

If we are right, the dictum "Let there be light" is indeed a very profound statement (as one might expect of its purported author). Inertia is the property of matter that gives it solidity; it's what gives things substance. The proposed connection between the zero-point field and inertia, in effect, suggests that the solid, stable world of matter is sustained at every instant by this underlying sea of quantum light.[7]

Haisch goes on to quote from a Jewish legend from the Haggadah (which he came across in yet another book, titled *The Other Bible*). He paraphrases:

The light created at the very beginning is not the same as the light emitted by the Sun, the Moon, and the stars, which appeared only on the fourth day. . . . The light of the first day was of a sort that would have enabled man to see the world at a glance from one end to the other. Anticipating the wickedness of the sinful generations of the deluge and the Tower of Babel, who were unworthy to enjoy the blessing of such light, God concealed it, but in the world to come it will appear to the pious in all its pristine glory.[8]

To become fully human in the Hermetic tradition is to become fully alive and awake—to exercise one's will to the point wherein nature obeys one's command, and to do so knowing that each of us is the "son [or daughter] of our deeds" and that universal justice cannot be avoided. If there is only one God, one creative force, then each of us is god in miniature and are self-created beings learning to live to our full potential. For Pike, this is the great secret of Freemasonry, clothed in the alchemical language of the Knight of the Sun.

Scottish Rite and the Rise of Esoteric Masonry: Key Points

1. Scottish Rite has its origins in eighteenth-century France and is linked to exiled Jacobite supporters of Bonnie Prince Charles.
2. Chevalier Andrew Michael Ramsay of Scotland asserted that Freemasonry was a direct descendant of chivalric and mystical societies brought to Europe by returning Crusaders. Most Masonic rites that appeared in France after 1737 were founded upon Ramsay's assertion, along with the added notion that it was connected to the Knights Templar.
3. Scottish Rite came to the New World with the appointment of Etienne Morin in 1761 as "Grand Inspector to all parts of the New World." Morin established a Rite of Perfection in the West Indies in 1763. From here, Scottish Rite spread to North America and grew into a worldwide practice.
4. Scottish Rite is the second largest rite, and like York Rite, it confers the three degrees of symbolic Masonry in Blue Lodge.
5. Albert Pike is the single most important leader in American Scottish Rite and is responsible for its renewal in the nineteenth

century. His work, *Morals and Dogma,* established an esoteric and occult interpretation for the degrees of Scottish Rite similar to what had occurred in the previous century.

6. *Morals and Dogma* is the unofficial textbook of the Southern Jurisdiction. Not all jurisdictions agree with Pike or support his views on the meaning of the degrees.

7. Pike was a scholar who understood the fundamental esoteric teachings present in Masonic symbolism that either went unnoticed or were misunderstood by most of its members.

8. Using the existing literature of his period, and drawing heavily upon the earlier works of the French occult revival and Eliphas Levi in particular, Pike sought to demonstrate that Masonry was more than just the gentlemen's social club it was morphing into but, instead, that it was the inheritor of a secret tradition of human unfoldment that was thousands of years old.

9. Freemasonry often refers to itself as the Royal Art, a name that has been around since 1693, when William III was initiated into the Craft, according to Albert Mackey. The term Royal Art is also used to describe alchemy, a similarity that would not have been lost on the earliest of Freemasons during the seventeenth and eighteenth centuries.

10. The purpose of both Freemasonry and alchemy is the Great Work, which is threefold in nature: religious, philosophical, and natural. It is above all the perfection of human capacity by an act of will of the individual upon themself and nature, and it is essentially magical in origin and function.

11. Levi and Pike point out that the ancient magi and alchemists believed in an underlying strata of light that created and sustains the physical universe, and that this underlying strata can be affected by human thought, thereby giving proof to the mystical doctrines of the ancients.

12. Modern theoretical physics refers to this underlying strata at the quantum level as zero-point energy existing in a zero-point field, and it is described in terms similar to those used in ancient alchemical and Qabalistic manuscripts to describe the nature and

function of the "Universal Agent," or astral light, as it is sometimes called.

Assignments for Chapter Seven

1. Imagine yourself in mid-eighteenth-century colonial America. What would it be like to travel to various cities, make contact with Masonic lodges, and discuss with them the establishment of a new rite or system?

2. Read an article or book on Albert Pike. Imagine yourself exchanging places with him, and try to understand what passion drove him to dedicate his life to explaining and expounding upon his interpretation of the teachings contained within Scottish Rite. What would it take for you in your current situation to undertake a similar course of action?

3. Meditate on what it would be like if you could consciously create and alter reality through the force of your mind. How would you use this ability? How would your life be different? What would this kind of power mean to you? What kind of person would you have to be before such a skill was given to you so that you could direct such power?

Scottish Rite and the Rise of Esoteric Masonry: Suggested Reading

A Glossary to Morals and Dogma, by Dr. Rex R. Hutchens, 33° (Supreme Council, Ancient and Accepted Scottish Rite of Freemasonry, Southern Jurisdiction of the United States of America, 1993). Exactly what it says: a glossary of the terms and words used by Pike that may be obscure or have a different meaning for the modern reader.

Morals and Dogma of the Ancient and Accepted Scottish Rite of Freemasonry, by Albert Pike (various editions; orig. pub. 1871). Pike's seminal work. Electronic editions can be found online.

Albert Pike's Esoterika: The Symbolism of the Blue Degrees of Freemasonry, transcribed and edited by Arturo de Hoyos (Scottish Rite Research Society, 2005). Pike's commentary on the symbolism of the three principal degrees of Masonic initiation and their meaning from the perspective of Scottish Rite.

8

Occult Masonry in the Eighteenth Century

At the first meetings, new disciples who have been invited to take part in the master's work will see the Thing accomplishing mysterious acts. They will leave the meeting fired with enthusiasm, yet terrified, like Saint-Martin, or drunk with pride and ambition, like the disciples of Paris. Apparitions have shown themselves and strange beings, different from earthly humans, have spoken.

PAPUS, COMMENTING UPON
MARTINEZ DE PASQUALES

MANY MODERN ANTI-MASONIC GROUPS, primarily the Roman Catholic Church and various fundamentalist Protestant churches, have used the writings of Pike as proof of an esoteric tradition within Masonry that goes counter to their established teachings and therefore makes Masonry incompatible with being Christian (as well as Muslim, according to some Islamic statements). Some Masons who have read Pike and do not like his conclusions have also attempted to distance themselves from the man who single-handedly revived Scottish Rite in the United States. However, this lack of appreciation for Pike's erudition, as well as the general ignorance of the many who achieve their 32nd or 33rd degree without having read him, is betrayed by a profound ignorance of the various genuinely occult rites connected with Freemasonry in Europe in the eighteenth and nineteenth centuries.

In the mid-eighteenth century an occult revival was under way in Europe. While focused mainly among the social elites, who had the means and leisure to pursue such topics, the ripple effect across society was clear and came mainly through Masonic and quasi-Masonic channels. The explosion of rites and grades being created gave rise to High-Grade Masonry in Europe was mainly centered around the search for the promise of secret knowledge that these rituals and groups were said to contain. While swindlers, frauds, and opportunists abounded—just as they do today among the New Age movement and even conventional religious scenes—there were in all likelihood some genuine teachings and practices that were of value. Unfortunately, one person's truth is another person's lie, and figuring out what was useful from what was trash is simply a matter of opinion. Clearly, Masons not interested in esotericism will find none of it of value, while others may see it as the only "true" form of Masonry.

Among the most important of these movements to both spring from as well as effect Freemasonry during the eighteenth century were Rosicrucianism, the Elus Cohen, and Egyptian Masonry.

ROSICRUCIANISM

No other topic in Western esotericism has produced so much awe, mystification, confusion, and even outright lying as has the subject of Christian Rosenkreutz, the society or fraternity he built, and the vault said to have contained his uncorrupted corpse. Manly P. Hall called Rosicrucianism "the most mysterious Secret Order of the modern world."[1]

The Rosicrucian Myth

When we say that the Rosicrucians are a myth, we do not mean that they are a fabrication or something unreal. We are simply pointing out that everything has a history, an interpretation of that history, and a belief that grows up around both of these. This belief can become more powerful than either of the previous two and constitutes a metaphysical structure for interpreting historical as well as personal experiences. It is this metaphysical structure that we refer to when we say "myth." Like all metaphysical constructs, a myth is a mix of history, belief, and wish fulfillment. It can be neither proved nor disproved, nor does it need to be, as its purpose is not to report history but rather to give meaning to it. This meaning is seen in light of invisible spiritual forces that affect and direct humanity toward a desired end. The role of the Rosicrucians, and their philosophy, known as Rosicrucianism, is clearly outlined in the *Fama Fraternitatis.*

Rosicrucian History

The Rosicrucian society appears on the scene of European history in the early seventeenth century. Its principle means of introduction was the publication of two announcements: the *Fama Fraternitatis* (1614) and *Confessio Fraternitatis* (1615). The *Fama* appeared in 1614, and the *Confessio* a year later. Both may have been circulated in manuscript form as early as 1610. Besides their anonymous authorship, what is most peculiar about these documents is that they use the term *Rosicrucian* for the first time.*

These manuscripts were supposedly written in five European languages, though today original copies are known to exist only in German and Latin. The English translation was made from a German original forty years after its publication. The issuance of *Fama Fraternitatis* in German was a significant statement in that it occurred over sixty years before German universities began to hold classes in vernacular German rather than Latin; thus, it marked a small step toward the mainstreaming of knowledge, rather than reserving it for the educated and privileged classes. *Fama Fraternitatis* relates the story of Christian Rosenkreutz, a youth of royal birth, but impoverished, and at five years of age sent away by his parent to live in a monastery. Ten years later he travels to the Middle East, where he learns the wisdom of the Arabic and Egyptian sages. Returning to Europe "Father CRC," as he is now called, gathers about himself a small group of pious men to form the

---

*In his *Encyclopaedia of Occultism,* Lewis Spence claims that the term *Rosicrucian* may have been around as early as 1598.

first Society of the Rosy Cross. These events occurred during the first half of the fifteenth century, according to the manuscript.

The "Invisible Fraternity"

Much has been said about the brotherhood of the Rosy Cross, or Rosicrucians, running the gamut from the ludicrous to the barely rational.

If we dismiss the documents outright as a sophomoric prank or the equivalent of a modern-day urban legend, then we have no further to go. If we seek to find behind them an established, international "invisible brotherhood" of perfected adepts guiding the development of humanity, then we will be equally disappointed, if not outright deluded. Since the rules of the society are said to state that "anyone who claims to be a Rosicrucian is not one," if the Rosicrucians actually exist, and one were to meet one, then either they would be recognized for who they were, or they would not.

As a result of the Rosicrucian manifestos in the early years of the seventeenth century, hundreds of lodges, organizations, and groups have sprung up, born fruit, and died, seeking to fulfill some part of the Rosicrucian ideal. This energy added to the strength of future movements, and as a result, we stand at the pinnacle of the "Rosicrucian movement" today. But it is time that we stop looking for the Rosicrucians in Tibet, Europe, or the Andes and instead seek the "Rosicrucian within" that we might bring it into the world.

Utopianism and the Principle Documents

While the core of the *Fama Fraternitatis* dealt with the biography of CRC and the rediscovery of lost wisdom represented by his burial vault, the *Confessio* presents us with an extension of this spiritual ideal in the material world—that of "universal reformation." As a result, many utopian ideals sprang up and utopian tracts were published, presenting solutions to the many ills that plagued humanity and proclamations of what the ideal state would look like. Francis Bacon, himself claimed by many to have been either a Rosicrucian or at least familiar with some form of Rosicrucian-inspired movement, authored the best known of these utopian treatises: *New Atlantis,* and a sort of companion work, *Novum Organum.*

Bacon's *New Atlantis* is often interpreted as a veiled description of ancient esoteric schools that are thought to have existed since after the biblical deluge to the present day. Others see it as a description of a secret society or "college," that Bacon either founded or headed. His description of the "College of Six Days Work" strongly resembles the "Pansophic University" of the Moravian alchemist John Amos Comenius.

While Bacon's work stands apart from the other utopian works of the period, they all held several points in common that are still relevant today: Education was stressed, and children were instructed in the arts and sciences, practical crafts, religion, morality, ethics, and social consciousness. Families were self-supporting, with work being viewed as honorable and the social leech as an outcast. Order, cleanliness, and sanitation were valued, and each individual fulfilled their obligations to society. Medicine was socialized and war rejected as a means of settling disputes.

How these ideals were implemented changed from author to author, with some advocating what would be considerably liberal even by modern standards, and others that were overly controlling and lacking in recognition of the individual. However, the basic ideas presented at that time, between 450 and 300 years ago, are still the object of much political action and speculation worldwide today, particularly in industrialized nations.

Yet when we speak of "reformation," it is clear that the authors of the manifestos were speaking of more than just political and religious changes, as dramatic as they were then and even to this day. They were also talking about changes in consciousness, for without changes in how people think and feel, there can be no lasting expansion in society and culture.

The worldview of the period was one of intense selfishness by the ruling classes. Varying degrees of determinism shaped the majority of people's beliefs, with God being the scriptwriter for everyone's life. Much of a person's life was seen to play out less as "cause and effect" and more from "God's will." Individuals sought simply to make their brief span on earth as comfortable as possible and wasted little or no time in attempting to push for reforms that would strip them of their birth rights or that they would never live long enough to see, let alone share in.

Given the climate, the Rosicrucian manifestos were truly revolutionary as well as evolutionary in their effect.

The nature and origin of Rosicrucianism is possibly the most opaque of topics in Western estotericism. While there is a fair amount of evidence to go on that the initial Rosicrucian manifestos were a satire on political and social reform, they apparently spread out of control and grew into something far larger than their youthful authors had ever intended, giving rise to numerous movements claiming the Rosicrucian mantle over the last four hundred years. That is, what began as little more than a collegiate prank became a phenomenon.

The first mention of the existence of a mystical fraternity practicing the arcane arts and calling itself Rosicrucian appears in 1614 with the publication of *Universal and General Reformation of the Whole Wide World*. This small booklet with a huge title was published in Cassel, Germany, by Wilhelm Wessel and consisted of a German translation of a chapter from Traiano Boccalini's *Ragguagli di Parnaso* (1612), which mocked the utopian ideas of the day. It was followed by the more famous *Fama Fraternitatis,* "Announcement of the Fraternity," which proclaimed the existence of the secret society or fraternity of the Rosy Cross. Therein the life of the fraternity's founder, Christian Rosenkreutz, was detailed, along with the discovery of a seven-sided vault containing his uncorrupted corpse, magical and alchemical implements, a book containing the fraternity's teachings, and an invitation to contact them. (Unfortunately, no mailing address was given, so those wishing to know the secrets of the universe were at a bit of a loss.)

The *Confessio Fraternitatis,* which followed in 1615, contained an essay on the magical philosophy found in John Dee's *Monas Hieroglyphica,* further linking, at least philosophically, Rosicrucianism with Dee and, as we saw earlier, linking Dee with pre-1717 Freemasonry via Elias Ashmole. These tangential links between the Hermetic defenders of Rosicrucianism and defenders of Dee would give rise to the idea that Freemasonry, or at least its reorganization from 1717 onward, was in fact an action by Rosicrucian superiors to further their goals of worldwide reformation.

The *Chymical Wedding of Christian Rosenkreutz,* published in 1616 in Strasburg, is an alchemical allegory describing CRC's journey as an old man to the wedding of a king and queen, and the trials he experiences along the way. The story climaxes with the death and resurrection of the bride and bridegroom, or the alchemical symbols for the mundane personality and the spiritual consciousness.

While it was the last chapter of the Rosicrucian trilogy to be published, the *Chymical Wedding* was the first to be written. Its author was the young Lutheran seminarian Johann Valentin Andreae. Andreae was deeply involved in the Hermetic society existing at the University of Teubingen. In addition, both his father and brother were practicing alchemists. It is in his autobiography, written near the end of his life but remaining unpublished until 1799, that Andreae mentions that he authored the *Chymical Wedding,* along with the *Fama Fraternitatis,* as a joke or mockery of the ideas of social reform that were current at the time. The word he uses is *ludibrium,* meaning "joke, mockery, comedy, or play."

It appears, however, that the original play took on a life of its own; Andreae himself noted that the actors had changed and the play lived on.

ELUS COHEN

Of all the quasi-Masonic orders of the eighteenth century, none better embodies the notion of a magical or operative occult lodge or system associated with Masonry than the Elus Cohen (and, one could also argue, Egyptian Freemasonry; see page 154).

The Elus Cohen, or "Elect Priests," was the short name for the Order of Knight Masons, Elect Priests of the Universe, which was established in 1767 by Martinez de Pasquales (also spelled Pasqually or Pasqualis). However, while this baroque-sounding Masonic title is typical, the roots of the Elus Cohen can be found in an earlier order, also founded by Pasquales: the Scottish Judges (Juges Ecossais), which claimed a connection to Scottish Rite. The first lodge of the Scottish Judges was established in Montpellier, France, in 1754; the first lodge of Elus Cohen (or Elus Coens) was established six years later in Toulouse.

Like many would-be adepts, Pasquales presented himself to the Grand Lodge of France in an effort to convert them, or at least interest them, in his rite. Like many before and after his, the effort failed, and he continued on this way regardless. It was during his visit to the Grand Lodge of France that Pasquales met Jean-Baptiste Willermoz. Willermoz, from Lyon, was a member of the Rite of Strict Observance and was influential in Masonic circles. It was through his assistance that Pasquales was able to establish the Elus Cohen across France.

The Elus Cohen system contained four grades. The first three were the same as Blue Lodge: Apprentice, Companion (just a different name for Fellowcraft), and Master. However, unlike standard Freemasonry, initiates of these degrees were given instructions and spiritual exercises to undertake. The fourth degree, that of the Elus Cohen, or Grand Profes, introduced the initiate to the inner magical teachings of the order and its entire reason for being. Here, at select times of the year, in concert with the equinoxes (when day and night are of equal length), extensive rituals were performed by Elus Cohen members in their private chambers. These rituals involved a plethora of magical circles and designs, many seen only within the Elus Cohen system, and the rituals often lasted up to six hours in length. Invisible entities, angels, and beings were invoked and brought to both visible and audible appearance. If all went well, this would culminate in the presence of La Chose, or "the Thing." Here, balls of light might be seen to flash or arc across the room, sweeps or "passes" would be experienced, and the presence of the redeeming power of Christ would be felt.

While the Elus Cohen placed a great deal of emphasis on the importance of these psychic phenomena and their reality, they were only signs and secondary to La Chose. For the fourth-degree Elus Cohen, the reintegration of his spiritual self into the cosmos, thereby correcting the errors and evils of the biblical fall from grace, was paramount, and this could be accomplished only by La Chose. This emphasis on the appearance of the divine glory, of the very power and presence of Christ, the repaired Adam Kadmon itself, makes Elus Cohen rituals unique in their nature as well as clearly different from either the Catholicism of the day and even Masonry.

The teachings of Pasquales were a complex mix of Roman Catholicism, Qabala, and Gnostic dualism within a Masonic framework utilizing the popular obsession with Scottish Rite in France as its vehicle of promulgation. Pasquales's only written work was an esoteric depiction of the Book of Genesis titled *Treatise on the Reintegration of Beings* (1769). Pasquales, said to have had poor command of written French, may have had assistance in compiling his book.

The key ideas in *Reintegration of Beings* are as follows: Like its Gnostic, and at times Roman Catholic, predecessors, the Elus Cohen saw the material world as evil, a place whose original purpose was to act as a prison for rebellious spirits. Adam Kadmon, the "First Man" or "Primordial Being," was placed upon the earth to act as a warden to keep the evil spirits from escaping. However, Adam was tempted by his desire to create, just as God had created, and in turn he "fell." His first creation was Eve, with whom he bore Cain, outside of divine blessing, and thereby brought evil into the world. The birth of their second son, Abel, was blessed by God, though Abel was later killed by Cain. Seth, the third child of Adam and Eve, was given access to all knowledge and wisdom. According to the Elus Cohen, the children of Seth mated with the children of Cain, giving rise to the human race. A small group of these humans were able to remember the divine teachings and occult arts and sought to attune themselves with divine will. They were called the "Friends of Wisdom," of which Pasquales claimed to be the final heir of their wisdom. Members of his order followed strict dietary rules, similar to those of the Levites, and abstained from specific animal products to purify themselves of evil and demonic influences.

The grade system, rituals, and initiations of the Elus Cohen were continually changing, evolving, and becoming more complex. Many of the initiations constituted a sort of ordination in the clerical sense, as advancing members of the Elus Cohen considered themselves to be priests in the line of the disciples of Christ and the patriarchs.

The first grouping shows four classes of a total of twelve degrees, with the second series of degrees being placed in four groups totaling eleven degrees. Much of the symbolism of these degrees focuses around Zerubbabel, who rebuilt the Temple of Solomon after it was destroyed by the Babylonians in the sixth century. As Masonic legend states Zerubbabel worked with a trowel in one hand and a sword in the other to defend himself from the threats of his idolatrous neighbors. Given that much of the preliminary work of the Elus Cohen is concerned with cleansing the earth's aura of the influences of demonic and evil influences—traditional sources of human error and confusion—it's fitting that both the Hebrew scriptures and High-Degree Freemasonry identify with this archetypal figure. Many of the Elus Cohen rituals are distinguished from the magic that was typical of the period in that no metal, ceremonial swords, or even wands are present, a proscription that may have been deeply influenced by the famous grimoire *The Book of the Sacred Magic of Abramelin the Mage*.

Pasquales died in 1774 in Haiti, and with no heir apparent, the order he had dedicated himself to fell apart. Some segments survived as Elus Cohen, others in the Rite of Strict Observance, some in the philosophical tenets of Louis Claude de Saint-Martin. Through Willermoz and the Rite of Strict Observance, some of the rituals were absorbed into Scottish Rite Freemasonry and exist in the Order of Knights Beneficent of the Holy City (Chevaliers Bienfaisants de la Cité Sainte), and as we will see, they became associated with the Knights Templar and York Rite. Through Saint-Martin the mystical philosophy of Pasquales would survive and be revived in the late nineteenth century by Dr. Gérard Encausse and his Martinist Order. The Elus Cohen was revived and reorganized during the darkest days of World War II and continues to operate to this day.

EGYPTIAN MASONRY

Just as the Elus Cohen was nearly inseparable from its founder, so is Egyptian Masonry intimately connected to the life and fate of its creator, the enigmatic Count Alessandro di Cagliostro. The two rites may even have been connected through an equally strange and enigmatic Irish Jesuit priest living in London: Father George Cofton, who is said to have been associated with the Elus Cohen. Cofton either copied the rituals of Egyptian Masonry or wrote them himself.

Cagliostro's *Secret Ritual of Egyptian Freemasonry* was originally published from a handwritten copy made in 1845 that he claimed to have discovered from a bookseller, and later published under the above title in English. In this rite we can see that within a generation after the formation of the Grand Lodge of France, the desire became intense to see more in Freemasonry than just a social club, fraternity, or charitable organization.

After due preparation and revelation of the signs of recognition, the candidate is instructed in a Hermetic-alchemical understanding of Masonry.

Seven are the passages to perfect the primal matter; seven are its colors. Seven are the effects required to complete the philosophical operations [i.e., the philosopher's stone].[2]

Further on,

Q. What do you mean by the Arcana [Secret] of Nature?

A. The recognition of that beautiful philosophy, both natural and supernatural, of which I have conversed previously and of which you found the principles confirmed in the emblems which represent the Order of Masonry and the tableau [i.e., tracing board] which was placed before your view in all the lodges.

Q. Is it possible for ordinary Masonry to furnish an idea of the sublime mysteries? Although I have been a Mason for thirty-three years and have passed through all the degrees during that long space of time, I had not the least suspicion of what you do me the favor to talk about. I have never considered that Masonry was anything other than a society of people who did not assemble to divert themselves and who for better unity have adopted some signs and a particular language. Deign, by your brilliant interpretations to uncover for me the solid and true end, which you promised me.

A. God inspire me and I will lift one of the corners of the veil which hid the truth; I will start to instruct you in the origin of Masonry; I will give you the philosophical explanation of the Masonic view and I shall finish when you have learned all of the meaning of the sublime and mystic aims of true Masonry.[3]

Numbers, Angels, and the Arcanum Arcanorum

The number seven plays a particularly important role in Egyptian Freemasonry and is often depicted as a seven-rayed star with the name Elohim written in the center and a Hebrew letter at the apex of each of the points, one for each of the seven angels of the classical planets. The catechism, or summary of teachings given at the end of each degree in a question and answer format, states, "Helohym signifies, I wish and I order that my will be done, and that it shall be done accordingly."

The Master Mason in the Egyptian rite wears green—associated with the number seven, as well as with Venus, the plant alchemilla, the regenerative powers of alchemy, Eastern philosophy, and Hermes— along with a red sash.

While the Elus Cohen were concerned with invoking the presence of the seven principal angelic powers and the reintegration of fallen humanity back into the perfect expression of divine will, Egyptian Masonry sought to contact the seven angelic beings who ruled the planetary energies, well known in Medieval and Renaissance magic, for the perfection of people while they were still on the earth and in the flesh. This alchemical emphasis can be seen most clearly in the teachings of the Arcana Arcanorum, or "Secret of Secrets." These teachings are said to have been derived from several orders and societies; they were part of Cagliostro's rite, they found their way into the Rite of Misraim in the 87th through 90th degrees, and, in the modern era, the Order of Hermes Thrice-Magistus, founded in 1927 by well-known European occultists and Freemasons, is said to employ them.

The Arcana Arcanorum is composed of three areas of interrelated work:

- Invocation of the angelic hierarchy of the elements, the planets, the levels of the Tree of Life, the angelic guide of the age, and the individual's own guardian angel or higher self
- Mineral alchemy working with antimony
- Interior alchemy, in which the external symbols and work find their correlation in the human body, thereby turning it into a perfect alchemical vessel

Four points are of particular interest to modern students of Masonry and esotericism:

1. The specific practices of the Arcana Arcanorum are similar to, and directly connected with, those of Rosicrucianism, including the Hermetic-alchemical practices of the Pietists of colonial Pennsylvania at Fairmount Park and later Ephrata and the need for a forty-day alchemical retreat for physical rejuvenation.
2. The Arcana Arcanorum declares that the philosopher's stone must be created directly from the distilled blood of the adept.[4]
3. It is connected to the enigmatic picture book known as *The Secret Symbols of the Rosicrucians of the 16th and 17th Centuries,* published in Altoona, Pennsylvania, in 1785.[5]
4. It is also connected to *The Book of the Sacred Magic of Abramelin the Mage,* the works of Agrippa, and those of Peter of Abano, including presumably the *Heptameron,* which is often bound with the *Fourth Book of Occult Philosophy,* attributed to Agrippa.[6]

ADOPTIVE MASONRY

In addition to their unique catechisms and instruction in operative methods of occult exploration, the esoteric lodges of the eighteenth century tended to share a common Masonic "heresy": they initiated women. Known as Adoptive Masonry, lodges of this nature were often separate from male lodges and run as parallel organizations for women. Within Cagliostro's rite his wife, Seraphina, ran a lodge composed exclusively of wealthy, upper-class women, whom she initiated into the mysteries of Isis, and wherein she was the grand mistress of the mysteries. Other systems allowed men and women to sit in lodge together. While "regular" Masonry is known to have had women members, often by default— they were caught overhearing or intentionally spying upon an initiation in progress and were "made Masons" to keep their obligations—it is not a common practice. While not all forms of Adoptive Masonry were or are esoteric, it is common, both historically and in the present, to see esoteric Masons and quasi-Masonic rites being adoptive in practice.

HERMETIC-ALCHEMICAL RITES AND THE ILLUMINATI

According to Albert Mackey, within the oldest Masonic records, Hermes Trismegistus is often called one of the founders of Freemasonry and recognized as the father of wisdom. He is said to have established two pillars of stone wherein were placed the arts and sciences to be preserved for future generations. We often see two Hermes occurring: Hermes the Thrice-Great, purported author of the Hermetic tracts, and Thoth-Hermes, also known as Hermes-Mercurius, the Egyptian god of magic and learning who so resembled his Greek and Roman counterparts that they simply combined. In truth, it is difficult to separate these figures from each other. Hermes the Thrice-Great has been associated with several historical priest-philosophers who lived in Egypt, and he has been seen as an incarnation of the gods themselves. As such, looking for a historical connection outside of the literature attributed to him is meaningless. The Hermetic writings have been among the most influential in the Western world, and their importance in Freemasonry has been overlooked by most Craft members for the last century.

As we have seen in most human spiritual pursuits, myth is often stronger and more important than history as it represents an ideal to be strived for—a truth yet to be attained. As such, myths guide us into the future rather than simply expound upon or shed light on the past.

For this reason, it's the mythology of Hermes that compels us. Within Masonry we find references to Hermes the Thrice-Great in the York Constitutions, a collection of manuscripts, in which the origin and rules of the York Rite are described. There are five York manuscripts, of which number four is missing, and they are referred to in the plural. The authors of this early document undoubtedly derived their knowledge of Hermes from popular legend and the philosophical, but clearly occult, writings of the period; chief among these, as far as Masonic interest is concerned, is the *Polychronicon*. Written by Ranulf Higden, a Benedictine monk, and translated from the Latin into English by John Trevisa, it was published by William Caxton in 1482, during the opening period of the Renaissance's Hermetic renewal. It is quoted extensively in the Cooke Manuscript, which came at the end of the fifteenth century and is the second oldest manuscript in Masonic history. It describes the origins of Freemasonry, and begins with a description of the several liberal arts and links geometry with Masonry.

Hermes the Thrice-Great, master of the magical and esoteric arts, of which alchemy is the crowning jewel, and author of the Corpus Hermeticum, appears most prominently in the writings of the intellectual elite of Europe prior to and slightly after the formation of the Grand Lodge of England in 1717. However, this should not suggest that interest in Hermes, Hermetic philosophy, and its practical application through magic was limited to the upper echelons of society. Dating back to the Middle Ages, there was extensive interest in Hermes even among the common populace. He was often depicted as being a contemporary of Moses, and he was featured in Christian churches and the art of the period and into the Renaissance. Prior to the initiation and flourishing of High-Degree Masonry on the Continent, we find no overt alchemical themes in Masonic rituals. But beginning in the eighteenth century, alchemical material can be seen in those rituals and rites with a specific Hermetic or philosophical theme. (At the time, *philosophical* was synonymous with *Hermetic*.) With this infusion of alchemical symbols, the Supreme Council of the Ancient and Accepted Scottish Rite in France introduced new initiations for the first three degrees with explicit alchemical symbolism. In 1785, for example, the Grand Lodge of France, known as the Grand Orient of France, ordered that small vials of salt and sulfur should be placed in the Chamber of Reflection, clearly suggestive of the alchemical milieu in which the candidate lived and the interpretation they were meant to extract from their initiations. We also find references to purification by fire and water, as well as the elements (herein the four elements of classical alchemy: fire, air, water and earth). In fact, the Chamber of Reflection is supposed to be underground, further suggesting pre-Christian initiations, as well as the element of earth. With this infusion of alchemical symbols, the Supreme Council of the Ancient and Accepted Scottish Rite in France introduced new initiations for the first three degrees with explicit alchemical symbolism.[7]

Specific alchemical instruction in a Masonic setting is clearly seen in the writings of Antoine-Joseph Pernety (1716–1800) and the Illuminati of Avignon. Pernety (also spelled Pernetii) was born in Roanne, France, in 1716 and while still young joined the Benedictine Congregation of Saint Maur. After a period of time he and twenty-eight of his brethren applied for dispensation from their monastic vows and left the order in 1765. Pernety traveled to Berlin, where he became the librarian of Frederick the Great of Prussia. Shortly thereafter, he left for France, where the archbishop of Paris attempted to convince him to return to the monastic life. It was around this time that Pernety encountered the writings and doctrines of Emanuel Swedenborg, the Swedish philosopher, and took a deep interest in his mystical speculations. He translated Swedenborg's *Heaven and Hell* into French and retired to Avignon.

Pernety formed the Illuminati of Avignon, the Masonic rite for which he is so well known, in 1770. The rite moved to Montpellier in 1778 under a new name: the Academy of True Masons.* This version of the rite contained four degrees, and the fourth, called True Mason, incorporated instruction in Hermeticism, laboratory alchemy,

---

*Regarding the year when the rite was founded, Waite states, "It has been referred erroneously to the year 1760 and alternatively to 1785," and goes on to quote one Masonic authority placing the rite in existence as late at 1812. See Waite, *A New Encyclopedia of Freemasonry*, vol. I (New York: Wings Books, 1996; orig. pub. 1921), 385.

and the teachings of Emmanuel Swedenborg. In *A New Encyclopedia of Freemasonry,* Waite states that Pernety was involved with "the investigation of future events by means of a peculiar Kabalistic oracle" that directed the members of the rite to "follow the teachings of Emmanuel Swedenborg."[8] Pernety created additional Masonic degrees, and he is believed to have authored the degree of the Knight of the Sun, Prince Adept (the 28th degree), within Scottish Rite. Derivations of this degree and that of the True Mason can be found in Martinism, which is the philosophic descendant of the Elus Cohen.

The degree of the Knight of the Sun, also known as Prince Adept, contains within it angelic magic, theurgic operations, hints of operative alchemy, and clear similarities to the works of the Elus Cohen. In his *Book of the Ancient and Accepted Scottish Rite of Freemasonry,* Charles T. McClenachan, 33rd-degree Mason and past master of ceremonies of the Supreme Council, writes:

> There is but one God, uncreated, eternal, infinite, and inaccessible: that the soul of man is immortal, and his existent life but a point in the centre of eternity: that harmony is in equilibrium, and equilibrium subsists by the analogy of contraries: that analogy is the key of all the secrets of nature, and the sole reason of being of all revelations: and, finally, that the *Absolute* is REASON, which exists through itself: that evil, and wrong, and misery are the necessary discords that unite with the concords of the universe to make one great harmony forever. Such is the argument of this the last philosophical [Hermetic] degree of the Ancient and Accepted Scottish Rite; its doctrine is derived from the Kabala, and is the same as that of the Hermetic philosophers who wrote on Alchemy.[9]

Elsewhere McClenachan describes the necessary symbols for the degree as a pentagram with an eye in its center and a hexagram in black in white, with black being uppermost, with an inverted Hebrew letter Shin in the center. This is peculiar, because normally white, the color of energy and purity, is uppermost, but here, black, the color of matter, solidity, and physicality, is pointed upward, forming the active or "male" triangle. A single triangle, with one side black, one white, and one red—the three principal colors of alchemy, symbolizing the three stages from dense matter (black) to purity (white) and finally perfection (red)—and the Hebrew letters Yod and Heh in the center of the hexagram.

In this degree we also find a triangular apron of white lambskin and a pentagram in vermilion. Vermilion, made from cinnabar or mercury sulfide, is used in alchemy. Red is the color of energy, power, and action and symbolizes the philosopher's stone as well as original man, or Adam. Here, the master is referred to as "Father Adam," and seven officers are also present, each representing one of the seven ancient planets and their angels, according to Masonic attribution. Other members wear a vermilion pentagram and are referred to as the "lions of God." Leo, the astrological sign who is ruled over by the Sun, and whose metal is gold, is represented by them as having attained to the end of the philosophers: the confection of the Philosopher's Stone. The same vermilion pentagram is found engraved upon a piece of square white marble placed upon the altar toward the north side.

Two pillars capped by a white dove and a black raven, the birds of initiation and alchemical work, are also present; although their interpretation is in terms of the fourth and fifth Sefirot of the Tree of Life, there is also a peculiarly Masonic interpretation of the dove being life and the raven divine justice. Seeing the raven as a symbol of death would be more appropriate, and it would fit with the alchemical attribute of the raven as the *caput mortum,* or "dead head," of the alchemical process.

As part of the Knight of the Sun degree, placed in the north of the lodge is a large image of Eliphas Levi's "Macrocosm," also known as "The Great Symbol of Solomon," from his book *Dogma and Ritual of High Magic.* This image is particularly interesting: It shows a crowned and bearded king with elbows raised and hands flat, with a mirror image below it; upon closer examination, the arms of both figures taken together form a hexagram. The figure is circled by the Hermetic saying "As above, so below" in Latin, and the whole image is surrounded by the ouroboros.

References are made to Egyptian initiation and trial by the four elements of fire, air, water, and earth, as found in classical magic and alchemy. In surviving these trials, the initiate was said to have mastered the elements and was raised to the status of an adept—the fifth point on the pentagram.

For Pike, McClenachan, and others, the symbolic meaning of alchemy within Masonry meant not the search for the elixir of life, potable gold, the panacea, or the philosopher's stone, as this would have been "unreasonable" by nineteenth-century standards, but instead, the quest to live a moral, upright, and well-ordered life in which one was a respected and productive member of their community, lodge, and family.

Pernety's principal contribution to the advancement of alchemy was his *Treatise on the Great Art: A System of Physics According to Hermetic Philosophy and Theory and Practice of the Magisterium,* which was first published in English in 1898 by the Occult Publishing Company of Boston, Massachusetts. The book was edited by Edouard Blitz, a Freemason and member of the Grand Council of the Martinist Order. In his treatise Pernety synthesizes the great writings on spagyrics and alchemy and presents one of the most lucid descriptions of the Great Work ever presented. For Pernety alchemy was "an operation of Nature, aided by art. It places in our hands the Key to Natural Magic or Physics, and renders us wonderful men, by elevating us above the masses."[10] This eighteenth-century idea of self-improvement and understanding the divine natural order of creation was in perfect harmony with the Masonic ideal that is expressed in "making good men better." Pernety was deeply influenced by classical mythology, and he dogmatically, as well as convincingly, interpreted the ancient myths from the perspective of them being variations of the Great Work.

In addition to his alchemical and Masonic interests, Pernety published numerous volumes on mythology, theology, philosophy, geography, the fine arts, and mathematics, both theoretical and applied. He died at Valence, in Dauphiné, in 1800.

Many other bodies, smaller than Pernety's, that worked operative alchemy may have existed, whereas for others, alchemical symbolism was used purely in a speculative sense to suggest a deeper meaning for the moral and ethical teachings of Masonry. One could look at it as a form of "Jungian alchemical psychotherapy" before its time. There also appears to have been a preoccupation with the Revelation of St. John (the Apocalypse) and its interpretation along initiatic, alchemical, and theurgic lines in many of these rites. It is the operative schools that are of the most interest, as they demonstrate either an actual connection between Masonry, the historical stone builders, and the Hermetic adepts or simply a belief that such a connection existed. This theme would be taken up a century and a half later, culminating in the writings of Isabel Cooper-Oakley and her *Masonry & Medieval Mysticism* and finding their capstone in Fulcanelli's *The Mystery of the Cathedrals*. Here, the mysterious alchemical adept of the twentieth century takes the position that within the stone facades of the great Gothic cathedrals, Chartres and Notre Dame in particular, the entire alchemical process is both revealed and concealed.

CONCLUSION

Despite the brief life span of many occult Masonic, or quasi-Masonic, orders of the eighteenth century, many would find themselves reinvigorated a century later during the Belle Epoque of the French occult revival. Some would even influence the British occult revival via the Societas Rosicruciana in Anglia (SRIA) and the formation of the Hermetic Order of the Golden Dawn. Yet despite claims of occult power and influence of affairs on the world stage, most would linger, die, and never be heard from again. Like a shooting star flashing across the night sky of the eighteenth century, the great occult rites attached to Scottish Rite Freemasonry would amuse, entertain, and distract many for an instant, only to fade into the cosmic darkness, out of sight and mind.

Occult Masonry in the Eighteenth Century:
Key Points

1. In the mid-eighteenth century interest in occultism was widespread across Europe. While focused mainly in the social elites, it was also widely popular among the middle class and peasants.

2. Many occult movements arose in and around Masonry, and Scottish Rite in particular.

3. While many anti-Masons have misquoted Pike, and many Masons have distanced themselves from him, he is more often than not simply misunderstood. Masonry is essentially afraid of its esoteric and occult origins, and modern reactions to Pike within Masonry are proof of this fear.

4. Rosicrucianism was central to the development of esotericism from the early seventeenth century onward. Many of the rites and degrees that appeared in eighteenth-century Scottish Rite claimed connection to or influence from Rosicrucian sources.

5. Rosicrucianism is focused around the story of Christian Rosenkreutz and his travels to the Middle East in search of wisdom and the fraternity he established upon his return. The key document in Rosicrucianism is the *Fama Fraternitatis,* published in 1614.

6. Utopian principles can be found in the *Fama Fraternitatis* and related documents. However, the documents themselves may have been written as a farce, poking fun at utopianism rather than advocating it.

7. The Elus Cohen, established by Martinez Pasquales, is one of the most important Masonic-styled bodies of the eighteenth century, linking operative medieval ritual magic, Catholic piety, and Masonic ritual. Its survival can be seen in the Rite of Strict Observance, modern Martinism, and modern Elus Cohen organizations.

8. Count Alessandro di Cagliostro established the rite known as Egyptian Masonry. A critical part of Cagliostro's system is the Arcanum Arcanorum, which deals with alchemical rejuvenation, communication with the seven planetary angels, and the perfection of the human body as an alchemical vessel. It is said to be based in part on a book titled *The Secret Symbols of the Rosicrucians of the 16th and 17th Centuries,* published in 1785.

9. French Benedictine monk Antoine-Joseph Pernety established the Illuminati of Avignon, one of the most well-known Hermetic Masonic rites. The rite was based upon the visions of Emmanuel Swedenborg, practical alchemy, Hermeticism, and Qabala and

eventually was absorbed into Scottish Rite, where its core ideas can be found in the 28th degree, Knight of the Sun, Prince Adept.

10. Pernety authored *Treatise on the Great Art: A System of Physics According to Hermetic Philosophy and Theory and Practice of the Magisterium.*

Assignments for Chapter Eight

1. Research the importance of Rosicrucianism in the development of Western esotericism.

2. Research the role of angels in Judaism and the various Christian faiths.

3. Read a book about alchemy and its attendant practices.

4. If you could live for 100, 150, or 200 years in good health, would you? What would you do with that time?

Occult Masonry in the Eighteenth Century: Suggested Reading

The Comte De Saint-Germain: Last Scion of the House of Rakoczy, by Jean Overton Fuller (East-West Publications, 1988). A look at the historical Count St. Germain, the pivotal figure linking Freemasonry with the mythologies presented by later esoteric movements. This is possibly the only book of its kind that does not rely on questionable sources to tell the tale of the remarkable and mysterious "man who would not die."

The Last Alchemist: Count Cagliostro, Master of Magic in the Age of Reason, by Iain McCalman (HarperCollins, 2003). A critical and informative look at Cagliostro that is fair in its treatment of this difficult and tangled subject.

The Rosicrucian Enlightenment, by Frances A. Yates (University of Chicago Press, 1972). With this book Yates made Rosicrucianism a field of study unto itself. Dated, but still critical reading.

The Rosicrucians: The History, Mythology, and Rituals of an Occult Order, by Christopher McIntosh (Weiser, 1997). Still one of the classics on this topic.

9

York Rite and the Survival of the Knights Templar

He reveals deep and hidden things; he knows what is in the darkness, and the light dwells with him.

DANIEL 2:22

YORK RITE, LIKE SCOTTISH RITE, requires that its members be Master Masons in good standing in a Blue Lodge. Also like Scottish Rite, the York Rite system is said to further elaborate on and explain, albeit symbolically, the material presented in the first three degrees. While Scottish Rite was forming and growing on the Continent, additional degrees were brought into England, and they eventually became known as York Rite. However, unlike Scottish Rite, York Rite is subdivided into three related groups: Royal Arch (aka Capitulary), Cryptic, and Chivalric Masonry, whose capstone is the Order of the Knights Templar. As can be discerned by now, the exact number of degrees and types of rituals vary among some jurisdictions, but the essential ideas remain the same.

The first of these new higher degrees were Royal Arch and Knights Templar. By the late 1730s, however, additional degrees that further expanded the system were being conferred, each one elaborating on the basic theme of Solomon's Temple, hidden treasure, and secrets long lost.

York Rite also diverges from typical Masonic protocol in that while any Mason may petition for membership in Royal Arch and Cryptic Masonry, in theory, only Christians may become members of the Chivalric degrees, particularly the Knights of Malta and Knights Templar, because of their distinct Christian orientation and emphasis. These degrees arose after the anti-Masonic period of the early eighteenth century and were in part an effort to make Masonry appear less like the anti-establishment, quasi-revolutionary, esoteric organization Scottish Rite was becoming in Europe, and more into a good mainstream Christian organization.

ROYAL ARCH: CAPSTONE OF MASONRY

Like many things bureaucratic, logic and the written word should be no obstacle to making something a fact in the eyes of the beholder. During the period of contention between the Antient and Modern grand lodges that began in the mid-1700s, the Antients considered the Royal Arch degree the philosophical completion of the making of a Master Mason. This was tricky because it was clear that there were only three degrees in Masonry, of which the Master Mason was the highest. However, in the eyes and ears of *tradition,* this did not matter, and the conferral of the Royal Arch degree was a major sticking point during the unification of the Antient and Modern grand lodges in 1813.

To make matters worse, as time went on, and as part of the compromise, Royal Arch went from being a single degree to its own administrative entity, and it now confers a total of four degrees: Mark Master, Past Master, Most Excellent Master, and Royal Arch. Cryptic degrees include Royal Master, Select Master, and Super-Excellent Master. Knights Templar degrees are the Illustrious Order of the Red Cross, Order of the Knights of Malta, and Order of the Knights Templar.

What makes these degrees fascinating, however, is not their convoluted and mind-numbing organizational concerns, but the messages they teach and the symbols they convey: the secrets of the Temple of Solomon.

CRYPTIC MASONRY AND THE LOST WORD

The Cryptic Rite degrees first appeared in Freemasonry between 1760 and 1780, and from appearances, they are among the best written and most informative of Masonic degrees. The degrees conferred in Cryptic Rite are based upon the biblical narratives and oral traditions of Enoch the Patriarch. Enoch is a particularly interesting figure. In addition to being Noah's great-grandfather, he also "walked with God and was no more" (Genesis 5:24), being transfigured into the archangel Metatron by some accounts. Metatron is of particular importance in Jewish folk magic and Qabalistic practices.

In *A Dictionary of Angels*, Gustav Davidson writes:

> The patriarch Enoch, on his translation to Heaven (Genesis 5:24), became Metatron, one of the greatest of the hierarchs, "king over all the angels." *Cf.* the Assyrian legend in the *Epic of Izdubar.* On earth, as a mortal, Enoch is said to have composed 366 books (the Enoch literature). Legend has it that Enoch-Metatron is twin-brother to Sandalphon (*q.v.*); that when he was glorified he was given 365,000 eyes and 36 pairs of wings. . . . The spectacular mode of Elijah's conveyance to heaven, as reported in II Kings 2, had, it seems, an earlier parallel in the case of Enoch, for the latter also was whisked away "in a fiery chariot drawn by fiery chargers," as related in *The Legend of the Jews* I, 130; however, a few pages farther on (p.138) it transpires that it wasn't a horse of a team of horses, but an angel (Anpiel) who transported the antediluvian patriarch from earth to Heaven. . . . To the Arabs, Enoch was Idris (Koran, *sura* 19, 56). In the *Pirke Rabbi Eliezer* the invention of astronomy and arithmetic is laid to Enoch. Legend connects Enoch-Metatron with Behemoth.[1]

The image of Metatron appears on the first talismanic image or pentacle of the sun in the *Clavicula Salomonis,* where it is given the description "The Countenance of the Almighty, at whose aspect all creatures obey, and the Angelic Spirits do reverence on bended knees."

Given that Enoch was ascended to heaven, wherein he was

transfigured in the archangel Metatron, the twin of the angel Sandalphon, ruler of the earth, it is peculiar that Masonic legend has him excavating a series of underground chambers, nine in total, each beneath the other, on the site where Solomon's Temple would be built.

Each of these vaults or chambers contained a specific secret, culminating in the ultimate secret of all—the Ineffable Name of God—in the ninth vault. Here, buried in the depths of matter, is the secret name YHVH. Here, in the most material of locations, is the truth each Mason seeks. Like the secret fire of the alchemists, the Lost Word is found in this world, not in the next. It is the key to our understanding and liberation from ignorance and suffering, but it is found within the rough rock of daily experience. God, it appears, is everywhere and hidden in everything, rather than only in the starry heavens. It would appear from the Masonic teachings of the Cryptic degrees that before we can ascend and be transfigured into divine beings of light, we must first dig deep within the world of matter and unlock the holy secrets it holds.

The Cryptic Degrees

Royal Master. The events portrayed in degree take place before the completion of Solomon's Temple. It provides the candidate with information about Hiram Abiff and his successor, Adoniram.

Select Master. This degree takes place between the first and second half of the previous degree. (It is common throughout Masonry for degrees to jump in periods of time, with degrees elaborating on events previously mentioned.) The main focus is on the depositing of secrets within the secret vaults and their location.

Super-Excellent Master. This degree takes place after the destruction of the Temple and the period of the Babylonian captivity.

In addition, the degree of the Thrice Illustrious Master is sometimes conferred to a select leadership position within Cryptic Rite. Hermeticists will note the similarity of the title to that of Hermes the Thrice Great, with Hermes and Enoch being interchangeable in some early Hermetic texts.

Enoch and Learning to Walk with God

Enoch is also associated with the angelic magic of Dr. John Dee and Edward Kelley, practices well known to several early and prominent Freemasons, Elias Ashmole in particular. While unrelated, a curious script known as "angelic" or "Enochian" writing appears on eighteenth-century Masonic trestle boards. This script, however, is distinct from the so-called Enochian alphabet used by Dee and Kelley.

While of little importance to modern Masons, in the eighteenth century, a period when biblical references and magical culture were still present, these references to Enoch and their attached significance would not have gone unnoticed.

Belief in magic and various occult practices was widespread in eighteenth- and nineteenth-century Europe and America, particularly during the period of Masonry's most prestigious growth. Harvard taught alchemy into the 1820s, and one of its presidents, Ezra Stiles (who headed the school from 1778 to 1795), explored alchemy and Qabala. Virginian aristocracy was well read in astrology and alchemical healing, though Benjamin Franklin openly satirized the public's obsession with all things occult, and Thomas Jefferson put it on par with the common belief in miracles. In England physicians were the force behind the occult revival of the 1780s.

Across Europe books on the occult were readily available to the lower classes, as noted by D. Michael Quinn:

Even by the early eighteenth century, at least one English clergyman complained that common people had widespread access to books promoting magic. Worse, he said, well-intentioned books condemning witchcraft and the occult actually provided enough details for readers to perform the forbidden rites: 'These books and narratives are in tradesman's shops, and farmer's houses, and are read with eagerness, and are continually leavening the minds of the youth, who delight in such subjects.' In nineteenth-century France, magic handbooks "abounded in the countryside" and judicial trials for sorcery often found that peasants owned occult books that had been out-of-print for two or three hundred years. This refutes the assumption that the common people were indifferent to academic magic, and also challenges that poor farmers had no access to published works and rare books.[2]

The widespread desire for books on the occult in rural and urban areas across the eighteenth and mid-nineteenth centuries is an established fact. In America the flood of books from Europe was endless, and itinerant rural book peddlers reported making enormous amounts of money from occult book sales. One peddler's records from 1809–10 showed that he had sold $24,000 worth of books door-to-door in the South, primarily to farmers. Given that the average price was seventy-five cents for a leather book, forty-four cents for a new book, and pennies for chapbooks, this documents a phenomenal interest in all things occult—and seemingly without concern for possible conflict with prevailing religious ideas of the period.

CHIVALRIC MASONRY

The Chivalric degrees constitute the height of Masonic initiation and its confusing mix of history and myth. While no historical connection exists between these actual orders and their non-Masonic successors, their existence does indicate that despite the egalitarian nature of Masonry, the need to have "further advancement" in the form of titles, separate meetings, and secrets appears to be inherent to human nature. If the common laborer had degrees that he could identify with, then it would not seem unusual for the upper class to have degrees with which it could identify with, and it could give the growing middle class a sense of belonging to something powerful and important.

The Chivalric degrees are:

Illustrious Order of the Red Cross. The theme of this degree links the Cryptic degrees with the Chivalric degrees, as well as Jewish and Christian scriptures. This degree is not conferred in all Templar systems. Some, like the British, confer only the following degrees.
Order of the Knights of Malta. Here the candidate is conferred with

a series of knightly titles, bundling together the Knights of St. Paul, Knights of Malta, and Knights Hospitaller.

Order of the Temple. In this degree the candidate will encounter what for many is the single most impressive series of ritual experiences in Masonry, as well as outside it. In addition to spending time in the Chamber of Reflection, here, each candidate meets with his brethren and shares the communal experience of the "draught of mortality." The rituals are clearly Christian in orientation, and those who take this degree state their willingness to defend the Christian faith if called upon to do so.

ORIGIN OF THE TEMPLARS

The Knights Templar came into being in 1118 CE, when Hugues de Payns, a minor noble, and eight fellow knights from northern France took oaths of poverty and obedience in connection with their military vows, becoming the first warrior-monks in Christendom. They took the name "Poor Fellows of the Knights of Christ" and chose as their symbol two poor knights sharing a horse. Their task was to protect pilgrims on the overland route from Jaffa to Jerusalem. Jerusalem had fallen to Christian armies in 1099, and the act of pilgrimage was extremely dangerous, as the roads were crawling with Muslim brigands and outlaws attacking both solitary travelers and armed caravans. It was believed that simply dying on the journey was enough in some instances to have one's sins remitted. Few in number, the Poor Fellows of the Knights of Christ could not hope to fulfill their mission without additional support.

In 1124 de Payns returned to France to receive an official sanction from the Roman Catholic Church at the Council of Troyes. While papal approval gave the order legitimacy, it was the endorsement of St. Bernard of Clairvaux that sealed their future and guaranteed extensive financial and political support. Within a generation the Poor Fellows would become the wealthiest and most powerful military force in history.

The name "Knights Templar" would come from the location of

their quarters in the palace complex of King Baldwin II of Jerusalem, a run-down section on the former site of King Solomon's Temple. It is often stated that the area they were given as quarters was previously used as a stable. This location was added to their name, and they were recognized as the "Poor Fellow Soldiers of Christ and the Templar of Solomon" or "Knights Templar" for short. In 1139 the Templars were given a power unknown by any other military order: They answered only to the pope, Innocent II. No other ecclesiastical authority could question their actions. They were exempt from taxes and virtually all civil authorities. This, coupled with their ability to keep all wealth captured during their campaigns, as well as commercial activities from lands and castles granted them, made them the wealthiest military order of the day—and possibly all of history.

While the Templars controlled large tracts of land in Palestine and Syria, their influence was not limited to the Holy Land. In 1131 Alfonso I of Aragon (modern-day Spain) drafted a will leaving his kingdom to the Templars, along with the Knights Hospitaller, and the Knights of the Holy Sepulchre. This was ultimately overruled upon his death in favor of more traditional routes of succession, but it speaks to the importance of the alliance of these orders to powerful Christian kingdoms. Templar priories, or chapter houses, and Templar churches (built in a unique circular design, reminiscent of the Arthurian Round Table and magical circles of medieval theurgy) were constructed across Europe and the Middle East. The Templars were a de facto state within the state of Catholic Europe.

Fall of the Templars and Their Survival

Defeat at Acre, near Haifa, in 1291 was the beginning of the fall of the Knights Templar. Under assault by Muslim forces numbering 160,000 with siege towers and catapults, the walls of the city were breached and Christian control of the region began to collapse. After leaving the Holy Land, the Templars went to Cyprus to reorganize. With nothing left for them in the East, they turned their attention west, to Europe and the massive holdings they had accumulated there. With their network in place and reputation for exchange well known, the Templars focused their energy on banking. Efforts by Pope Clement V to peacefully merge the Templars with the Hospitallers failed, which was a sign that Rome had little use for them with Jerusalem under Muslim control. After the destruction of the Templars and the execution of their Grand Master, the remaining property and members of the Order would be merged with the Hospitallers. Kings who were indebted to them had their own reasons for wanting to see the all-powerful and nearly untouchable Templars reined in once and for all.

Unfortunately for the Templars, they found their archenemy in a man they had once helped, and who in turn would destroy them. King Philip IV of France, also known as Philip the Fair, was a scoundrel by all measure. He expelled the Jews from France in 1306 in order to steal their property, stole money from Italian bankers in 1311, and debased the national currency, thereby weakening it and increasing the national debt. Philip even attempted to kidnap Pope Boniface VIII. In 1306, during riots in Paris, Philip was given sanctuary and protection in the Templar preceptory. There, Philip would have seen just a fraction of the Templar wealth, and that was enough to set him scheming.

Two events would eventually provide Philip with the opportunity he was seeking: accusations of sodomy, idolatry, and blasphemy within the Templars by a former member named Esquiu de Floyrian, and the contentious election of Pope Clement V, which took a year to conclude. To facilitate his election Clement had arranged with Philip that, upon his election as pope, he would repeal previous laws passed by the Vatican against France. This was the beginning of a friendship between a weak pope and an avaricious king that would end with the destruction of the Knights Templar.

At sunrise on Friday, October 13, 1307, the Knights Templar were arrested in a series of coordinated raids across France. In all, two thousand members of the order were imprisoned. The coordination for this kind of large-scale arrest is astonishing given the period and the sheer manpower it required. Copies of arrest warrants, all copied by hand, had to be produced and delivered with official seals and under Philip's authority. Men had to be organized and deployed. The fact that no one sympathetic to the Templars tipped them off about the forthcoming arrests is in itself telling of both the jealousy they may have fostered and the fear of church punishment should one be found guilty of assisting the doomed Knights of the Temple. Less than a year later, Pope Clement V would authorize additional arrests wherever the Roman Catholic Church held authority.

Charges brought against the Templars included heresy, denying the divinity of Christ, spitting on the cross, sodomy and homosexuality (giving an anal kiss to one's initiator in the order), and the most famous of all, worshipping an idol in the shape of a strange head known as Baphomet. (And while Baphomet has taken on many strange and peculiar meanings over the years, it is in all likelihood a misspelling of Mohammed in medieval French.)

Trials and interrogations were a mockery of justice; confessions extracted under torture were routine. Leading questions were the order of the day. No evidence, outside of that extracted through torture, was ever produced to support the accusations brought against the Templars. No Baphomets were ever found. Yet, in the end, about sixty knights who had been arrested either died under torture or were executed after a puppet trial. Fifty-four of the sixty recanted their confessions and were burned at the stake in 1310 under the charge of being relapsed heretics. The methods established for the destruction of the Templars would be perfected a century later during the beginning of the "Burning Times," or persecution of those perceived as practicing witchcraft.

Among those to die was the order's grand master, Jacques de Molay. After being imprisoned for seven years, on March 18, 1314, Molay was burned at the stake. Before his death he predicted that King Philip and Pope Clement would soon follow him. Within a year both were dead.

After their trials most Templars were released and either joined other orders or retired to civilian life. Outside of France the arrests and persecutions were not as vigorous.

Templars in York Rite Masonry

Just as Chevalier Andrew Michael Ramsay's Templar mythology stirred the imagination of what would become Scottish Rite, it also planted the seeds for what would become York Rite. French and German obsession with this purported connection was the most fabulous and productive in the spawning of new degrees and even entire rites. While there was no evidence to support the notion that Templars had fled to Scotland, along with esoteric wisdom gleaned from their stay in the Holy Land, their massive treasure, or both, this did nothing to slow the explosion of the myth of a Templar connection to Freemasonry. By 1769 Templar degrees were being given in the American colonies and by 1778 in England. However, a distinct difference, even at this stage, was apparent between American and British Templar rites and those of German and France, and in the Rite of Strict Observance in particular. In Europe a clear and direct connection was made between Masonry, Templars, esoteric studies, and occult practices such as alchemy, astrology, and Qabala. In Anglo-Saxon Templarism this connection was absent, and, in fact, Templar degrees were little more than an additional degree to be had on the ever-expanding Masonic ladder.

Templars and the Occult

In Templar mythology and Strict Observance Masonry, we find the notion that the Templars were heirs of an Eastern treasure of a spiritual rather than material nature, that included the secrets of Qabala, alchemy, and Arabic magic. While such an idea may have existed earlier, it is not until the development of the Masonic grades that this notion appears full-blown and in a coherent manner, complete with rituals, rites, and teachings that suggest a continuity of teaching reaching back to Templars themselves.

The traditional history behind Strict Observance states that Pierre d'Aumont, grand marshal of the Knights Templar, who succeeded Jacques de Molay as grand master, and seven knights fled to Scotland, disguising themselves as stonemasons. There, the tradition claims, the Templars established Freemasonry in its present form. However, like all traditional histories, facts to support these statements are lacking, and the "history" is better understood as mythology, or a teaching story, rather than an actual history. Unfortunately, traditional histories are often positioned as actual facts rather than suggestive retellings. This has created a hornet's nest of confusion within Masonic circles and for Masonic research up to the present day.

Founded in Germany circa 1754 by Johann Gottlieb von Hund, the Rite of Strict Observance was based upon von Hund's assertion that he had been initiated into a Masonic Templar lodge twelve years earlier and entrusted with the mission of spreading this rite. His authority and knowledge, he said, were derived from "Unknown Superiors" who required perfect obedience. While it is possible that von Hund was initiated into a Templar degree or rite, it is unlikely—or he may simply have been fooled. The notion of "Unknown Superiors," those invisible masters of human destiny found in the writings of Madame Blavatsky and throughout the occult revival of the nineteenth and early twentieth centuries, finds its origins in part in this "history" of Strict Observance. Unlike later reports of these superbeings, von Hund would state that he received his investiture and was left to his own devices on how to proceed; thus, Strict Observance is a vehicle of his own creation. Later occultists and Masons with occult interests would pick up where von Hund left off and state that they were in continued, often telepathic, contact with their invisible masters and tutors.

With only his word of honor to go on, von Hund and his rite languished and fell into disrepair. With his death the Lodge of Philalethes absorbed much of the rite. What remained of Strict Observance, like most things Masonic, was destroyed or scattered by the French Revolution.

Among the most important of Strict Observance brethren was Jean-Baptiste Willermoz (1730–1824). Willermoz was a well-known Mason from Lyon and a cofounder of the Rectified Scottish Rite. Interestingly, the Rectified Rite denied any connection to the Knights Templar and contained elements of ritual magic. Willermoz was also an ardent disciple of Martinez de Pasquales, founder of the Elus Cohen (see chapter 8), and one of his two heirs: Louis Claude de Saint-Martin being his mystical son, and Willermoz his magical one. In this way, the stage was set at the end of the eighteenth century for the Elus Cohen to be absorbed in the cross-fertilization of ideas and practices of High-Grade Masonry and, through Strict Observance, connected to the myth of the Templars and their esoteric wisdom.

Despite Strict Observance rejecting Rosicrucianism and its Hermetic-alchemical philosophy in favor of the Elus Cohen and their theurgy in 1782, Willermoz was responsible for establishing a chapter of the Black Eagle of the Rose-Croix nearly twenty years earlier.

York Rite and the Survival of the Knights Templar: Key Points

1. Members of York Rite must be a Master Mason in good standing. Like Scottish Rite, York Rite is a system that elaborates on the first three degrees. York Rite consists of several related groups, each of which confers a specific set of degrees, culminating in the Order of the Knights Templar.

2. The first higher degrees in York Rite history were Royal Arch and Knights Templar. By 1730 additional degrees were being conferred, each elaborating on the basic theme of Solomon's Temple, hidden treasure, and lost secrets.

3. For many, Royal Arch is considered the pinnacle of Masonic achievement, and any subsequent degrees are simply explanatory.

4. Unlike Blue Lodge or Scottish Rite, York Rite is distinctly Christian in its tone and membership requirements.

5. The Cryptic degrees of York Rite first appeared between 1760 and 1780 and were based upon the theme of nine crypts or vaults existing beneath the Temple of Solomon. In the lowest vault is the Lost Word, placed there by Enoch the Patriarch.

6. Enoch is a critical figure in Masonry; he is also strongly identified with ritual magic and Qabala through his association with, or rather transformation into the archangel Metatron.

7. Chivalric degrees confer knightly titles, but there is no evidence that they are historically linked to the actual orders those titles refer to. The Chivalric degrees culminate in the Knights Templar.

8. The Knights Templar were founded in 1118 CE when Hughes de Payns, a minor nobleman, and eight fellow knights from France took vows of poverty and obedience in connection with their military vows. In doing so, they became the first warrior-monks in Christendom.

9. The knights, known as the Poor Fellows of the Knights of Christ, were given residence in a dilapidated section of Solomon's Temple in Jerusalem and thereafter changed their name, calling themselves Knights Templar for short.

10. The self-appointed task of the Templars was to guard Christian pilgrims on their journey to the Holy Land. They quickly rose to become the most powerful military and economic entity in the region, reporting only to the Pope.

11. In 1307 the Templars were arrested and their leaders executed on trumped-up charges of heresy, sodomy, and worshipping an idol called the Baphomet. Torture was widely used to extract confessions, and on March 18, 1314, after seven years in prison, Jacques de Molay, the last grand master of the Knights Templar, was burned at the stake.

12. In part due to Chevalier Andrew Michael Ramsay's Templar mythology in the eighteenth century, extensive myth and lore has grown up around the Templars over the last two centuries. Most of these stories link the Templars to ancient treasures or secret wisdom of an alchemical, Qabalistic, or Arabic nature.

Assignments for Chapter Nine

1. What can you learn about the Lost Word or the divine secret hidden in creation? What does this mean to you? How do you believe it can be experienced?

2. When you contemplate the story of Enoch transforming into Metatron and being taken bodily into heaven, what ideas arise in your mind? What similar ideas exist in other faiths, philosophies, and esoteric traditions?

York Rite and the Survival of the Knights Templar: Suggested Reading

The Templars and the Assassins: The Militia of Heaven, by James Wasserman (Inner Traditions, 2001). An exploration of the strange and exciting history of one of history's greatest rivalries.

An Illustrated History of the Knights Templar, by James Wasserman

(Inner Traditions, 2006). History with pictures, and beautiful ones at that, as Wasserman adds his erudition to the mix.

The Templars: Knights of God, by Edward Burman (Destiny Books, 1986). A concise look at the history of the Templars.

The Knights Templar and Their Myth, by Peter Partner (Destiny Books, 1990). A critical examination of the various myths that have shaped our view of the Knights Templar.

10

Freemasonry
and the European
Occult Revival

*Know then, O Aspirant, that the Mysteries of the Rose and
the Cross have existed from time immemorial, and that
the Rites were practiced, and the Wisdom taught in Egypt,
Eleusis, Samothrace, Persia, Chaldea and India, and far
more ancient lands. The story of the introduction of these
mysteries into medieval Europe has thus been handed
down to us.*

FROM THE THIRD ADEPT'S LECTURE, ADEPTUS MINOR
RITUAL, HERMETIC ORDER OF THE GOLDEN DAWN

BY THE END OF THE NINETEENTH CENTURY, fringe Masonic
and Masonic-style groups had become the focal point of the occult
revival. Even organizations such as the Theosophical Society incorporated Masonic elements into sections of their work, becoming, as we
shall see, the principal champion for a mixed-Masonic order known as
Co-Masonry. This period of time is of considerable interest to students
of esotericism as well as mainstream Masonry because of the rich field
of personalities, rites, charters, claims and counterclaims to authenticity, lawsuits, and outright hostility and occasional violence that dominated movements based on the philosophical ideal of the brotherhood
of man and spiritual values. The irony cannot be missed by anyone who

explores this period and is, in fact, its main attraction for more than one author.

Despite this, from the compost pile of human endeavors gone awry, the core groups from this period continued to exert an influence on esotericism in the United States and Europe long after their fires had burned their brightest. The seeds they planted, just as the seeds of their seventeenth- and eighteenth-century ancestors had done, would grow quietly, their fruits to be discovered by future generations long after the personalities had become footnotes in history.

In some respects it is these fringe groups that demonstrate what is best and worst with Freemasonry, and with human ideals and activities as a whole. Strong ideals require strong character. The temptation to sneak around giving the devil his due is a powerful one, and even more so when titles and promises of material and spiritual power are attached. While many people (this author included) have benefited tremendously from participation in some of the groups listed below, it is also clear that movements can become a lightning rod for those seeking fulfillment and satisfaction through so-called spirituality when they have failed to find these qualities in material life. In traditional Masonry membership was allowed only on or after the age of twenty-one—that's nearly middle age for the average person living in the eighteenth century—and Qabala was permitted only for men of "the age of wisdom," or forty. Clearly, a firm grounding and establishment in material life was expected by these points in life, and this was meant to be brought into a member's activities within the Fraternity. If there is a lesson to be learned from the following brief study of modern fringe Masonic groups, it is that human ideals, no matter how noble, still require the imperfect vehicle of humanity to carry them out. Perfection is an ideal strived for but possibly never attained.

CO-MASONRY AND
THE INVISIBLE ADEPTS REVISITED

Co-Masonry, among the most recent of Masonic bodies, is the direct offspring of the nineteenth-century occult revival. Founded in 1900,

Co-Masonry claims its authority through a variety of Masonic entities that seceded from the Supreme Council of France in 1879. The first Co-Masonic lodge was opened in London in September 1902, with Dr. Annie Besant acting as vice president grand master of the Supreme Council and deputy for Great Britain and its dependencies.

What makes this of interest is that while Co-Masonry admitted women into its ranks (and still does, as it is alive and well) on an equal basis with men in an era where the women's suffrage movement was beginning to take on tremendous force in Europe and America, its members saw in this nothing irregular.

- The fundamental tenet of Co-Masonry is that women were admitted to the ancient mysteries prior to the ascent of the Christian era, and, as such, admitting them into Freemasonry was a restoration of something that was lost.
- Given this tenet, it is clear that Co-Masonry views Freemasonry as a whole as a continuation of the ancient Middle Eastern and Asian mystery schools under the guise of the stonecutters guild, rather than as a social entity.
- The leadership and members of Co-Masonry from its origin to this day are in some fashion involved with Theosophy. They see Christianity as a dying religion that will be replaced by a single universal system of belief and believe that the world will be united under a single government, and from this, universal peace and brotherhood established—thereby completing the political expression of the esoteric mission of Freemasonry.
- Behind the established movements of Theosophy and Co-Masonry stand the "Unknown Superiors" or invisible masters who guide humanity, leading it to its goal of unity under an enlightened leadership.

The rituals of Co-Masonry were eventually revised to reflect the perception that the original initiations and working degrees of the Craft contained esoteric wisdom that had been lost since their inception. These revisions, completed in 1916, were based on English and

Scottish rituals. More ideas were introduced from French rituals, as well as innovations emphasizing esoteric ideas peculiar to the leadership of the period. Additional degrees were eventually modified over the years as well, allowing Co-Masonry to work its own unique understanding of Craft, Royal Arch, and Scottish Rite Freemasonry.

The most influential leaders in Co-Masonry were Annie Besant (1847–1933) and Charles Webster Leadbeater (1847–1934), both well known and established in the Theosophical community. Besant was a phenomenal woman involved in many of the most important social movements of the period, moving through atheism, socialism, the promotion of Indian nationalism, feminism, and the promotion of birth control at a time when one in six women died in childbirth and urban poverty in the industrialized nations was rampant. Leadbeater was a clergyman in the Church of England whose interests in Theosophy caused him to eventually leave the church; later in life he stated publicly that he was a practicing Buddhist. He authored several important Theosophical books, as well as two on the esoteric nature of Freemasonry: *The Hidden Life in Freemasonry* and *Glimpses of Masonic History,* whose weight rest upon Leadbeater's status as a 32nd-degree Mason and his reputed clairvoyant abilities. Leadbeater's life, however, was filled with controversy, and he was forced to resign from the Theosophical Society in disgrace after allegations of homosexual liaisons with young boys began to surface and were substantiated. Various actions allowed him to eventually rejoin the Theosophical Society and lead its Indian section, until the old charges of pedophilia reemerged. Leadbeater then was forced from India, settling in Australia. Next to Blavatsky, he is the most controversial figure in the Theosophical movement.

Theosophy itself is a peculiar term meaning "knowledge of God," and while often applied to unique streams of European mystical and esoteric speculation from the Renaissance onward, it has become identified almost exclusively with the writings of Russian seer and adventurer Helena Petrovna Blavatsky. Blavatsky (1831–1891) was born in the Ukraine to the daughter of a provincial official of German extraction and minor nobility. She was reared by her maternal grandparents, both nobles, and in this environment exposed to many esoteric and philosophic ideas, including Freemasonry, Strict Observance, and the ideas of Pasquales and Saint-Martin. At the age of seventeen, she was married to Nikifor Blavatsky, a Russian military officer very much her senior, and she ran off after a few months of marriage.

For the next decade she traveled widely—her travels would form the basis for the mythology constructed around her life story in later years. The official "history" from Theosophists proclaims that she ventured to Tibet, where she lived with the *mahatmas,* "great souls," those enlightened beings who guide humanity on its spiritual quest. Evidence suggests that she was more of an adventurer, sometime a circus performer, possibly a spy, and, of course, as is typical for the period, a fraudulent medium. It is unclear if she had any children, and during her later years she refused to discuss her wanderings despite the great body of lore they had produced during her lifetime.

It is known that Blavatsky spent time in Egypt, something that played an important part in the development of Co-Masonry under Annie Besant. Blavatsky was always involved in some fashion with fringe Masonry, Hermetic and quasi-Hermetic societies, and Eastern mystical groups in all of their forms, using these contacts to claim access to some form of secret or hidden wisdom—a theme that reappears in Co-Masonry. Blavatsky was among the survivors of the shipwreck of the vessel carrying her to Cairo in 1871. While in Cairo she founded a Spiritualist organization, aided by Emma Coulomb, an English woman Blavatsky employed as her housekeeper. Blavatsky's relationship with Coulomb would be long-lasting and fateful, as Coulomb would become one of her bitterest critics. The organization, known as the Société Spirite, was based upon the theories of author and founder of Spiritism Allan Kardec and was established for the investigation of spiritualistic phenomena. It lasted a short time, however (one report put it at as little as two weeks); it ruptured under the usual charges of fraud and embezzlement of funds from scammed patrons. Blavatsky left the group early and focused her attention on Hermeticism and its accompanying practices of magic, astrology, and Qabala. She traveled to Paris by way of eastern Europe and arrived in Paris by spring of 1873. Her travels would eventually take her to the United States.

Using her travels and writings as a guide, it is clear that Blavatsky's life had two distinct periods: one Western and Hermetic, the other Eastern and Buddhist. Her Hermetic period dominated the early years of the Theosophical Society, from its inception in 1875, and reached its zenith with the publication of *Isis Unveiled* in 1877. With Blavatsky's journey to Bombay two years later, the philosophical direction of the Theosophical Society changed was well, and a strong Indo-Tibetan approach became the norm. Then, while in Egypt, Blavatsky met and claimed membership in the Hermetic Brotherhood of Luxor, and she learned enough details of Masonic ritual and teachings to suitably impress Parisian Masonic authorities.

Madame Blavatsky's past would begin to haunt her during her Indian period. In 1884, while Blavatsky was in London with her longtime friend and supporter Colonel Henry Steel Olcott, two Theosophical Society staff members, Emma Coulomb and her husband, Alexis, stated that they had assisted Blavatsky in the perpetuation of fraudulent mediumistic séances. The resulting publicity of these accusations created a split between Blavatsky and Olcott. With Blavatsky's death in 1891, leadership of the Theosophical Society fell to Annie Besant, after which it began to suffer from a series of schisms. While Besant's personality and apparent lack of tact and diplomacy played no small role in stoking the fires of revolt, her desire to promote Co-Masonry was also at fault, as Theosophists felt that Co-Masonry and Leadbeater's Liberal Catholic Church were not appropriate topics given the clearly Indo-Tibetan direction of the organization.

MARTINISM AND ROSICRUCIANS REBORN

The popularity of Eliphas Levi's works *Dogma and Ritual of High Magic* and *The History of Magic* can be seen as the seed behind what would eventually be termed the *occult revival* of the nineteenth and early twentieth centuries. Not a single movement remained untouched by their contents, and in many ways they gave birth to entire occult orders—not the least among them modern rebirths of Martinism, Rosicrucianism, and, as we have seen, Pike's interpretation of the degrees of Scottish Rite.

In this twilight milieu that pervaded the Belle Epoque, we see the emergence, or reemergence, of the doctrines of Louis Claude de Saint-Martin, student and disciple of Martinez Pasquales, under the umbrella of Martinism. In 1884 Dr. Gérard Encausse (1865–1916) united with Augustin Chaboseau to found the Martinist Order. Writing under the pen name Papus, Encausse became one of the leading figures of European occultism, even venturing into the court of Czar Nicholas II and becoming the spiritual archrival of Rasputin. Papus has often been called the "Balzac of occultism" because of the number of books he published—over two hundred. While many are short and of little scholarly value, they point to his pivotal role and the popular desire for such works, and many of them are still available well over a century after they were written. Papus published his first book, *Elementary Treatise of Occult Science,* in 1888 and his most famous work, *The Tarot of the Bohemians,* the following year. Dozens of titles were to follow until his untimely death in 1916 while serving as a physician at the front in World War I.

Prior to his involvement in Martinism (and later the establishing of several Rosicrucian groups), Papus was active in the Parisian Theosophical scene, but like Rudolf Steiner, he left when it turned from Hermeticism toward Eastern mysticism.

In 1891 the Supreme Council of the Martinist Order was established, and efforts were made to bring into the fold the many diverse groups, circles, and independent initiators and teachers that had grown out of the work of Saint-Martin, Pasquales, and Willermoz's Strict Observance Masonry. Four degrees were utilized, with similarity in structure to Freemasonry. The fourth degree, that of Independent Superior Inconnu ("Free Unknown Superior," or, later, L.I. or Free Initiator), gave its holder the authority to initiate others and to form lodges composed of the lower three degrees of Associate, Mystic (also Brother), and Superior Inconnu ("Unknown Superior"). As a result, Martinism spread quickly, even far beyond the shores of Europe, and as a result of such rapid growth gave rise to personal innovations and schisms. Several attempts were made by Papus and others to use Martinism as a means of returning Freemasonry to its esoteric roots. These overtures were firmly rejected by regular Masonic authorities, and many even incorrectly saw Martinism as a form of irregular or clandestine Masonry based upon the superficial similarities of its degree structure. Like many of the occult orders of the day, the Martinist Order admitted women on equal footing with men, although later attempts to change this and force a Masonic requirement on Martinist members led to the formation of yet another schismatic Martinist body.

A natural organizer, Encausse linked up with numerous well-known personalities in Parisian occultism to form the Kabbalistic Order of the Rose-Cross. This order was in part the brainchild of Stanislaus de Guaita (1860–1898). A flamboyant artist and poet, de Guaita made his mark by creating a sinister persona around himself, reveling in the decadence of period. He slept during the day, worked at night, and destroyed his health through addiction to morphine and cocaine, dying at the age of thirty-eight of a drug overdose in a public urinal. Like many dreamers of all ages and periods, Guaita saw art as the means of transforming the world, and he participated in well-attended salons with esoteric themes. Similar to the New Age movement of the late twentieth century, spirituality, occultism, and counterculture linked together in nineteenth-century Paris to form a fashionable narcissism wherein the elect could find illumination in the arms of their mistresses under the influence of drugs and justify it in the language of revolution. Also like its New Age counterpart, its impact on society at large appears to have been negligible.

However, as was the case for so many idealistic movements, the illuminati of the Paris brothels were unable to hold their dream together. In 1890 one of the founding members of the Kabbalistic Order of the Rose-Cross left to found the Catholic Order of the Rose-Cross, an attempt to reunite art, mysticism, and traditional Catholic theology under a single initiatic movement. A series of letter-writing campaigns, known as the War of the Roses, ensued, wherein each side attempted to justify its position while decrying the treason of the other.

Like so many things esoteric, with only a few rare exceptions this infighting had little impact outside of the limited circles wherein it occurred; day-to-day life went on for the man on the street. The siege of Paris and the battles of Verdun, Saint-Mihiel, Ypres, and others too numerous to remember, along with death on a massive scale in the trenches of World War I, was only a generation away. By 1919 most of the founding members of these orders would be dead, too old, or simply too tired to care any longer. The ancient feuds of authenticity were seen for what they were then and are now: a convenient distraction born out of luxury of both time and money. Invoking the shades of the dead went from fashionable to commonplace as mourners sought solace in the glimpse of a loved one in the darkened chamber of the spiritualist medium or in the magic mirror of the magus. There was no longer a need to talk of the demons of the abyss in the abstract. They were now neighbors.

From the period of the French occult revival, with its glory and its decadence, a spirit would arise and give birth, even if more in inspiration than in direct substance, to the single most important initiatic mystical fraternity of the twentieth century: the Ancient Mystical Order Rosea Crucis (AMORC), better known as the Rosicrucian Order. Within AMORC the ideal of a single unified international esoteric movement open to men and women of all races within a quasi-Masonic framework of initiation, ritual, and instruction would be realized. Drawing upon the inspiration of his contemporaries as well as Cagliostro and Egyptian Freemasonry, Harvey Spencer Lewis (1883–1939) achieved through AMORC what many esoteric and occult movements had attempted but failed: permanence beyond the death of its founder, physical temples worldwide, and a profound impact on popular culture and understanding of traditionally secret and highly veiled themes and ideas.

At different periods and with varying enforcement from jurisdiction to jurisdiction, members of AMORC were at times refused Masonic membership, as during its early years the Rosicrucian Order was seen as a clandestine Masonic body. This never seems to have become a widespread notion and was more of a local peculiarity. However, Lewis, the organization's founder, was refused initiation as a Master Mason by the Grand Lodge of New York after having completed his Entered

Apprentice and Fellowcraft degrees. This slight appears to have been retribution in part for Lewis's lack of tact in the early promotion of his fledgling movement and in part due to a personal grudge against him from a former AMORC member who was also a member of the lodge where Lewis was being initiated.

THE HERMETIC ORDER OF THE GOLDEN DAWN

Martinism drew upon Freemasonry for some of its members and even, if ever so briefly, sought to change the face of Freemasonry itself, and Co-Masonry saw itself as the rightful esoteric heir of the occult truth within Masonic ritual and form. Yet it is the Hermetic Order of the Golden Dawn that has had the most impact on the twentieth- and twenty-first-century occult scene and is most clearly connected to Masonic and semi-Masonic movements.

The two principal founders of the Hermetic Order of the Golden Dawn were William Wynn Westcott (1848–1925) and Samuel Liddell Mathers (1854–1918). Both men were deeply entrenched in the Masonic and esoteric world of Victorian England and brought with them connections and skills that would fuse together in the creation of the single most important magical order in over a century.

While the actual origins of the Golden Dawn are murky at best, it is known that in 1886 Westcott found, received, or created a set of documents in a unique code or cipher. These became known as the "Cypher Manuscripts." These documents contained teachings and rituals in outline form for an organization calling itself the Hermetic Order of the Golden Dawn. The structure of the order was identical to the eighteenth-century quasi-Masonic and alchemical Orden des Gold- und Rosenkreuz (Order of the Golden and Rosy Cross).

Westcott says that Reverend A. F. A. Woodford (1821–1887), a fellow Mason with occult interests, found the documents in a bookseller's stall—just as Cagliostro had claimed of the texts for his Egyptian Rite. This is not improbable, but neither can it be substantiated, which caused many to question the authenticity of the story.

Accusations of forgery also accrued, pointing mainly to the fact that letters later produced by Westcott and supposedly from a Fräulein Sprengel in Germany were clearly written by someone with a limited command of German. Westcott was no stranger to the problems of making claims of succession without documentation to support them. As a member of the Societas Rosicruciana in Anglia (SRIA), or Rosicrucian Society of England, he had investigated claims by the society's founder, Robert Wentworth Little, that the SRIA was founded on documents discovered in Freemasons' Hall in London and found nothing to support this claim.

Westcott had risen quickly through the ranks of the SRIA; he joined in 1880 and became Supreme Magus in 1891. Mathers was also a member of the SRIA. Perhaps not surprisingly, the grade structure of the SRIA was identical to that used earlier by the Orden des Gold- und Rosenkreuz and later by the Hermetic Order of the Golden Dawn.

Westcott formally established the Hermetic Order of the Golden Dawn in March 1888 with the assistance of Mathers and William Robert Woodman—the other two Freemasons he recruited for the task. As to be expected, initial membership drew from the associates of the founders, and eventually it grew to around three hundred members and at least nine temples, six in Britain, two in the United States, and one in Paris. The first public announcement was in the form of a reply from Westcott to a letter published in the British literature and folklore journal *Notes and Queries* in December 1888. The letter inquired about the continued existence of a Qabalistic society that supposedly included Eliphas Levi and famous Qabalist and alchemist Hayyim Samuel Jacob Falk among its members. Westcott stated in the affirmative, though Levi and Falk were not official members, but inspirational and literary influences. This answer prompted additional questions and soon the Golden Dawn's membership increased significantly.

As the Hermetic Order of the Golden Dawn grew, its members desired more practical material than was issued in the lower grades of Neophyte, Zelator, Theoricus, Practicus, and Philosophus, and under the skilled hand of Mathers they were obliged. With the creation of the Portal and the Adeptus Minor rituals, a second or inner order called the

Ordo Rosae Rubeae et Aureae Crucis was formed. Additional grades were planned, but their completion was disputed as a result of the Golden Dawn's breakup in 1900.

It was here in the second order that the practical magical teachings for which the Golden Dawn would become famous were actually taught and practiced, and it is with the order's self-destruction in its twelfth year that these practices were cast to the winds of fortune. While several organizations were created to continue the teachings of the Golden Dawn, including Mathers's own Order of Alpha et Omega, most of them dwindled and died or were succeeded by second-generation students, such as Dion Fortune's Fraternity of the Inner Light (which later changed its name to the Society of the Inner Light) and Paul Foster Case's Builders of the Adytum, to name just two. Fortune's society originally used several grades derived from Co-Masonry for its lesser mysteries. This ended, however, in 1961 when the work was reduced to one degree and took on a distinctly Christian tone. Case's organization, often known only by its initials, or BOTA, works the Golden Dawn rituals but without the use of Enochian magic. The practical work of the Golden Dawn survived in most part as a result of its rituals being published—first by Aleister Crowley, a former student and close associate of Mathers, and then again by his student Israel Regardie between 1937 and 1940, in several volumes.

Oddly, some of the Golden Dawn material also found itself in the SRIA. When Westcott was forced to choose between resigning his membership in the Golden Dawn or his position as a public official, he chose to leave the Golden Dawn but retained his Masonic activities. In 1907 the American branch of the SRIA (known as the Societas Rosicruciana in Civitatibus Foederatis) experienced a schism from members wishing to remove the Masonic membership requirement. The schismatic body adopted the name Societas Rosicruciana in America (SRIA—again). It was initially headed by Sylvester C. Gould, though he was succeeded two years later by Dr. George Winslow Plummer. Under Plummer's leadership the Societas Rosicruciana in America grew and, using the methods of the day, established a correspondence course that contained much of the teachings of the Golden Dawn. Upon Plummer's death in 1944, leadership of the organization fell to his wife, Gladys Plummer, better known as Mother Serena, who was succeeded by Sister Lucia Grosch, and later by Soror M.A.* The SRIA continues to offer courses of instruction online and is run by Sandra Tabatha Cicero, a well-known author within the Hermetic Order of the Golden Dawn tradition with its authority coming directly through their connection to Israel Regardie. Both the Hermetic Order of the Golden Dawn (which she runs with her husband, Chic) and the SRIA are headquartered in Florida.

KNIGHTS TEMPLAR ANEW

One of the most controversial and influential figures in what could be called "magical fringe Masonry" of the early twentieth century is Aleister Crowley (1875–1947). Born into a wealthy family that practiced an unusually severe form of Puritanism, the Plymouth Brethren, Crowley was reared with a small fortune, a first-rate education, and a significant amount of psychological baggage. Crowley saw himself as the prophet of the New Aeon, a messiah come to liberate humanity from its moral and ethical constraints and find its own "true will" through magic (which he spelled *magick*). Crowley turned to magic while at college, after finding a copy of A. E. Waite's *Book of Black Magic and of Pacts*. In 1898 he became a member of the Golden Dawn, taking on a leadership role under the direction of Mathers. Crowley, however, would turn his talents against both Waite (who, after the schism of 1900, established his own Fellowship of the Rosy Cross, which worked the Golden Dawn scheme in a purely mystical manner) and Mathers, engaging in vitriolic diatribes against both in his writings. At their

---

*Courtesy of Sandra Tabatha Cicero: Gladys Miller Plummer (later Gladys Plummer de Witow) known in the Society as Mother Serena served as Imperatrix from 1969 to 1989.

Sister Lucia Albers Grosch, 1989–1997

Maria Babwahsingh, 1997–2010

Sandra Tabatha Cicero, 2010–present.

Whether male or female, the head of the order is known as a Supreme Magus. Or as an Imperator or Imperatrix, whichever the case may be.

lowest point Mathers and Crowley were engaged in a running magical war against one another, sending astral vampires to attack the other.

While in Cairo in April 1904, Crowley had a series of experiences that involved communications from an entity calling itself Aiwass. Over the course of three days, he wrote down these messages in a volume that became known as the *Book of the Law,* which among other things proclaimed Crowley as the Antichrist, the Beast of the Book of Revelation. Using up what was left of his inheritance, he published *The Equinox,* a magazine through which he brought the teachings of the Golden Dawn to a wider occult public. Soon afterward he joined the Ordo Templi Orientis (OTO), a quasi-Masonic group run by Theodor Reuss (1855–1923).

The Ordo Templi Orientis had been established by Reuss and Karl Kellner (1851–1905). Both men were entrenched in the occult world and its fringe Masonic movements that dominated central Europe prior to World War I. In 1902 both men contacted John Yarker (1833–1913), an English Freemason and occultist who possessed a massive library, along with numerous occult lineages. From him they purchased a charter to establish a lodge of the Rite of Memphis and Misraim, a Masonic rite consisting of ninety-nine degrees. The following year they published a prospectus for the establishment of the OTO. The order made little headway over the next few years and only began to grow significantly with Crowley's membership. Eventually, as with all things Crowley touched, he would have a falling out with Reuss as it became clear that Reuss was reinventing the OTO in his own image.

Despite Reuss's questionable character, several well-known occultists of the period had brief encounters with the OTO, including Papus, Rudolf Steiner, and Harvey Spencer Lewis. Lewis's connection to Ruess would fuel another running legal battle for Crowley when he attempted to take over Lewis's AMORC in the 1930s—just as AMORC became established and prosperous and Crowley's own money had long been squandered on drugs, alcohol, sex, and vanities of the highest order.

Under Crowley's leadership the OTO adopted the *Book of the Law* as its principal text, and members—both men and women—undertook a series of initiations imparting magical knowledge, and emphasizing sexual magic, something both Kellner and Reuss were obsessed with. However, by the time of Crowley's death in 1947, the only active OTO body left in the world was Agape Lodge located in California. The lodge would not last long after Crowley's death. In 1969, however, Grady McMurtry (1918–1985), an American who had partly run Agape Lodge, announced that he had his own OTO charter from Crowley and had received it when visiting the Beast in London in 1943. Despite claims and counterclaims the legal authority of McMurtry was established in court, and trademarks and copyrights were awarded to his branch of the OTO. Under his leadership the OTO reached a far larger audience than it ever had under either Reuss or Crowley, and currently it is one of the most influential, as well as controversial, fringe Masonic movements in existence.

Freemasonry and the European Occult Revival: Key Points

1. By the end of the nineteenth and beginning of the twentieth century, Masonry and fringe Masonic and Masonic-style movements were the focal point of an occult revival.

2. Despite claims of promoting equality and fraternity, many of these groups were torn apart by schisms and personality conflicts.

3. Co-Masonry moved into prominence thanks to the connection of several of its leaders to the Theosophical Society. Co-Masonry admitted women on equal ground as men and promoted an esoteric understanding of Masonic ritual and initiation.

4. Co-Masonry saw Freemasonry as a continuation of the ancient mystery schools and medieval occultism. It saw Christianity as a dying religion that would be replaced by a single universal system of belief and believed that the world would be united under a single government, thereby promoting universal peace.

5. Co-Masonry and the Theosophical Society claimed that perfect beings, known as "Unknown Superiors," "Masters," or "Adepts," guided the movement's leadership, making them nearly infallible.

6. Eliphas Levi's writings were the impetus for the French occult

revival and directly as well as indirectly gave birth to several organizations, including Rosicrucian and Martinist movements.

7. Gérard Encausse, better known by his pen name Papus, was a central force in Parisian occultism. He was a prolific author and tireless organizer. He is responsible for modern Martinism, and to a lesser degree Rosicrucianism.

8. The "War of the Roses" between two conflicting French Rosicrucian movements demonstrated the human weakness behind the ideals of the time. Whatever those internal squabbles did not destroy, the First and Second World Wars did, making many modern esoteric movements irrelevant in day-to-day life.

9. The Hermetic Order of the Golden Dawn is the single most influential modern magical order to have appeared during this period. It lasted only twelve years, but its influence is felt more strongly than ever. Several of its founders were High-Degree Masons and members of a Masonic Rosicrucian group.

10. Aleister Crowley was among the most famous, or infamous, of the Golden Dawn's members. He played a pivotal role in the order's demise and eventually published its teachings in his journal, *The Equinox,* thereby bringing them to the attention of the broader public for the first time.

11. Crowley later became a leading member of Karl Kellner's Ordo Templi Orientis, a Knights Templar–styled initiatic order claiming Masonic status. The OTO practiced a variety of forms of sex magic. At the time of Crowley's death in 1947, there was only one functioning OTO lodge in the world.

12. Starting in 1969, under the leadership of Grady McMurtry, a student of Aleister Crowley, the OTO underwent a renewal process that would within three decades make it one of the largest movements of its kind, with active lodges across the globe.

Exercises for Chapter Ten

1. If you were to organize a movement, be it esoteric, charitable, or educational, what would its core ideals be? What organizational structure would you use as a model for your organization?

2. How would you address the problems that can arise from differing personalities and leadership responsibilities?

3. Based on your knowledge of fraternal and secret societies, what are the main problems that seem to arise within movements of these types, and how can they be avoided?

Freemasonry and the European Occult Revival: Suggested Reading

Fulcanelli and the Alchemical Revival: The Man behind the Mystery of the Cathedrals, by Geneviève Dubois (Inner Traditions, 2006). One of several books that attempts to solve the riddle of the mysterious French alchemist Fulcanelli.

Al-Kemi: A Memoir: Hermetic, Occult, Political, and Private Aspects of R. A. Schwaller de Lubicz, by Andre Vandenbroeck (Lindisfarne Press, 1987). A specialized look at one of the twentieth century's most influential and, at times, least understood esotericist.

Eliphas Levi and the French Occult Revival, by Christopher McIntosh (Weiser, 1972). Slightly dated, but still a classic in the field of French occultism.

Access to Western Esotericism, by Antoine Faivre (State University of New York Press, 1994). A detailed examination of the problems and possibilities in the academic research of esotericism.

Modern Esoteric Spirituality, edited by Antoine Faivre and Jacob Needleman (Crossroad, 1992). Essays on key figures and movements. Well worth reading to gain insight into other areas of possible interest.

Modern Masonry

IIIIIIIIIIIIIIIIIIIIIIIIIIIIIIIIIIIIIIIIIIIIIIIIIIIIIII

Much Ado about Nothing,
or the Revival of the Lost Word?

Example is not the main thing in influencing others. It is the only thing.

ALBERT SCHWEITZER

ONE OF THE MORE INTERESTING OBSERVATIONS about Freemasonry is that while it has a series of landmarks, traditions, and rituals that make it recognizable from age to age and across jurisdictions, it is in many ways a malleable entity, changing to meet the particular aspirations of it members. As we have seen, since the very inception of the first grand lodge, there has persisted the idea that something is missing from Freemasonry—that it holds the deepest of mystical secrets within its breast but cannot find the key to unlocking them. Simultaneously, we see Freemasonry growing and expanding as a social entity, as a leveler of class differences, as a vehicle for men of good will, regardless of social and economic status, to come together. Each candidate brings what they have to the door of the temple—not in money or status, as that will be at least temporarily stripped from them, but in terms of who they are and what they hope to become. For some, this aspiration will express itself through charity, for others it is social climbing, and for a small group, it is philosophical or even esoteric and occult

199

speculations and practices. As noted in the introduction to this book, it becomes difficult to speak of Freemasonry as a monolithic subject for there are as many variations of Freemasonry as there are Freemasons. Each chooses to make of it what they will, and in turn, the fraternity both shapes and is shaped by its members.

The world of the seventeenth and early eighteenth centuries from which Freemasonry emerged was not much different from our own. Many of the same ideas that flourished then are popular now—utopianism, Atlantis and lost continents, the feeling that the world is in chaos and the center has collapsed. (As I reread this conclusion in 2020, fourteen years after its first publication, this strange feeling of near constant instability has only been amplified by the Covid-19 virus and other current events. And yet the similarities to the early 2000s and the earlier periods mentioned remain the same.)

In the time when Freemasonry stepped onto the world stage as a highly organized entity with centralized grand lodge, religious sectarianism and violence had broken the morale of the population, decimated economies, and all but destroyed cultures built up over hundreds of years or more. The Thirty Years' War (1618–1648) would set German unification back two hundred years. That is, it would take Germany two hundred years to rebuild its infrastructure as a result of the damage done. England would recover more quickly from the Catholic-Protestant divide, but only as a result of its limited size and geographic isolation. Severe dictatorships, both secular and sectarian, also assisted in getting things done much more quickly in the small land that would become the seat of the British empire, and of Freemasonry.

In our own lifetime, Freemasonry, like all civic organizations, has seen a constant and steady decline in membership since the mid-1960s. However, for Freemasonry, or more specifically regular Freemasonry, the impact has been harder and is more difficult to resolve. The Craft in many instances is finding itself confronted with culture shock—not unlike the rift between the Antients and the Moderns in the early years of the first grand lodge. Today, many of the young men joining regular Masonry find that their expectations of meeting men of learning, culture, and self-improvement are not being met. Instead, they are greeted by members of twenty, thirty, and even fifty years, for whom the Craft has been a lifetime of fraternity, social contacts, and civic service, but not a philosophical or particularly highbrow organization. Masonic education has come to consist of generous and impressive amounts of memorization, particularly for the rituals, but includes nothing in terms of their symbolic meaning and possible origins, let alone an active study of the seven liberal arts and sciences. Esotericism is all but unknown to 90 percent of the brethren. This emphasis on form over essence has meant that Freemasonry has lost one if not two generations of potential members.

And yet, despite the downturn, many of the young men joining Masonry who are seeking those very things are working with other brethren and bringing them into reality. Lodges of Research, lodges of the College of Rites (or Grand College), or the most recent Traditional Observance movement, and a host of printed and electronic resources mean that Freemasons are better able to connect with each other, exchanging more information on what Masonry means to them than ever before. Social media has made it easier than ever to get embroiled in Masonic disputes or to get involved with brethren from across the world who are actively living the Masonic principles as best they can. I am particularly proud of the work done by the Grand Lodge of Pennsylvania and its Academy of Masonic Knowledge. Programs are held twice yearly, spring and fall, and include world authorities on all areas of Freemasonry. These programs have been recorded and can be watched by Masons and non-Masons alike. Combined with the academy's certification program and Masonic Scholars awards, they ensure that any Mason in Pennsylvania is able to extract the best in personal development from their Masonic experiences—the choice is simply up to them to participate to the degree they are comfortable with. This is true for many jurisdictions; extensive online and in-person programs that go beyond memorization of the rituals are available, and members derive from Freemasonry what they are willing to put into it.

Esoteric Freemasonry does not exist in every lodge, but it does exist and is growing quickly among regular Freemasons who see in the fraternity the ideals of the eighteenth century as vital to the twenty-first century. In many jurisdictions, Traditional Observance lodges, in which members must prove intellectual and philosophical proficiency before advancing to the next degree, and wherein esotericism plays a primary or strong secondary role in the interpretation of the Craft's meaning, will be the norm and not the exception within a generation or less. Many of the works prized by those involved in Traditional Observance Masonry have been mentioned elsewhere in this book, but we mention them again, as both those who are members of the Craft and those who are not will benefit from reading them:

"A Classical Vision of Masonic Restoration: Three Key Principles of Traditional Observance," by Shawn Eyer, in *Philalethes: The Journal for Masonic Research and Letters* 66, no. 4 (2013): 147–59; https://scholar.harvard.edu/seyer/three-principles-of-traditional-observance
Freemasonry: The Reality, by Tobias Churton (Lewis Masonic Publishers, 2007)
The Masonic Initiation, by W. L. Wilmshurst (Plumbstone, 2007; orig. pub. 1924)
Observing the Craft: The Pursuit of Excellence in Masonic Labour and Observance, by Andrew Hammer (Mindhive Books, 2010)
The Way of the Craftsman: A Search for the Spiritual Essence of Craft Freemasonry, by W. Kirk MacNulty (Plumbstone, 2017)

In addition, Co-Masonry, Le Droit Humain, and a host of other rites that are open to both men and women and are unequivocally esoteric in their orientation are finding their membership increasing and discussions with regular Masons flourishing.

In terms of membership, Masonry is at the same point it was in the first half of the eighteenth century: the number of Freemasons is dropping and will continue to do so as the current generation dies off over the next ten years. However, the hundreds of billions of dollars of resources available to various grand lodges means that Masonry will never die and its charitable work is guaranteed by its investments; this gives Masonry the opportunity to focus now on rebuilding the philosophical aspect of the Craft—if it is to be called an actual fraternity, and not simply a social club. Freemasonry is shifting back into a small, socially connected, elite organization composed of people who choose to be members. rather than those who are members simply because their father or grandfather was a Mason. This membership-by-choice means that Freemasonry is being reshaped to meet the desires of the current and future generations for education, involvement, and personal growth along spiritual lines. Regular Freemasons who find these things in their fraternity stay and support their lodges. Those who do not find what they are seeking leave and join other organizations that can provide it.

Despite this change of direction in the Craft's orientation, it is amazing to see how Masons of all ages greet each other upon meeting, even for the first time. Anger has been softened to patience, hurried gruffness to an apologizing nod and a pause to exchange sincere pleasantries, and distracted self-absorption into selfless assistance and even sacrifice at the sight of a ring on a brother's finger or lapel.

Just as its members change Masonry, Masonry changes its members. It is an organization whose ideals are eternal and that are needed now more than ever.

Afterword

Charles S. Canning, 33°

IN LIFE'S PILGRIMAGE we travel many highways and byways. You have now completed the reading of *The Path of Freemasonry*, whereby you have taken a detour on your journey and have ventured into a fascinating and intriguing world. This world of Freemasonry has as its goal self-improvement. Do not be disappointed if you feel confused or puzzled about Freemasonry. I have been an active member and student for over fifty-five years and find myself suddenly becoming aware of a new way of looking at a symbol or motif that gave me a new understanding. Some readers may dismiss this text as another reading that may have had some interest for them and they will now move on to another novel. Some may be interested in the overall picture of Freemasonry and, having completed the lessons and readings, felt satisfied with their understanding of Masonry and its relationship to esoteric philosophy. Others may have been interested in Freemasonry as a Western magic tradition phenomena, while some may be members of Freemasonry and now find a new way of thinking about the fraternity. There may also be a small group who, having gone this far, may wish to fully understand the mysteries of the Craft by petitioning a Masonic lodge for membership.

In the last decades more and more attention has been focused on the esoteric aspects of Freemasonry. While we do not expect to find any documents that would have existed in the formative years of symbolic Masonry and would attest to the use of esoteric symbolism and procedures in developing Masonic ritual, we may draw implications from a reasoned study of the historic periods and probable influences. There have been publications on the study of the degrees of the Masonic lodge and their interpretation of the Qabala's "Tree of Life" and various aspects of Hermeticism. Yet few authors have gone beneath the surface of the Masonic ritual, its motif and allegory, to examine the hidden symbolism that points to a past centered around ritual magic that can be traced back through the Age of Reason, the Enlightenment, the Renaissance, and into early traditional mysticism. *The Path of Freemasonry* has turned the corner in presenting the esoteric roots of Freemasonry in a comprehensive and understandable manner.

Mark Stavish has taken a very complex subject and presented it with a common viewpoint. He did not illustrate this using only "regular and official" Freemasonry, made up of the traditional grand lodges with pedigrees from some other recognized grand authority, but used the overall picture of Masonry, which includes various origins, affiliations, and makeup. In this context, he examined the esoteric roots and their applications, looking back through the eighteenth century. *The Path of Freemasonry* has been organized in a study-workbook format, giving the reader an opportunity to search out and come to their own understanding of the subject.

As you traveled this path of Freemasonry, you were taken to the period of the operative craft, the builders of classical temples and Gothic cathedrals. You were informed of the spirituality seen in architecture and found additional mystery in the initiatic illustrations throughout your readings. You learned that there is a spiritual potential that may transform one's environment beyond time and space. To venture into the cosmology of Freemasonry, one may find a world that some believe takes them nearer to God.

As you journeyed through the transition of Masonry from an operative to a speculative art, you were introduced to elements that reflected an esoteric origin. You may have asked if the hidden mystery of Freemasonry is to be found in Hermetic philosophy, alchemy, or the Qabala. That should become a personal quest, and through meditation and study, you may better be able to understand the nature of man and the improvement of self.

In the text Stavish presented the popular mindset of various eras and built upon the magical and alchemical practices found there to project the development of Freemasonry for the reader's mental reception, while at the same time giving clues and guiding the reader in making an esoteric connection to the present.

Freemasonry has many facets and is the focus of over seventy-five thousand books. The student who only reads about Freemasonry is at the same level of understanding as the member who only watches the ritual. The richness of Freemasonry is given an even greater assessment when one develops a wider appreciation for its heritage through an inward journey to seek understanding of its esoteric background and interpretation. Through this venture the two-dimensional experience of words, signs, and motifs becomes multidimensional. The "word," which is central to much of ritual, resonates with new vibration and meaning and yields a deeper and personal experience. Freemasonry as it once existed in the past is given renewed vision. While the recognized secrets of Freemasonry are in the modes of recognition—signs, passwords, and handgrips—the real secret and esoteric meaning of Freemasonry is in the personal journey each member must take in reflecting upon their own self and their travel in the deeper cosmology of that mystical timeless landscape. Here the member must confront their own archetypes and become their own operative Mason, who will find the true word in their collective unconscious. Whatever path you take, the destination is the same: becoming a more polished living stone for a "house not made with hands, eternal in the heavens."

CHARLES S. CANNING, 33°,
KNIGHT YORK GRAND CROSS OF HONOR
DIRECTOR, HARRY C. TREXLER MASONIC LIBRARY

Sacred Geometry and the Masonic Tradition

John Michael Greer

THE IDEA THAT MASONRY AND GEOMETRY have quite a bit to do with each other is a hard one to miss. Brothers who familarize themselves with the rituals of our fraternity, or simply attend the Fellowcraft degree more than a few times, will remember that geometry is there described as the first and noblest of sciences and the basis on which the superstructure of Freemasonry is erected. Most of the use made of geometry in modern Masonry is moral and symbolic. Just as the lectures on the working tools draw a distinction between the practical use of those tools and the "more noble and glorious purposes" of moral allegory, the common attitude toward geometry among today's speculative Masons seems to be that it is to be contemplated in the abstract, rather than studied and practiced in any more concrete sense.

This is certainly one way to approach Masonry, and an entirely valid way on its own terms. Yet historical interest, at least, would suggest that if the entire edifice of Freemasonry is built on the basis of geometry, a look at the foundations may occasionally be in order. Furthermore, the idea that operative Masonry is necessarily less noble and glorious than the speculative form of the institution may be questioned by anyone who has experienced the noble and glorious creations of ancient, medieval, and Renaissance architecture. Buildings such as the temples of ancient Greece and the Gothic cathedrals are as much works of mind and spirit as of stone and mortar. They were designed and built not merely for practical purposes but to uplift the hearts and enrich the lives of those who worshipped in them. To give such beauty and such inspiration to the world was no small thing, and it involved more than merely physical labor. Our ritual reminds us that our ancient brethren wrought in both operative and speculative Masonry, but I'm not sure how many modern Masons realize that these two were not seen as two separate things. Rather, our ancient brethren wrought in both forms of Masonry at the same time and in the same actions.

It's rarely realized just how close company practical geometry and philosophy kept before the scientific revolution. In an important 2001 study, philosopher Robert Hahn documented that the origins of Greek philosophy itself are closely woven together with early developments in the history of Greek architecture, and in particular with the adoption of Egyptian architectural methods for the first Greek temples of stone.[1] Thales and Anaximander, the first Greek philosophers known to history, were also famous for their accomplishments in geometry, engineering, and the sciences; ancient testimonies name Thales as the man who first brought geometry from Egypt to Greece. Pythagoras, who invented the word *philosopher* and was arguably the first known historical figure in the development of the esoteric traditions of the West, is still remembered today for his theorem on the relationship of the sides of a right triangle—a theorem we will be exploring in some detail a little later on.

Thus the art of sacred geometry needs to be understood in its proper context. It is certainly true, as a useful article about sacred geometry in Masonry suggests, that the principles of sacred geometry are based on "profound meditations upon geometric space and form"[2] rather than the deductive logic of Euclid or, for that matter, of modern schoolroom geometry. Yet these meditations did not remain in the realms of abstract thought and mystical perception; they came down the planes, as modern occult terminology would put it, all the way to the plane of dense matter—the plane of operative Masonry, of stone, timber, and mortar. Our ancient brethren, if we may call the master builders of ancient, medieval, and Renaissance times by that term, applied the principles of strength, wisdom, and beauty to their work. A mastery of strength enabled them, despite what we might consider very simple technical means, to raise buildings, some of which still stand tall more than three thousand years after they were built. A mastery of beauty enabled them to design and ornament those buildings with an elegance and grace that still evokes wonder today. These two are obvious; less immediately visible, but just as central to the ancient achievement, is the presence of wisdom.

That wisdom was founded above all on a mastery of proportion. Plenty of factors contribute to make today's buildings as mindlessly ugly as they are, but one of the most important is that their parts and dimensions have no relation to one another; convenience and the whim of the architect govern all. The temples of pagan Greece, the cathedrals of the Middle Ages, and the palaces and paintings of the Renaissance were cast in a different mold. Vitruvius, whose textbook of architecture is the only classical work on that subject to have survived the wreck of the ancient world, explains that the six essential principles of architecture are order, disposition, eurhythmy, symmetry, decorum, and economy.[3] Only the last deals with the practical concerns that now ride roughshod over all other issues in building. The next to last deals with issues of style and decoration, which occupy all the attention modern architects can spare from purely pragmatic issues. The other four deal with the missing dimension of modern architecture: proportion, relation, balance, and harmony, set out by geometry and woven into every detail of the building from the ground plan to the fine points of decoration.

Formed in ancient Egypt and passed on to Greece and Rome, this fusion of what we would now call operative and speculative approaches to geometry continued without a break into the Middle Ages, reinforced by the patronage of the early and medieval Christian church. The church's hostility to esoteric traditions from the end of the Renaissance on has made it hard for modern scholars—and often, even harder for modern Masons—to recognize that this state of affairs was a new departure of the early modern period, and that things had been different earlier on. Valerie Flint's study *The Rise of Magic in Early Medieval Europe* documents that the church, far from being hostile to esoteric spirituality, played a crucial role in preserving, transmitting, and disseminating it in the centuries following the collapse of the Roman Empire.[4] So long as people invoked the Trinity rather than pagan gods and stayed clear of obvious moral difficulties, almost anything was acceptable. This easy tolerance remained part of medieval Christian culture until the first witch panics at the end of the fourteenth century, and was not finally forced underground until the scientific revolution of the seventeenth century made the entire subject too hot to handle.

Thus the sacred geometries of classical pagan temples, copied by the builders of early Christian churches, became part of the stock in trade of medieval operative Masons and survived in poorly understood forms in the fabric of modern speculative Masonry. This connection can be shown readily enough, for specific details of modern Masonic symbolism can be shown to link back to medieval building practice and demonstrate an unexpected meaning in that context.

A parallel example from another tradition will help clarify this. In some modern Druid orders, initiates of a certain grade wear a rope belt divided by thirteen equally spaced knots. Very few of those who wear such a belt have any idea of the origins of this custom. The knotted belt has in turn been borrowed by other traditions outside of Druidry, some of which have evolved their own interpretations of the knots, explaining them by way of mythological and spiritual symbolism. Yet the actual meaning of the knotted rope is wholly practical, or as we would say Masonically, operative.

Thirteen evenly spaced knots divide the rope into twelve equal sections. Given one of these rope belts, three wooden stakes, and no other equipment, it is possible to lay out an exact right angle on the ground, using the simplest whole-number Pythagorean triangle: three units for the short base, four for the long base, and five for the hypotenuse. According to Greek sources the ancient Egyptians used exactly this method to lay out the foundations of their pyramids and temples, and it has been suggested by modern scholars that similar methods were used centuries earlier in Britain and Ireland to lay out the great stone circles such as Stonehenge and Avebury. These Druid orders, which curiously enough were founded at about the same time as the Grand Lodge of England, almost certainly borrowed the idea for their knotted ropes from the same Greek sources—there is no reason whatsoever to think that the building methods used at Stonehenge were passed down intact to the present—but the transformation from operative tool to speculative emblem is worth noticing, for this same method of laying out right angles by way of Pythagorean triangles has left its mark on Masonry as well.

I'm sure that everyone present will remember the place of the forty-seventh proposition of Euclid in the rituals of our Craft; it is presented in the ritual used in the state of Washington as "a discovery of our ancient friend and Brother, the great Pythagoras." There are plenty of propositions from Euclid, and any of them could have been singled out and interpreted in the moral terms standard in modern speculative Masonry. Yet this one alone has a place in the ritual. Why? I suggest that the reason for its inclusion is the role of this proposition in the practical geometry of our medieval operative brethren.

We are not forced to speculate about the methods used by the medieval stonemasons; the testimony of archaeologists and historians is ready to hand, and relevant. For example, in the year 1134, the monks of the newly founded Priory of St. Bertelin at Norton, not far from Liverpool, commissioned a stone church and hired the master mason Hugh de Cathewik to design it and superintend the work. His design methods have been reconstructed by the archaeologists who excavated the ruins of the priory in the 1970s and 1980s.[5] These methods were as elegant and exact as they were simple. First, Hugh laid out a straight line from east-northeast to west-southwest, angling it so that the rising sun would shine straight down the nave of the church on St. Bertelin's feast day. The alignment was probably laid out with the skirret, a Masonic working tool no longer included in our Washington ritual but still mentioned in some English rituals, which consists of a marked rope or chalk cord on a reel.[6] A skirret, two straight staves, a trained apprentice or fellow of the craft, and a practiced eye are the only pieces of equipment needed. Such a carefully selected solar orientation was nearly universal in churches before the Reformation and has echoes in the symbolic orientation of Masonic lodges to the rising, noonday, and setting sun.

Next, Hugh measured out three Pythagorean triangles, again using the skirret. The first two, starting from the west, were 25 medieval feet on the short base, 60 feet on the long base, and 65 feet on the hypotenuse; the last, on the east, was 25 feet on the short base, 30 feet on the long base, and 39 feet on the hypotenuse. The 25-foot bases determined the width of the nave, made the walls of the church precisely parallel with each other, and allowed exact right angles to be marked out for the east and west walls, the pulpit screen, and the west end of the chancel. Two overlapping squares, which again could be traced out quickly with the skirret on the bare ground, defined the transepts to north and south and the dimensions of the choir. Once that was done, fine details could be put in at will, using similar methods. The entire process could be completed in a few hours, and work on the foundation started on the same day.[7]

The entire process depends on a mastery of whole-number Pythagorean triangles. Surveying equipment of the modern sort did not exist when the church of St. Bertelin was built, nor for many centuries thereafter, nor was there yet a source paper large enough to draw up building plans to a workable scale. The skillful application of practical geometry was the only option available to the medieval master builder, and Pythagorean triangles one of the few efficient answers to the problem of laying out exact right angles and parallel lines. It seems unlikely to be accidental that the geometrical principle central to this method of laying out buildings remains the one piece of actual geometry in our current Masonic ritual.

These Pythagorean triangles did not make up the whole of the medieval operative mason's geometrical stock in trade. They formed one of the basic elements of the builder's art, an element suited, in fact, to fellowcrafts who had not yet earned the rank of master. More important were the subtle geometrical patterns by which those first four principles of Vitruvius—order, disposition, eurhythmy, and symmetry—were woven into the fabric of sacred and secular architecture alike. These patterns form the core of sacred geometry as known to its modern practitioners. Each had its special meaning. The square root of 2, derived geometrically from the relationship between the square and its diagonal, represented generation and the fourfold world of nature. The square root of 3, derived geometrically from the equilateral triangle, represented integration and the threefold world of the spirit.[8]

Two different systems of sacred architecture, the *ad quadratum* and *ad triangulum* systems, unfolded respectively from one or the other of these basic proportions, and there were quarrels—on occasion descending to the level of fistfights—between the adherents of the two systems. Yet there was also a third proportion, the master proportion of all sacred geometry: the golden proportion or golden section. Its mathematical properties are fascinating, its geometry complex; experiments have shown that a majority of people instinctively find shapes based on it more beautiful than any other.[9] Researchers have traced it in the forms of the Parthenon, the great cathedrals, and many other masterpieces of the builder's art.

Contemporary documentation for the golden proportion's use as a design principle in ancient, medieval, and Renaissance architecture is all but absent, but this can be understood in more ways than one. Operative Masons in the Middle Ages and Renaissance are known to have kept certain of their practical methods secret, passing them on only to qualified members of their guild, under oath, on the attainment of master's rank. For example, the Regensburg ordinances, a set of rules established by an assembly of German Master Masons in 1459, forbade any Mason from communicating their secret method of working out the elevation of a structure from the ground plan to anyone but a qualified candidate for mastership.[10] Medieval guilds of all kinds had secrets of this sort. Yet the transmission of such secrets in the Middle Ages and Renaissance posed problems unfamiliar from a modern perspective. Most medieval Masons were illiterate—Mason's marks, those elegant geometrical patterns that mark the work of individual stoneworkers in the fabric of the great Gothic cathedrals, came into use because their owners were not able to write their own names. How could exacting methods of geometrical construction be passed on to each newly made Master Mason in a way that was memorable enough to preserve the crucial information intact over the generations?

One way of doing this, practiced in the Middle Ages as much as in earlier periods, was to convert the details of a practical method into the events of a narrative, a story in which the central incidents served as reminders to the trained memory. Such a narrative, I suggest, conceals an operative secret at the core of speculative Masonry: the legend of the Master Mason degree.

We can begin exploring this dimension of Masonic sacred geometry with the familiar title of "Widow's Son." This has been interpreted in many different ways by Masonic theorists and students of comparative mythology, but as far as I know it has not yet been noted that this famous title has a straightforward geometrical interpretation.

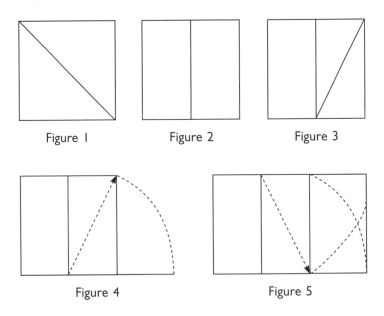

Figure I   Figure 2   Figure 3

Figure 4   Figure 5

As mentioned already, the square with its diagonal forms the geometrical symbol of generation (fig. 1). A widow, as half of a married couple—the human symbol of generation—might be represented by half a square, divided by a vertical line rather than the diagonal from which the larger square is generated (fig. 2). Yet for the widow to have her own son, she must have a diagonal of her own, so we draw a diagonal from the midpoint of the square to the opposite corner, as shown in the diagram (fig. 3).

For the widow to generate her son, the upper end of the diagonal then rotates downward until it's parallel to the bottom line of the square (fig. 4); in practice, this is done with a compass on paper or with a skirret on the bare ground of a medieval building site. Next, the upper line of the square is extended the same distance, again using the compass or skirret (fig. 5). The ends of the two extended lines are then connected with a vertical line.

The result is a golden proportion rectangle (fig. 6). If the side of the original square is equal to 1, the long side of the new rectangle is the irrational number Φ, equal to $(\sqrt{5} + 1)/2$ or approximately 1.618. The ratio 1:Φ gives the golden proportion, the "precious jewel" of sacred geometry. If the argument presented here is correct, this proportion is also referred to Masonically as the Widow's Son, who sets out the patterns used by the workmen building the holy temple.

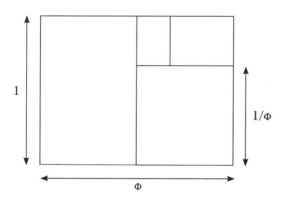

Figure 6

The construction just given is familiar to anyone with a good general knowledge of plane geometry. It has certain disadvantages for practical use in medieval architecture, however. The most important of these problems is that it starts with a smaller measurement and creates a larger one. In medieval practice, as shown in the design of the church of St. Bertelin, the largest dimensions were usually set out first and all smaller dimensions produced as fractions of one or

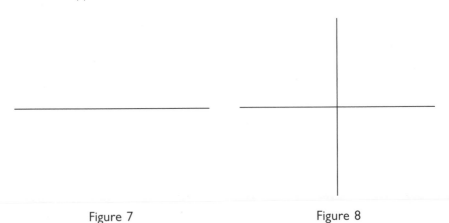

Figure 7   Figure 8

another of these primary measurements. Masonically, we can say that our operative brethren were left in a quandary once these first measurements were traced out, for the Widow's Son was nowhere to be found, and without him the work could not go forward. The methods they used to search out this missing proportion will be familiar to any Master Mason.

The search for the Widow's Son begins with a line of any length (fig. 7), which is symbolically the empty worksite, with no sign of the Widow's Son. The first step is to look for him in the four directions. This is done by drawing a second line perpendicular to the first and passing through its center (fig. 8).

Next, using compass or skirret, an arc is traced with the intersection of the two lines as its center, and the distance from the intersection to the end of the first line (that is, half the first line's length) as the radius. This reveals the shape of a hill. It also resembles the upper part of a human face, and the medieval fondness for puns might suggest a term such as *the brow of a hill* for this diagram (fig. 9). Then a line is drawn from one end of the original line to the point where the curve intersects the perpendicular line. This line, which will be removed to another place in the course of the construction, might be likened to the branch of some symbolically appropriate tree.

The branch is removed by setting the compass or skirret equal to its length and drawing a line of the same length perpendicularly from the

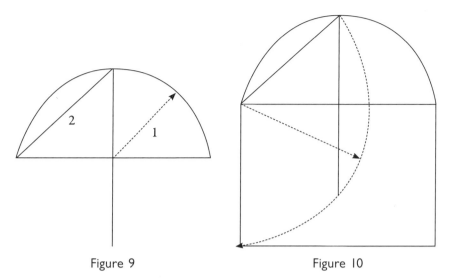

Figure 9   Figure 10

end of the original line, using the square on paper or knotted ropes and Pythagorean triangles on the ground of a medieval building site. Another line of the same length is extended in the same way from the other end of the original line, and their ends are connected with a straight line parallel to the original line to form a rectangle (fig. 10). This rectangle might well be compared to a grave, particularly since the original line on the building site of a medieval church was usually lined up on the rising sun, as was the ground plan of the church of St. Bertelin described above; the symbolic "grave" thus lies due east and west.

Next comes the excavation of the grave, which is done by drawing diagonal lines connecting the opposite corners of the rectangle. But the Widow's Son hidden in the grave cannot be drawn out of it quite so simply. It takes three additional actions, which might be called three attempts, to do so. First, setting the compass or skirret to a radius equal to the original line, and taking one end of the original line as the center, make a short arc on the diagonal line extending from the same end of the original line to the opposite corner of the rectangle, measuring the length of the original line onto the diagonal. Next, with the compass or skirret set to the same measure, take the other end of the original line as the center and repeat the process along the other diagonal line. Finally, using either of these two short arcs as the center and the compass or

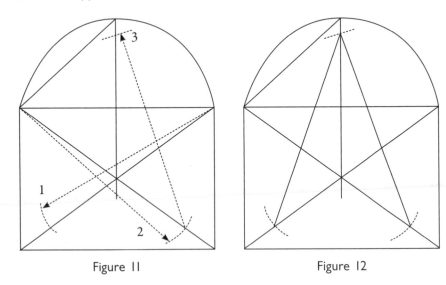

Figure 11   Figure 12

skirret still set to the same measure, make a third short arc on the perpendicular line drawn across the original line, as shown in the diagram (fig. 11).

At this point the Widow's Son can be drawn out of the grave. The two ends of the original line and the three short arcs mark out the points of a pentagram (fig. 12). The five points of this figure will readily remind any Master Mason of the five points by which he was raised from a similar state of concealment. It also forms a symbol that may be found in a position of honor in every Masonic lodge.

Geometrically, the pentagram divides the original line by the golden proportion in no fewer than six different ways, as shown in figure 13. The ratio between AD and AB is 1:Φ, and so is the ratio between CB and AB. Furthermore, the ratio between AC and CB and that between DB and AD are also equal to 1:Φ, and so are the ratios between CD and AC, on the one hand, and CD and DB on the other. The remarkable geometrical properties of the golden proportion weave each of these relationships together by way of F relationships as well; for example, the ratio between AC and AB is 1:Φ^2, and that between CD and AB is 1:Φ^3. Thus the operative master mason using this construction could produce a cascading series of Φ-based proportions from a single initial measurement, such as the intended length of a building.

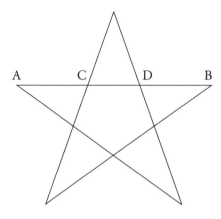

Figure 13

To continue the same series of proportions down to even smaller scales, he could repeat the same construction using CD as the initial line, say, or do the same thing even more simply by connecting the five points of the pentagon at the center of the pentagram, creating a new pentagram with sides equal to AC or DB. Either process could be repeated as many times as necessary, so that everything down to the fine details of windows and string courses follows the same elegant system of proportion.

Can it be proven that this construction and its uses are what the narrative of the 3rd degree was originally meant to conceal? Almost certainly such a proof is beyond reach. As far as we know, among the Scottish or English operative Masons from whose craft modern Masonry descends, not one betrayed his trust and revealed the practical secrets of the Royal Art. Barring such a disclosure, the diagrams and explanations I have presented are speculative—this time in the everyday sense of the word. Yet one point worth mentioning is that I have never encountered the construction just outlined in any ancient, medieval, or modern source. It is not found in the works of Euclid. I did not know of it when I began the investigation that led to this paper; it unfolded, step by step, as I tried to work out how the narrative of the Master Mason degree might make geometrical sense. It is also simpler, more elegant, and more practical for architectural uses than any alternate construction I have encountered for the same proportion.

It is also worth taking a moment to stress that, even if this was the operative secret behind the story of the Widow's Son, that story is not limited to a purely geometric or architectural relevance. Its moral, philosophical, and spiritual meanings remain, and they were in all probability known to the same operative Masons who also used it to remember a central secret of their practical art. As mentioned earlier in this essay, the art of the medieval operative masons was not simply a matter of piling up stones, and it took shape in a culture that still remembered that a symbol or a story can have many meanings.

Like the rest of medieval culture, and like the ancient cultures that came before, the operative Masonry of our early brethren fused the physical and the metaphysical through the medium of a geometry that united matter and mind. It taught the building of both temples, that made with hands in the realm of time and change, and that made without hands, eternal in the heavens. We live in an age in which the very concept of such a unity of being is labeled an anachronism, in which a Berlin Wall of the mind has been raised between the material and the spiritual sides of reality. Yet Freemasonry, among its many other virtues, is a time capsule that comes to us from an age before that wall was raised, and it suggests another and, perhaps, a better way of embracing reality. Like so many other spiritual traditions, it calls us to seek, as Socrates is said to have prayed, that the outward and the inward man may be as one.[11]

NOTES TO APPENDIX A

1. Robert Hahn, *Anaximander and the Architects: The Contributions of Egyptian and Greek Architectural Technologies to the Origins of Greek Philosophy* (Albany: SUNY, 2001).

2. Herbert P. Bangs, "The Geometry of the Visible Lodge," *Heredom* 7 (1998): 115.

3. Cited in Richard Padovan, *Proportion* (London: E & FN Spon, 1999), 158.

4. Valerie Flint, *The Rise of Magic in Early Medieval Europe* (Princeton: Princeton University Press, 1991).

5. J. Patrick Greene, *Norton Priory: The Archaeology of a Medieval Religious House* (Cambridge: Cambridge University Press, 1989).

6. See Stephen R. Greenberg, "The Ultimate Implement of Freemasonry," *Proceedings of the Illinois Lodge of Research,* no. 10 (n.d.), and Bob J. Jensen, "The Missing Working Tools in American Masonry," *Walter F. Meier Lodge of Research Masonic Papers,* vol. 6, no. 12 (December 1992).

7. The description of the laying out of the Norton Priory church is from Greene, *Norton Priory,* 81–83.

8. See Robert Lawlor, *Sacred Geometry: Philosophy and Practice* (London: Thames and Hudson, 1982), for a discussion of these proportions.

9. See Padovan, *Proportion,* 308–16, and Matila Ghyka, *The Geometry of Art and Life* (New York: Dover, 1977).

10. See Nigel Hiscock, *The Wise Master Builder: Platonic Geometry in Plans of Medieval Abbeys and Cathedrals* (Aldershot: Ashgate, 2000), 186–95.

11. Plato, *Phaedrus,* 279b.

Symbols of the Tracing Boards and the Degrees

THE VARIOUS TRACING BOARDS, also known as trestle boards, of Freemasonry vary from period to period as well as between jurisdictions and rites. The following synopsis of the symbols and their basic meaning is given as a guide rather than a definitive list or set of interpretations. A careful study of the symbols and the boards they appear on, as well as actively drawing them with chalk or pencil, will help those of a more mystical orientation to understand how the mundane tools of the builder can be transformed into the inner teachings of morality and ethics—the foundation for all genuine spiritual unfoldment. From this newfound perception it becomes possible to transform any aspect of life into a spiritual teaching, allowing us to see the divine in everything and everyone.

ENTERED APPRENTICE DEGREE

Apron. The apron connects Masons to one another in the fraternity and to the ancient building guilds of the past. It represents work, both material and spiritual, for the improvement of one's self and humanity.

Ornaments of the Lodge. These include the checkerboard floor or mosaic pavement, the indented tessel, and Blazing Star. The mosaic pavement represents the duality of this world or good and evil; the tesselated border is fellowship and union; the Blazing Star is the divinity in man. These ornaments are not mentioned in the old rituals or in biblical references within Masonic rituals; as such, their origin in Masonic ritual is unclear.

Burning Tapers. Each lodge has three lights around the altar, which represent the light of the sun that rules the day, the moon that rules the night, and the master that rules the lodge.

Three Immovable Jewels. These are the three stationed officers of a lodge—the master, senior warden, and junior warden, who wear the square, level, and plumb, respectively. They represent morality, equality, and personal integrity. They are called "immovable" because these three officers must be present for a lodge to be opened.

Movable Jewels. These are the rough ashlar, perfect ashlar, and trestle or tracing board. They are called "movable" because they may be absent and a lodge still opened by the officers present. The rough ashlar represents the crude and base nature of a man who is yet unrefined. The perfect or smooth ashlar represents the educated man who raises himself above the unthinking and common. He has done this by using the tools of the Entered Apprentice to smooth down the rough edges of his personality and character and refined them through the teachings of the liberal arts and sciences, as instructed in the Fellowcraft degree. The tracing board represents the application of reason, planning, and foresight to one's life so that it may mirror the truths learned through Masonic fellowship.

Holy Saints John. Saint John the Baptist and St. John the Evangelist are the two patron saints to whom Masonic lodges are dedicated. It is unclear why they were chosen over other saints or even King Solomon; it may have to do with their feast days falling near the summer and winter solstices. Saint John the Baptist's is June 24 and St. John the Evangelist's is December 27. Both dates play important roles in Freemasonry.

Point within a Circle. The point within a circle placed between two parallel lines (said to represent the two Saint Johns) reminds Masons to keep their actions circumscribed and guided by the Volume of the Sacred Law that rests above it. Building construction requires the ability to make a perfect square and is tested by using the center point of the circle, and this method was considered a secret known only by operative Master Masons. Albert Mackey states that the point is Will, the creative energy of God and the divine power in each person, the circle is all that comes under its domain, and the parallel lines are wisdom and power.

Working Tools of the Entered Apprentice. The working tools explained to a newly made Entered Apprentice are the twenty-four-inch gauge and a common gavel. The gauge is representative of the hours in a day, the passing of time, and how we use it. The gavel is representative of power and its rightful and constructive use in life.

FELLOWCRAFT DEGREE

Three Jewels—In the Entered Apprentice degree, the Three Immovable Jewels are present but not explained. In the Fellowcraft degree the meanings of the square, level, and plumb are given. They are the tools of a craftsman, who must exhibit a higher level of skill than the laborer.

Twin Pillars—The pillar of Jachin is revealed to the Entered Apprentice, and now the pillar of Boaz is revealed to the Fellowcraft. Combined, they represent the Pillars of the Porch, set outside the Temple of Solomon, and mean, "I will establish (Jachin) in strength (Boaz)." This is a reference to the power and presence of divine power, the kingdom of God. By understanding the importance of power and control or self-discipline, the Fellowcraft then encounters the Winding Staircase.

Winding Staircase. The staircase consists of fifteen steps, although some illustrations show seven. The first three steps represent the working tools of the Fellowcraft, the following five the five orders of architecture and the five senses, and the last seven are the seven liberal arts and sciences. Combined, these steps lead the Fellowcraft to the middle chamber.

Orders of Architecture. These are Tuscan, Doric, Ionic, Corinthian, and Composite.

Liberal Arts and Sciences. The seven liberal arts and sciences are required if a person is to be well rounded in their education as well as able to solve the practical problems of daily life. They consist of grammar, rhetoric, logic, arithmetic, geometry, music, and astronomy (or astrology).

Middle Chamber. The middle chamber represents the resulting reward for our labors. In life, Masons are told, we will receive exactly the payment we request. If we ask more from life, we will receive more; if we ask but little, we will receive but little. As the architect and builder of our own life, it is up to each of us to decide what we will get from it.

Wages of the Fellowcraft. Wine, corn, and oil are given as the wages of the Fellowcraft. Corn was unknown to the ancients, as it was native to the Americas, and so wheat is often used in its place and is more likely the actual foodstuff given in payment for work. Corn or wheat represents abundance and the goddess Ceres; wine represents refreshment from a day's work; and oil represents joy and happiness in life.

Attentive Ear, Instructive Tongue, and Faithful Heart. These symbols represent the need of Fellowcraft Masons to be attentive in listening to instructions from the master, constructive in their words to their fellows and those Entered Apprentices under their care, and faithful in their adherence to what they have received. They demonstrate the tradition of oral instruction in Masonic ritual.

MASTER MASON DEGREE

The Square and Compass. With these tools the Master Mason can square a circle, creating a firm and perfect foundation for building his inner spiritual life while being of service to his family and community. The compass draws the circle, whose point reminds us to be centered and balanced if we are to successfully build the life we want. The square provides us with the means of making a straight line—that is, a firm decision, and the compass serves as a means of testing its strength.

The Trinity of Lights. These three lights form a triangle around the altar that each Mason passes and kneels before three times in their journey. It is the ancient symbol of deity and the divine inspiration each Freemason seeks.

The Working Tools of the Master Mason. These are all of the tools of Masonry combined, and the trowel in particular. The trowel spreads cement to bind stones together, just as the Master Mason spreads brotherly love and affection to support and uphold his brethren and maintain harmony in the lodge.

Skull and Crossbones. According to Jewish lore all that is needed for physical resurrection of a person are the skull and thighbones of that person. Here they represent the death of Hiram, as well as the selfishness and egotism that prevent each person from experiencing the mastery of life they seek.

Sprig of Acacia. Acacia represents the evergreen or eternal life and the immortality of the soul or consciousness of the Master Mason.

Inner Chamber and Veil. This is the temple built without hands—the deepest part of our selves and our connection to God.

Excerpts from *Morals and Dogma* on the Three Degrees of Masonry

THE FOLLOWING EXCERPTS from Albert Pike's *Morals and Dogma* can be found in many of the Bibles given to members of the Scottish Rite. Additional sections are used to further illuminate the importance of the degrees of York and Scottish Rite and thereby to encourage study of the symbols presented.

I. APPRENTICE

FORCE, unregulated or ill-regulated, is not only wasted in the void, like that of gunpowder burned in the open air, and steam unconfined by science; but, striking in the dark, and its blows meeting only the air, they recoil, and bruise itself. It is destruction and ruin. It is the volcano, the earthquake, the cyclone;—not growth and progress. It is Polyphemus blinded, striking at random, and falling headlong among the sharp rocks by the impetus of his own blows.

The blind Force of the people is a Force that must be economized, and also managed, as the blind Force of steam, lifting the ponderous iron arms and turning the large wheels, is made to bore and rifle the cannon and to weave the most delicate lace. It must be regulated by Intellect. Intellect is to the people and the people's Force, what the slender needle of the compass is to the ship—its soul, always counseling the huge mass of wood and iron, and always pointing to the north. To attack the citadels built up on all sides against the human race by superstitions, despotisms, and prejudices, the Force must have a brain and a law. Then its deeds of daring produce permanent results, and there is real progress. Then there are sublime conquests. Thought is a force, and philosophy should be an energy, finding its aim and its effects in the amelioration of mankind. The two great motors are Truth and Love. When all these Forces are combined, and guided by the Intellect, and regulated by the RULE of Right, and Justice, and of combined and systematic movement and effort, the great revolution prepared for by the ages will begin to march. The POWER of the Deity Himself is in equilibrium with His WISDOM. Hence [the] only results [are] HARMONY.

* * *

Though Masonry neither usurps the place of, nor apes religion, prayer is an essential part of our ceremonies. It is the aspiration of the soul toward the Absolute and Infinite Intelligence, which is the One Supreme Deity, most feebly and misunderstandingly characterized as an "ARCHITECT." Certain faculties of man are directed toward the Unknown—thought, meditation, prayer. The unknown is an ocean, of which conscience is the compass. Thought, meditation, prayer, are the great mysterious pointings of the needle. It is a spiritual magnetism that thus connects the human soul with the Deity. These majestic irradiations of the soul pierce through the shadow toward the light.

* * *

A "Lodge" is defined to be "an assemblage of Freemasons, duly congregated, having the sacred writings, square, and compass, and a charter, or warrant of constitution, authorizing them to work." The room or place in which they meet, representing some part of King Solomon's Temple, is also called the Lodge; and it is that we are now considering.

It is said to be supported by three great columns, WISDOM, FORCE or STRENGTH, and BEAUTY, represented by the Master, the Senior Warden, and the Junior Warden; and these are said to be the columns that support the Lodge.

II. THE FELLOWCRAFT

IN THE ANCIENT ORIENT, all religion was more or less a mystery and there was no divorce from it of philosophy. The popular theology, taking the multitude of allegories and symbols for realities, degenerated into a worship of the celestial luminaries, of imaginary Deities with human feelings, passions, appetites, and lusts, of idols, stones, animals, reptiles. The onion was sacred to the Egyptians, because its different layers were a symbol of the concentric heavenly spheres. Of course the popular religion could not satisfy the deeper longings and thoughts, the loftier aspirations of the Spirit, or the logic of reason. The first, therefore, was taught to the Initiated in the mysteries. There, also, it was taught by symbols. The vagueness of symbolism, capable of many interpretations, reached what the palpable and conventional creed could not. Its indefiniteness acknowledged the abstruseness of the subject: it treated that mysterious subject mystically: it endeavored to illustrate what it could not explain; to excite an appropriate *feeling*, if it could not develop an adequate *idea*; and to make the image a mere subordinate conveyance for the conception, which itself never became obvious or familiar.

Thus the knowledge now imparted by books and letters, was of old conveyed by symbols; and the priests invented or perpetuated a display of rites and exhibitions, which were not only more attractive to the eye than words, but often more suggestive and more pregnant with meaning to the mind.

Masonry, successor of the mysteries, still follows the ancient manner of teaching. Her ceremonies are like the ancient mystic shows,—not the reading of an essay, but the opening of a problem, requiring research, and constituting philosophy the arch-expounder. Her symbols are the instruction she gives. The lectures are endeavors, often partial and one-sided, to interpret these symbols. He who would become an accomplished Mason must not be content merely to hear, or even to understand, the lectures; he must, aided by them, and they having, as it were, marked out the way for him, study, interpret, and develop these symbols for himself.

* * *

Christianity taught the doctrine of FRATERNITY; but repudiated that of political EQUALITY, by continually inculcating obedience to Caesar, and to those lawfully in authority. Masonry was the first apostle of EQUALITY. In the Monastery there is *fraternity* and *equality,* but no *liberty.* Masonry added that also, and claimed for man the three-fold heritage, LIBERTY, EQUALITY, and FRATERNITY.

III. THE MASTER

TO UNDERSTAND literally the symbols and allegories of Oriental books as to ante-historical matters, is willfully to close our eyes against the Light. To translate the symbols into the trivial and commonplace, is the blundering of mediocrity.

All religious expression is symbolism; since we can *describe* only what we *see,* and the true objects of religion are THE SEEN. The earliest instruments of education were symbols; and they and all other religious forms differed and still differ according to external circumstances and imagery, and according to differences of knowledge and mental cultivation. All language is symbolic, so far as it is applied to mental and spiritual phenomena and action. All *words* have, primarily, a *material* sense, howsoever they may afterward get, for the ignorant, a spiritual *non*-sense. "To retract," for example, is to *draw back,* and when applied to a *statement,* is symbolic, as much so as a picture of an arm drawn back, to express the same thing, would be. The very word "*spirit*" means "*breath,*" from the Latin verb *spiro,* breathe.

To present a visible symbol to the eye of another, is not necessarily to inform him of the meaning which that symbol has to you. Hence the philosopher soon superadded to the symbols explanations addressed to the ear, susceptible of more precision, but less effective and impressive than the painted or sculptured forms which he endeavored to explain. Out of these explanations grew by degrees a variety of narrations, whose true object and meaning were gradually forgotten, or lost in contradictions and incongruities. And when these were abandoned, and Philosophy resorted to definitions and formulas, its language was but a more complicated symbolism, attempting in the dark to grapple with and picture ideas impossible to be expressed. For as with the visible symbol, so with the word: to utter it to you does not inform you of the *exact* meaning which it has to *me;* and thus religion and philosophy became to a great extent disputes as to the meaning of words. The most abstract expression for DEITY, which language can supply, is but a *sign* or *symbol* for an object beyond our comprehension, and not more truthful and adequate than the images of OSIRIS and VISHNU, or their names, except as being less sensuous and explicit. We avoid sensuousness, only by resorting to simple negation. We come at last to define spirit by saying that it is not matter. Spirit is—spirit.

Notes

DEEPER INTO THE WONDERFUL MYSTERY:
FOREWORD TO THE 2021 EDITION

1. John Locke, "An Essay Concerning Human Understanding," (1689).
2. Arturo de Hoyos, *Albert Pike's Morals and Dogma: Annotated Edition,* 2nd ed. (Washington, D.C.: Supreme Council, 33°, 2013), essay 2, p. 34.
3. de Hoyos, *Albert Pike's Morals and Dogma,* essay 32, 81.
4. Arturo de Hoyos, *Albert Pike's Esoterika: The Symbolism of the Blue Degrees of Freemasonry* (Washington, D.C.: Scottish Rite Research Society, 2005, 2008), xxx.
5. de Hoyos, *Albert Pike's Esoterika,* xxxvi.

INTRODUCTION:
WHAT IS THE SECRET OF FREEMASONRY?

1. John Anthony West, foreword to *The Return of Sacred Architecture: The Golden Ratio and the End of Modernism,* by Herbert Bangs (Rochester, Vt.: Inner Traditions, 2007), x.

2. THE TEMPLE OF SOLOMON AND
THE LEGEND OF HIRAM ABIFF

1. John Michell, *The Temple at Jerusalem: A Revelation* (York Beach, Me.: Samuel Weiser, Inc., 2000), 46.
2. Michell, *The Temple at Jerusalem,* 60.

3. Flavius Josephus, *Antiquities of the Jews,* vol. 7, in *The Works of Flavius Josephus,* vol. 1, trans. William Whiston (London: Chatto & Windus, 1897), 329.

4. Edward Rice, *Captain Sir Richard Francis Burton: The Secret Agent Who Made the Pilgrimage to Mecca, Discovered the Kama Sutra, and Brought the* Arabian Nights *to the West* (New York: Charles Scribner's Sons, 1990), 462–63.

5. Possibly of Babylonian origin. Rice, *Captain Sir Richard Francis Burton,* 160.

6. Frances A. Yates, *Giordano Bruno and the Hermetic Tradition* (Chicago: University of Chicago Press, 1964), 50.

7. Gershom Scholem, *Kabbalah* (New York: Meridian Books, 1974), 186.

8. Scholem, *Kabbalah,* 362.

9. Scholem, *Kabbalah,* 362.

10. Scholem, *Kabbalah,* 365.

11. Scholem, *Kabbalah,* 367–68.

12. A. E. Waite, *A New Encyclopedia of Freemasonry,* vol. 1 (New York: Weathervane Books, 1970; orig. pub. 1921), 366–67.

3. MASONIC INITIATION AND THE BLUE LODGE

1. Joscelyn Godwin, *The Pagan Dream of the Renaissance* (Grand Rapids, Mi.: Phanes Press, 2002), 85.

2. Albert G. Mackey, *Encyclopedia of Freemasonry,* rev. ed. edited by W. J. Hughan and E. L. Hawkins (New York: Masonic History Company, 1924), 141.

3. Andre Nataf, *The Wordsworth Dictionary of the Occult* (Hertfordshire, UK: Wordsworth Editions, 1991), 67.

4. Waite, *New Encyclopedia of Freemasonry,* 108–9.

4. THE WORLDVIEW OF THE RENAISSANCE: THE WORLD IS ALIVE, AND MAGIC IS AFOOT

1. Quoted in Jolande Jacobi, ed., *Paracelsus: Selected Writings,* vol. 27, Bollingen Series (Princeton, N.J.: Princeton University Press, 1951), xxviii.

2. Mark Stavish, "Modern Shamanic and Hermetic Practices," on the website www.hermeticinstitute.org.

3. Quoted in Carl Jung, *Psychological Types*, vol. 6, *Collected Works of C. G. Jung* (Princeton, N.J.: Princeton University Press, 1971), 256.

4. Mark Stavish, "Wisdom's Bliss: Developing Compassion in Western Esotericism," on the website www.hermeticinstitute.org.

5. Valerie Flint, *The Rise of Magic in Early Medieval Europe* (Princeton, N.J.: Princeton University Press, 1991).

6. Caitlin and John Matthews, *The Western Way: A Practical Guide to the Western Mystery Tradition* (London: Arkana/Penguin Books, 1986), 290.

7. Matthews, *The Western Way*, 294.

8. Peter Dawkins, *Arcadia*, 5 vols (Stratford-upon-Avon: Francis Bacon Research Trust, 1988).

9. See Noel Cobb, *Prospero's Island: The Secret Alchemy at the Heart of the Tempest* (London: Coventure, 1984).

5. SACRED GEOMETRY, GOTHIC CATHEDRALS, AND THE HERMETIC ARTS IN STONE

1. Titus Burckhardt, *Sacred Art in East and West* (Louisville, Ky.: Fons Vitae, 2002), 61.

2. Arthur Edward Waite, trans., *The Hermetic and Alchemical Writings of Paracelsus the Great* (London: James Elliott, 1894), 138, 140.

3. Heinrich Cornelius Agrippa, *The Three Books of Occult Philosophy*, ed. Donald Tyson, trans. James Freake (Saint Paul, Minn.: Llewellyn, 1993), 233.

4. See Andre Vandenbroeck, *Al-Kemi: A Memoir: Hermetic, Occult, Political, and Private Aspects of R. A. Schwaller de Lubicz* (Great Barrington, Mass.: Lindisfarne Press, 1987), and Geneviève Dubois, *Fulcanelli and the Alchemical Revival: The Man behind the Mystery of the Cathedrals* (Rochester, Vt.: Inner Traditions, 2006).

5. Fulcanelli, *Fulcanelli, Master Alchemist: Le Mystère des Cathédrales*, trans. Mary Sworder (Albuquerque, N.M.: Brotherhood of Life, 1984), 36–37.

6. Frater Achad, *The Egyptian Revival; or, The Ever-Coming Son*

in the Light of the Tarot (York Beach, Maine: Weiser, 1974), chapter 8.

7. Frances Yates, *Occult Philosophy in the Elizabethan Age* (Routledge, 1979), 127.

8. Edmund Spenser, *The Faerie Queene* (1590), bk. 2, canto 9, stanza 22.

9. Claude Lecouteux, *Witches, Werewolves and Fairies: Shapeshifters and Astral Doubles in the Middle Ages* (Rochester, Vt.: Inner Traditions, 2003), vii–viii.

10. D. Michael Quinn, *Early Mormonism and the Magic World View* (Salt Lake City, Utah: Signature Books, 1998).

11. Agrippa, *The Fourth Book of Occult Philosophy,* ed. with commentary by Stephen Skinner (Berwich, Maine: Ibis Press, 2005) 34–35.

12. Michell, *Temple at Jerusalem,* 11.

13. Agrippa, *Three Books of Occult Philosophy,* 330.

14. Charles T. McClenachan, *The Book of the Ancient and Accepted Scottish Rite of Freemasonry* (New York: Masonic Publishing Co., 1884), 412–13.

6. THE LOST WORD AND
THE MASONIC QUEST

1. Charles T. McClenachan, *The Book of the Ancient and Accepted Scottish Rite of Freemasonry* (New York: Masonic Publishing Co., 1884), 186.

2. Johann Reuchlin, *On the Art of the Kabbalah,* trans. Martin and Sarah Goodman (Lincoln: University of Nebraska Press, 1983), xix.

3. Scholem, *Kabbalah,* 177.

4. Christopher McIntosh, *The Rosicrucians: The History, Mythology, and Rituals of an Esoteric Order* (York Beach, Maine: Weiser, 1997), 40–41.

5. Albert Mackey, *The Symbolism of Freemasonry* (1882), chapter 31.

6. Mackey, *Encyclopedia of Freemasonry,* 856.

7. Pike, 697.

8. Mackey, *Encyclopedia of Freemasonry,* 33.

9. Jean Dubuis, *The Fundamentals of Esotericism,* Philosophers of Nature, book 1, trans. Brigitte Donvez (Wheaton, Ill.: Triad Publishing, 2000), 10–11.

7. SCOTTISH RITE AND THE RISE OF ESOTERIC MASONRY

1. Mackey, *Encyclopedia of Freemasonry*, 649.
2. Mackey, *Encyclopedia of Freemasonry*, 44.
3. Albert Pike, *Morals and Dogma of the Ancient and Accepted Scottish Rite of Freemasonry*, 775.
4. Eliphas Levi, as quoted by Jean Dubuis in *Qabala*, Philosophers of Nature, book 4, trans. Brigitte Donvez (Wheaton, Ill.: Triad Publishing, 2000), lesson 61, page 4.
5. Michel Caron and Serge Hutin, *The Alchemists*, trans. Helen R. Lane (New York: Grove Press, 1961), 163–64.
6. Dubuis, *Qabala*, lesson 60, 2.
7. Bernard Haisch, *The God Theory* (York Beach, Maine: Weiser, 2006), 93.
8. Haisch, *The God Theory*, 98–99.

8. OCCULT MASONRY IN THE EIGHTEENTH CENTURY

1. Manly P. Hall, *The Riddle of the Rosicrucians* (1941).
2. Comte de Cagliostro, *Secret Ritual of Egyptian Rite Freemasonry* (Whitefish, Mont.: Kessinger Publishing, n.d.).
3. Comte de Cagliostro, *Secret Ritual of Egyptian Rite Freemasonry* (Whitefish, Mont.: Kessinger Publishing, n.d.).
4. Jean Dubuis, *Mineral Alchemy*, Philosophers of Nature, book 3, trans. Brigitte Donvez (Wheaton, Ill.: Triad Publishing, 1987), lesson 30.
5. *Codex Rosae Crucis D.O.M.A.*, with commentary by Manly P. Hall (Los Angeles: Philosophical Research Society); *Cosmology*, by Franz Hartman (Pomeroy, Wash.: Health Research; contains color plates); and *Secret Symbols of the Rosicrucians of the 16th and 17th Centuries* (San Jose: Rosicrucian Order/AMORC).
6. Agrippa, *Fourth Book of Occult Philosophy*.
7. Antoine Faivre and Jacob Needleman, eds., *Modern Esoteric Spirituality* (New York: Crossroad, 1992), 268–69.
8. Waite, *New Encyclopedia of Freemasonry*, 385.
9. McClenachan, *Book of the Ancient and Accepted Scottish Rite*, 400.

10. Antoine-Joseph Pernety, *An Alchemical Treatise on the Great Art,* foreword by Todd Pratum (York Beach, Me.: Weiser, 1995), 127.

9. YORK RITE AND THE SURVIVAL OF THE KNIGHTS TEMPLAR

1. Gustav Davidson, *A Dictionary of Angels, Including the Fallen Angels* (New York: Free Press, 1971; orig. pub. 1967), 106.
2. D. Michael Quinn, *Early Mormonism and the Magic World View,* 21.

Bibliography

Abbé N. de Montfaucon de Villars. *Comte de Gabalis*. Paterson, N. J.: The Brothers, 1914.

Achad, Frater. *The Egyptian Revival; or, The Ever-Coming Son in the Light of the Tarot*. New York: Weiser, 1974.

Agrippa, Cornelius. *The Fourth Book of Occult Philosophy*. Edited by Stephen Skinner. Newburyport, Mass.: Ibis Press, 2005.

Agrippa, Heinrich Cornelius. *The Three Books of Occult Philosophy*. Edited by Donald Tyson; translated by James Freake. St. Paul, Minn.: Llewellyn, 1993.

Anonymous. *Secret Symbols of the Rosicrucians of the 16th and 17th Centuries*. Various editions; orig. pub. 1785.

Aveni, Anthony. *Behind the Crystal Ball: Magic, Science, and the Occult from Antiquity through the New Age*. Boulder: University Press of Colorado, 1996.

Baigent, Michael, and Richard Leigh. *The Temple and the Lodge*. Arcade Publishing, 2011.

Beresniak, Daniel. *Symbols of Freemasonry*. Editions Assouline, 1997.

Berman, Ric. *Schism: The Battle That Forged Freemasonry*. Sussex Academic Press, 2013.

Birch, Una. *Secret Societies: Illuminati, Freemasons and the French Revolution*. Edited by James Wasserman. Newburyport, Mass.: Ibis Press, 2007.

Burckhardt, Titus. *Sacred Art in East and West*. Fons Vitae, 2002.

Burman, Edward. *The Templars: Knights of God*. Rochester, Vt.: Destiny Books, 1986.

Caron, Michel, and Serge Hutin. *The Alchemists.* Translated by Helen R. Lane. New York: Grove Press, 1961.

Churchward, Albert. *The Arcana of Freemasonry: A History of Masonic Signs and Symbols.* New York: Red Wheel/Weiser, 2005; orig. pub. 1915.

Churton, Tobias. *Gnostic Philosophy: From Ancient Persia to Modern Times.* Rochester, Vt.: Inner Traditions, 2005.

Churton, Tobias. *The Golden Builders: Alchemists, Rosicrucians, and the First Freemasons.* New York: Red Wheel/Weiser, 2005.

Churton, Tobias. *The Magus of Freemasonry: The Mysterious Life of Elias Ashmole—Scientist, Alchemist, and Founder of the Royal Society.* Rochester, Vt.: Inner Traditions, 2006.

Cobb, Noel. *Prospero's Island: The Secret Alchemy at the Heart of the Tempest.* London: Coventure, 1984.

Collins, Andrew. *From the Ashes of Angels: The Forbidden Legacy of a Fallen Race.* Rochester, Vt.: Bear & Co., 1996.

Cooper-Oakley, Isabel. *The Comte de St. Germain.* Various editions; orig. pub. 1912.

Couliano, Ioan P. *Eros and Magic in the Renaissance.* Chicago: University of Chicago Press, 1987.

Davidson, Gustav. *A Dictionary of Angels, Including the Fallen Angels.* Free Press, 1971; orig. pub. 1967.

Dawkins, Peter. *Arcadia.* 5 vols. Francis Bacon Research Trust, 1988.

Dawkins, Peter. *A Commentary on the Great Instauration: The Universal and General Reformation of the Whole Wide World through the Renewal of All Arts and Sciences.* Francis Bacon Research Trust, 1983.

Day, Christopher. *Places of the Soul: Architecture and Environmental Design as a Healing Art.* Aquarian Press, 1990.

de Hoyos, Arturo, ed. *Albert Pike's Esoterika: The Symbolism of the Blue Degrees of Freemasonry.* Scottish Rite Research Society, 2005.

de Hoyos, Arturo. *Albert Pike's Morals and Dogma: Annotated Edition*, 2nd ed. Supreme Council, 33°, 2013.

Dubois, Geneviève. *Fulcanelli and the Alchemical Revival: The Man behind the Mystery of the Cathedrals.* Rochester, Vt.: Inner Traditions, 2006.

Dubuis, Jean. *The Fundamentals of Esoteric Knowledge.* Philosophers of Nature, book 1. Translated by Brigitte Donvez. Triad Publishing, 2000.

Dubuis, Jean. *Mineral Alchemy*. Philosophers of Nature, book 3. Translated by Brigitte Donvez. Triad Publishing, 1987.

Dubuis, Jean. *Qabala*. Philosophers of Nature, book 4. Translated by Brigitte Donvez. Triad Publishing, 2000.

Dubuis, Jean. *Spagyrics*. A Practical Course in Plant Alchemy (2 vols.). Translated by Brigitte Donevez. Triad Publishing, 1987.

DuQuette, Lon Milo. *The Key to Solomon's Key: Secrets of Magic and Masonry*. CCC Publishing, 2006.

Faivre, Antoine. *Access to Western Esotericism*. New York: State University of New York, 1994.

Faivre, Antoine, and Jacob Needleman, eds. *Modern Esoteric Spirituality*. Crossroad, 1992.

Fix, William. *Lake of Memory Rising: Return of the Five Ancient Truths at the Heart of Religion*. Council Oak Books, 2000.

Fleming, John V. *The Dark Side of the Enlightenment: Wizards, Alchemists, and Spiritual Seekers in the Age of Reason*. Norton, 2013.

Flint, Valerie. *The Rise of Magic in Early Medieval Europe*. New Jersey: Princeton University Press, 1991.

Fulcanelli. *The Dwellings of the Philosophers*. Translated by Brigitte Donvez and Lionel Perrin. Archive Press and Communications, 1999.

Fulcanelli. *Fulcanelli, Master Alchemist: Le Mystère des Cathédrales*. Translated by Mary Sworder. Brotherhood of Life, 1984.

Fuller, Jean Overton. *The Comte De Saint-Germain: Last Scion of the House of Rakoczy*. East-West Publications, 1988.

Gelb, Michael J. *How to Think Like Leonardo da Vinci*. Delacorte Press, 1998.

Godwin, Joscelyn. *The Pagan Dream of the Renaissance*. Phanes Press, 2002.

Godwin, Joscelyn. *The Theosophical Enlightenment*. New York: State University of New York, 1994.

Grand Lodge of California. *California Cipher: A Valuable Aid to Memory*. F & A. M., 1990.

Guénon, René. *Perspectives on Initiation*. Sophia Perennis, San Rafael, Calif., 2002.

Haisch, Bernard. *The God Theory: Universes, Zero-Point Fields, and What's Behind It All*. Weiser, 2006.

Hall, Manly P. *Codex Rosae Crucis D.O.M.A.* Los Angeles: Philosophical Research Society, 1938.

Hall, Manly P. *Freemasonry of the Ancient Egyptians.* Los Angeles: Philosophical Research Society, 1937.

Hall, Manly P. *The Lost Keys of Freemasonry.* Los Angeles: Philosophical Research Society, 1923.

Hall, Manly P. *Masonic Orders of Fraternity.* Los Angeles: Philosophical Research Society, 1950.

Hall, Manly P. *The Most Holy Trinosophia of the Comte de St. Germain.* The Phoenix Press, Los Angeles, Calif., 1933.

Hall, Manly P. *The Riddle of the Rosicrucians.* Los Angeles: Philosophical Research Society, 1941.

Hartmann, Franz. *Cosmology.* Health Research, 1969.

Howe, James Robinson. *Marlowe, Tamburlaine and Magic.* Ohio University Press, 1976.

Hutchens, Rex. *A Glossary to* Morals and Dogma. Supreme Council, Ancient and Accepted Scottish Rite of Freemasonry, Southern Jurisdiction of the United States of America, 1993.

Jacobi, Jolande, ed. *Paracelsus: Selected Writings*, vol. 27. Bollingen Series. New Jersey: Princeton University Press, 1951.

Jacobs, Margaret C. *The Origins of Freemasonry: Facts and Fictions.* University of Pennsylvania Press, 2006.

Jameux, Charles B. *Memory Palaces and Masonic Lodges: Esoteric Secrets of the Art of Memory.* Rochester, Vt.: Inner Traditions, 2019.

Josephus, Flavius. *Antiquities of the Jews.* Translated by William Whiston. Chatto & Windus, 1897.

Jung, Carl. *Psychological Types.* Volume 6 in *Collected Works of C. G. Jung.* New Jersey: Princeton University Press, 1971.

Kernan, Alvin, ed. *Two Renaissance Mythmakers: Christopher Marlowe and Ben Jonson.* Baltimore: Johns Hopkins University Press, 1977.

Kristeller, Paul Oskar. *Renaissance Thought and Its Sources.* New York: Columbia University Press, 1979.

Lawlor, Robert. *Sacred Geometry: Philosophy & Practice.* London: Thames and Hudson, 1982.

Leadbeater, C. W. *Freemasonry and Its Ancient Mystic Rites.* New York: Gramercy Books, 1998.

Lecouteux, Claude. *Witches, Werewolves and Fairies: Shapeshifters and Astral Doubles in the Middle Ages.* Rochester, Vt.: Inner Traditions, 2003.

Line, Jill. *Shakespeare and the Ideal of Love.* Rochester, Vt.: Inner Traditions, 2006.

Lomas, Robert. *Freemasonry and the Birth of Modern Science.* Fair Winds Press, 2003.

Lomas, Robert. *Turning the Hiram Key: Rituals of Freemasonry Revealed.* Fair Winds Press, 2005.

Mackey, Albert. *Encyclopedia of Freemasonry*, rev. ed. Edited by W. J. Hughan and E. L. Hawkins. Masonic History Co., 1921.

Markale, Jean. *Cathedral of the Black Madonna: The Druids and the Mysteries of Chartres.* Rochester, Vt.: Inner Traditions, 2004.

Marshall, Peter. *The Magic Circle of Rudolf II: Alchemy and Astrology in Renaissance Prague.* Walker & Company, 2006.

Matthews, Caitlin and John. *The Western Way: A Practical Guide to the Western Mystery Tradition.* Arkana/Penguin Books, 1986.

McCalman, Iain. *The Last Alchemist: Count Cagliostro, Master of Magic in the Age of Reason.* HarperCollins, 2003.

McClenachan, Charles T. *The Book of the Ancient and Accepted Scottish Rite of Freemasonry.* Masonic Publishing Co., 1884.

McIntosh, Christopher. *Eliphas Levi and the French Occult Revival.* New York: Weiser, 1972.

McIntosh, Christopher. *The Rose Cross and the Age of Reason: Eighteenth-Century Rosicrucianism in Central Europe and Its Relationship to the Enlightenment.* E. J. Brill, 1992.

McIntosh, Christopher. *The Rosicrucians: The History, Mythology, and Rituals of an Occult Order.* New York: Weiser, 1997.

McLean, Adam, ed. *A Compendium on the Rosicrucian Vault.* Hermetic Research Series, 1985.

Mebane, John S. *Renaissance Magic and the Return of the Golden Age: The Occult Traditions and Marlowe, Jonson, and Shakespeare.* University of Nebraska Press, 1992.

Michell, John. *The Temple at Jerusalem: A Revelation.* New York: Samuel Weiser, Inc.: 2000.

Moore, Thomas. *The Planets Within: The Astrological Psychology of Marsilio Ficino*. Lindisfarne Press, 1993.

Murphy, Christopher, and Shawn Eyer, eds. *Exploring Early Grand Lodge Freemasonry: Studies in Honor of the Tricentennial of the Establishment of the Grand Lodge of England*. Plumbstone, 2017.

Nataf, Andre. *The Wordsworth Dictionary of the Occult*. Wordsworth Editions, 1991.

Naudon, Paul. *The Secret History of Freemasonry: Its Origins and Connection to the Knights Templar*. Rochester, Vt.: Inner Traditions, 2005.

Naydler, Jeremy. *Temple of the Cosmos: The Ancient Egyptian Experience of the Sacred*. Rochester, Vt.: Inner Traditions, 1996.

Ophiel. *The Art & Practice of Creative Visualization*. New York: Red Wheel/Weiser, 1997.

Parker, Geoffrey, ed. *The Thirty Years' War*, 2nd ed. Routledge, 1997.

Partner, Peter. *The Knights Templar and Their Myth*. Rochester, Vt.: Destiny Books, 1990.

Patai, Raphael. *The Hebrew Goddess*. Wayne State University Press, 1990; orig. pub. 1967.

Pike, Albert. *Morals and Dogma of the Ancient and Accepted Scottish Rite of Freemasonry*. Various editions; orig. pub. 1871.

Pincus-Witten, Robert. *Occult Symbolism in France*. Garland Publishing, 1976.

Purce, Jill. *The Mystic Spiral: Journey of the Soul*. London: Thames and Hudson, 1980.

Quinn, D. Michael. *Early Mormonism and the Magic World View*. Signature Books, 1998.

Reuchlin, Johann. *On the Art of the Kabbalah*. Translated by Martin and Sarah Goodman. University of Nebraska Press, 1983.

Rice, Edward. *Captain Sir Richard Francis Burton: The Secret Agent Who Made the Pilgrimage to Mecca, Discovered the Kama Sutra, and Brought the Arabian Nights to the West*. Charles Scribner's Sons, 1990.

Ridley, Jasper. *The Freemasons: A History of the World's Most Powerful Secret Society*. Arcade Publishing, 2011.

Saint-Martin, Louis Claude de. *Theosophic Correspondence 1792–1797*.

Translated by Edward Burton Penny. Theosophical University Press, 1982.

Scholem, Gershom. *Kabbalah*. Meridian Books, 1974.

Schuchard, Marsha Keith. *Restoring the Temple of Vision: Cabalistic Freemasonry and Stuart Culture*. Brill, 2002.

Schwaller de Lubicz, R. A. *The Temple of Man*. Rochester, Vt.: Inner Traditions, 1998.

Seligmann, Kurt. *The History of Magic and the Occult*. Gramercy Books, 1997.

Seznec, Jean. *The Survival of the Pagan Gods: The Mythological Tradition and Its Place in Renaissance Humanism and Art*. New Jersey: Princeton University Press, 1995; orig. pub. 1940.

Shesso, Renna. *Math for Mystics: From the Fibonacci Sequence to Luna's Labyrinth to the Golden Section and Other Secrets of Sacred Geometry*. New York: Red Wheel/Weiser, 2007.

Sitwell, Sacheverell. *Gothic Europe*. Holt, Rinehart, and Winston, 1969.

Smoley, Richard, and Jay Kinney. *Hidden Wisdom: A Guide to the Western Inner Traditions*. Wheaton, Ill.: Quest Books, 2006.

Stoddard, Whitney S. *Art and Architecture in Medieval France*. New York: Icon, 1972.

Tourniac, Jean. *Principes et problèmes spirituels du rite écossais rectifié et de sa chevalerie templière* [The Principles and Spiritual Problems of the Revised Scottish Rite]. Paris: Dervy, 1969.

Trowbridge, W. R. H. *Cagliostro: The Splendour and Misery of a Master of Magic*. Boston: E. P. Dutton & Co., 1910.

Vandenbroeck, Andre. *Al-Kemi: A Memoir: Hermetic, Occult, Political, and Private Aspects of R. A. Schwaller de Lubicz*. Stockbridge, Mass.: Lindisfarne Press, 1987.

Waite, Arthur Edward. *The Brotherhood of the Rosy Cross*. University Books, 1973.

Waite, Arthur Edward, trans. *The Hermetic and Alchemical Writings of Paracelsus the Great*. London: James Elliott, 1894.

Waite, Arthur Edward. *A New Encyclopedia of Freemasonry*. Various editions; orig. pub. 1921.

Waite, Arthur Edward. *The Unknown Philosopher: Louis Claude de St. Martin*. Hudson, N.Y.: SteinerBooks, 1987; orig. pub. 1901.

Wallace-Murphy, Tim, and Marilyn Hopkins. *Templars in America: From the Crusades to the New World.* New York: Red Wheel/Weiser, 2004.

Wasserman, James. *An Illustrated History of the Knights Templar.* Rochester, Vt.: Inner Traditions, 2006.

Wasserman, James. *The Templars and the Assassins: The Militia of Heaven.* Rochester, Vt.: Inner Traditions, 2001.

White, Michael. *The Pope and the Heretic: The True Story of Giordano Bruno, the Man Who Dared to Defy the Roman Inquisition.* New York: William Morrow, 2002.

Wilson, Colin. *The Occult.* London: Watkins, 2006.

Wilmhurst, W. `L. *Meaning of Masonry.* Various editions; orig. pub. 1922.

Wittemans, Fr. *A New and Authentic History of the Rosicrucians.* London: Rider and Company, 1938.

Wolf, Fred Alan. *The Spiritual Universe: One Physicist's Vision of Spirit, Soul, Matter, and Self.* Portsmouth, N.H.: Moment Point Press, 1999.

Yates, Frances A. *The Art of Memory.* Chicago: University of Chicago Press, 1966.

Yates, Frances A. *Giordano Bruno and the Hermetic Tradition.* Chicago: University of Chicago Press, 1964.

Yates, Frances A. *The Occult Philosophy in the Elizabethan Age.* Oxfordshire, UK: Routledge, 1979.

Yates, Frances A. *The Rosicrucian Enlightenment.* Chicago: University of Chicago Press, 1972.

Index